Contents

4

Geographical studies in

NORTH AMERICA

B. E. Price BA, MSc

Senior Lecturer in Geography and American Studies,
Crewe and Alsager College of Higher Education

E. Tweed BSc, MA

Senior Lecturer in Geography and Educational Studies,
Crewe and Alsager College of Higher Education

Editorial Adviser: **T. W. Randle**

Principle Lecturer in Geography, Sheffield City Polytechnic

Maps and Diagrams by Tim Smith and Margaret Watson

Oliver & Boyd

ACKNOWLEDGMENTS

The authors and publishers would like to thank the following for permission to reproduce the following photographs (numbers indicate plate numbers):

Aerial Photos of New England Inc. 16; Alabama Bureau of Publicity and Information 32; Baton Rouge Chamber of Commerce 35; Bethlehem Steel Corp. 17; Chris Birrell 4; British Petroleum Co. Ltd. 69; Brock University, Ontario 86; Camera Press 37 (photo: Richard Harrison), 66; Canada National 84; Canadian Information Services, London 5, 71; Colorific! 24; Dresser Industries Inc. 25; Ford Motor Co. 26, 28; General Motors of Canada 91; Government of British Columbia 79, 81; John Hillelson Agency Ltd, 19 (photo: Bruce Davidson), 31 (photo: Martin J. Dain); Information Canada Phototheque 82 (photo: G. Hunter); International Nickel Co. of Canada 76; Kenbarry Productions 11; Kennecott Copper Corp., Utah 42; Los Angeles Times 53, 55, 56, 57; Mansell Collection 13, 30; Mississippi Agricultural and Industrial Board 33; National Film Board of Canada Phototheque 1, 6, 70, 72, 73, 78, 89, 92, 93; Nova Scotia Information Services 94; Ontario Hydro 87; Ontario Ministry of Information and Tourism 74, 85, 88; San Francisco Convention and Visitors' Bureau 47, 58, 59; Seattle Times 64; Charles Swithinbank 67; Tennessee Valley Authority 34a/b; John Topham Picture Library 23; US Bureau of Mines 43; US Bureau of Reclamation 48, 65; US Geological Survey 60; US Travel Service 18, 46, 61; USDA—Soil Conservation Service 21, 22, 38, 49, 50; R. Gerald Wand 15.

The publishers would also like to thank the following organisations for permission to reproduce extracts from their publications:
BBC Publications (for *The Restless Earth* by Nigel Calder); Jarrold & Sons Ltd, Norwich; National Geographic Magazine; Evelyn Singer Agency Ltd (for *The Face of North America* by Peter Farb, Harper & Row).

Oliver & Boyd
Robert Stevenson House,
1–3 Baxter's Place,
Leith Walk,
Edinburgh EH1 3BB

A Division of the Longman Group Limited

ISBN 0 05 003013 2
First published 1979

Printed in Hong Kong by
Sheck Wah Tong Printing Press Limited

Introduction

A survey of O-level and CSE syllabuses soon reveals a variety of approaches to the study of North America: some favour the exhaustive study of selected regions; others follow a systematic approach and yet others combine the two.

In this book, the authors have adopted a broad regional framework as a setting within which to develop selected topics in some depth—a format which allows teachers to follow whichever approach they wish. They may study the USA and Canada and their component regions in detail; follow a systematic thread; or select groups of topics to illustrate broad themes. For example, they could develop the theme of technological change in agriculture with reference to selected areas, or examine the problems of inner cities in the USA and Canada.

This flexibility of approach is also assisted by the division of each chapter into short topics, each of which concludes with a set of questions. The questions vary in difficulty to enable teachers to select those most appropriate to the needs of their pupils.

Note on nomenclature and statistics

In this book, 'North America' is used as a collective term for the United States and Canada. 'American' is used specifically with reference to the United States.

Where possible, all statistics give the latest available figures at the time of publication.

U S S R

NORWAY

L

Edin.

Greenwich Meridian 0°

120°E 90°E 60°E

North Pole

SIBERIA

180°

Arctic Ocean

120°W 60°W

90°W

GREENLAND
(Danish)

Arctic Circle

C

ALASKA (USA)

66½°N

Anchorage

to Yokohama
5600 km

Frobisher Bay

C A N A D A

Hudson
Bay

50°N

to Liverpool
3500 km

B

St John's

Vancouver

K   J   A

river G

OTTAWA

river E

New York

The Great Lakes

WASHINGTON

Pacific Ocean

Atlantic Ocean

San Francisco

I

UNITED STATES

M

to Panama
3700 km

To Rio de Janeiro
8700 km

to Sydney
(via Honolulu)
12 000 km

L

OF AMERICA

H

N

river F

Gulf of Mexico

D Miami

BAHAMAS

23½°N — Tropic of Cancer

MEXICO

A

WEST INDIES

0   km   2000

CENTRAL AMERICA

The Continental Framework 1:
The Physical Background

Relative size and population of the USA and Canada

Questions

Figure 1 ana an atlas

1. Name the following features:
   (*i*) islands A and B; (*ii*) straits C and D; (*iii*) rivers E, F and G; (*iv*) states or provinces H. I and J; (*v*) cities K, L, M and N.

Figure 1

2. *a*) Compare the distance between Edinburgh and London with that between:
   (*i*) Miami and New York; and (*ii*) Miami and Frobisher Bay.
   b) Between which lines of longitude approximately does North America lie? (*hint:* use the lines shown on Fig. 1.) What fraction of 360° is this?

Table 1   Political units: comparisons

Country	Area (km²)	Population (millions)
Canada	9 970 000	23·00
United States	9 360 000	215·00
*Greenland	2 180 000	0·06
*Mexico	1 970 000	58·00
United Kingdom	230 000	56·00

*Sometimes included in North America.

(Europa Year Book, 1977)

Table 1

3. *a*) Approximately how many times larger than the UK is the USA: (*i*) by area; (*ii*) by population?
   b) Which of the listed countries has: (*i*) the greatest; (*ii*) the smallest population density per square kilometre?

Figure 2 and Table 1

4. One way of showing population density is by constructing a triangle using population and area statistics. For example, the triangle for the United States would appear like Figure 2, using information from Table 1.

The population density of the United States is represented by the angle *x*, which can be measured; the larger the angle the greater the population density. Note also that the particular size and shape can be compared with other triangles.

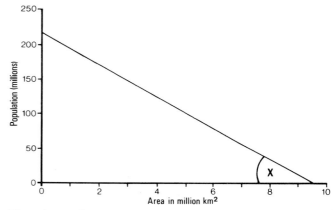

Figure 2   *North America: population triangle*

a) Copy Figure 2 in your notebook.
b) Using the same scale, and the information from Table 1, draw the triangles to represent Canada, Mexico and the United Kingdom. In each case measure angle *x*.
c) List the four countries in order of population density.
d) Compare the shapes of the triangles against that of the United States. How might the differences be explained?

An atlas

5. *a*) Rearrange the following cities in a column and beside each one, write in the name of the country in which it is found and its latitude. Begin with the most northerly city and end with the city nearest the equator: Cairo, London, Los Angeles, Madrid, Miami, New Delhi, New Orleans, New York, Peking, Rome, Seattle and Tokyo.
   b) Underline the American cities and comment on their positions relative to the others.

TIME AND DISTANCE

The earth rotates on its axis once every 24 hours, and time changes as the 'daylight hemisphere' crosses the continent from east to west. When dawn is breaking over the Atlantic coast, the people of the Pacific region are sleeping through the middle of the night. To overcome this problem North America is divided into a number of *Time Zones*. Each zone is basically 15° of longitude in width and the difference between each time zone is one hour.

7

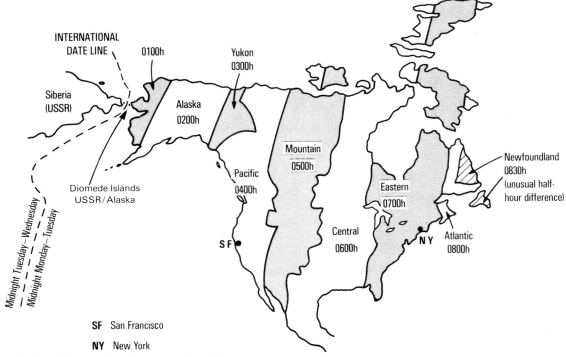

Figure 3 *Time Zones and the International Date Line*

SF San Francisco

NY New York

INTERNATIONAL DATE LINE

Another problem occurs at the line where the date changes. The 180° meridian is both 12 hours ahead *and* 12 hours behind the Greenwich meridian. Thus the 24-hour change from one date to the next is usually made as one crosses longitude 180°. This meridian is regarded as the *International Date Line*, except where it deviates to pass between Asia and North America and to avoid splitting groups of islands which are under one government. In the rather special case of the Diomede Islands, the International Date Line separates the Alaskan island from the Russian one. As the Alaskans begin work on their island they can see the Russians beginning work on the next day!

Questions

Figure 3 and the account

1. *a)* How long does the earth take to rotate through 360°?
   b) Through how many degrees of longitude does the earth rotate in one hour?
   c) Explain why each time zone is 15° of longitude in width.

2. Why do the boundaries between North America's time zones not always exactly follow each 15° line of longitude?

3. Explain, in detail, why a business executive telephoning from San Francisco at 16.30 (Pacific Time) would be unable to contact an office in New York.

Figure 3

4. *a)* From the evidence on the map, what day and time is it at Greenwich?
   b) If you fly from Alaska to Siberia does the date move forward or back?

Atlas and the account

5. *a)* Explain in your own words why the International Date Line does not follow the 180° meridian exactly.
   b) List the land areas that cause the Date Line to 'bend'.

Structure and relief

I THE CANADIAN SHIELD

The huge Canadian Shield forms the structural core of the North American continent and is composed of Pre-Cambrian igneous and metamorphic rocks, many of which are 500 000 000 years or more in age. Since its formation it has been worn down and has undergone countless other changes, including very recent ice scouring. Even so, the Shield is one of the great stable blocks of the earth's crust. In particular, it has acted as the buffer zone against which subsequent fold mountains have been formed.

II THE APPALACHIANS

The eastern side of North America is dominated by the remnants of an ancient fold mountain range of Palaeozoic age. Once loftier than the Himalayas, the Appalachians have been much reduced in height since their formation and are generally more subdued and rounded than the mountains in the west.

III THE WESTERN CORDILLERA

The young fold mountains of the Western Cordillera were created in the most recent mountain building period, the Alpine—a mere 20 000 000 to 30 000 000 years ago! Faulting, together with the work of ice and running water, has already destroyed much of their original structure; but they remain the continent's dominant relief zone, steep slopes and jagged crests being commonplace.

Plateau areas separate the Rocky Mountains from the westernmost ranges. Within the plateau country there are many kinds of distinctive landscapes, including canyons and lava flows. The large rivers of the west seem to disregard the present relief and cross, often dramatically, many kinds of surface to reach the ocean. The region is still a relatively unstable part of the earth's crust, with active volcanoes, destructive earthquakes, and frequent gaseous outpourings.

IV THE CENTRAL LOWLANDS

The Central Lowlands form the youngest part of North America and extend from the Arctic Ocean to the Gulf of Mexico. Most of the region consists of gently folded sedimentary rocks forming lowlands of almost flat or rolling relief, in which the river valleys are often the most notable features.

Plate 1   *The Canadian Shield*

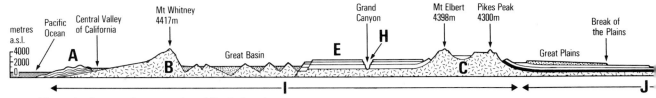

Figure 4 *Structural cross-section of North America*

Questions

Figure 4, Figure 5 and atlas

1. Name the features shown on Figure 4: (*i*) mountain ranges A, B, C and D; (*ii*) plateaus E, F and G; (*iii*) river H; (*iv*) structural regions I, J, K and L.

Figure 4

2. *a*) Examine the vertical and horizontal scales, then calculate the approximate vertical exaggeration.

b) What are your general conclusions about the comparative height of relief features in a continental area like North America?

3. *a*) Using the same scale as Figure 4: (*i*) draw a simple cross-section of Canada following line X–Y (Figure 5); (*ii*) annotate the cross-section.

b) Compare your cross-section with Figure 4 and account for any major differences.

Figure 5 *Structure and relief features of North America*

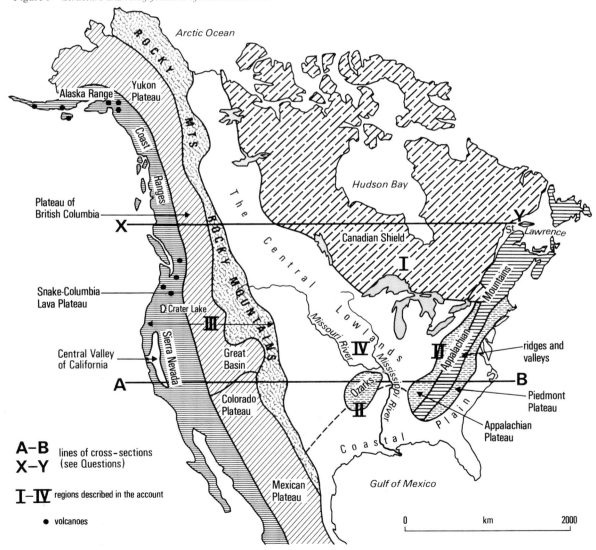

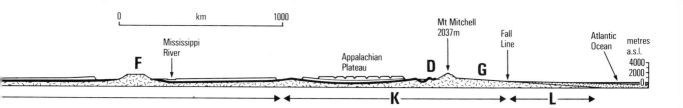

Plate 2 *Grand Tetons*

Plates 1, 2 and 3, Figure 5 and the account

4. *a*) Describe the outstanding features of the landscape in each photograph.
   b) Name the major structural region to which each landscape belongs.

The account and general

5. List as many differences as possible:

a) between the physical features of the Rockies and those of the Appalachians;
b) between the physical features of the Canadian Shield and those of the Central Lowlands.

Atlas

6. 'The continental divide, the watershed between east and west-flowing rivers, follows the axis of the Rockies'. Elaborate on this statement.

Plate 3 *Great Plains*

THE GRAND CANYON

A VISITOR'S ACCOUNT

'Of the few things in this world which are beyond description by poets or painters, surely the Grand Canyon is one. There has never been a line written about it that matches its profound depths, or a painting that captures its full range of colours. One can look at the canyon, one can measure it, but it eludes comprehension. . . . It is the most humbling scene on the continent, the greatest visual shock a human being can experience. . . . Standing on the rim, one can clearly see twelve major layers of rock, which form distinct bands of colour. The vertical cliffs are layers of limestone and sandstone; the crumbling slopes are usually shales. . . . The top layer is the one most recently formed; the layers become successively more ancient towards the bottom of the canyon. These layers are like pages in a book of earth history. Many of the pages are wrinkled and creased, and whole chapters are missing. But those that remain provide a clear picture of the succession of life on the continent. . . . The rocks bordering the muddy river are the basement upon which the layers of sediment were deposited, and are among the most ancient rocks to be seen anywhere in the world. . . . They are reminders of the antiquity of the continent, for they represent a sequence of mountain building in which ramparts were uplifted and then ground down, rose again and were ground down for the second time, leaving only their roots. Thousands of metres of rock were thus twice removed, particle by particle, over hundreds of millions of years. And all of this was accomplished before even a single layer of sediment was deposited.'

(From *The Face of North America* by Peter Farb, Harper & Row, 1963)

Questions

General

1. *a*) How are the following types of rocks formed: (*i*) sedimentary, (*ii*) igneous, (*iii*) metamorphic?
   b) Name one example of each type.

The account and general

2. *a*) Explain how the sedimentary rocks provide a clear picture of the succession of life on the continent.
   b) Suggest why no fossils exist in the basement rocks.

Plate 4　*Grand Canyon*

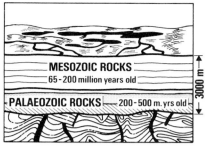 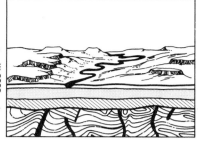 

1. Ancient basement of Pre-Cambrian rocks (igneous and metamorphic) 500-2000 million years old, above which sedimentary layers accumulated.

2. Most of the younger sedimentary rocks have been removed. The Colorado River established a west-ward course, flowing at speeds up to 35 k/h and carrying sand and silt averaging 500 000 tonnes per day.

3. Gradual uplift of the plateau surface matched by downcutting of the river, forming the Grand Canyon. Weathering has very slowly lowered the plateau areas.

Figure 6   *Formation of the Grand Canyon*

Atlas and Figure 6

3. *a*) Name (*i*) the region where the Colorado River has its source, and (*ii*) the gulf where it enters the sea.
   b) Approximately how long is the river?
   c) What factors have given the river such formidable erosive powers?

Plate 4 and general

4. *a*) Explain why most of the Canyon walls have a step-like appearance.
   b) How does aridity contribute to the grandeur of the Canyon?

Figure 6

5. The length of the Grand Canyon is 350 km and it has an average width of 14·5 km. Estimate its depth.

THE GREAT ICE AGE

Geologists now believe that enormous sheets of ice accumulated, then advanced and retreated a dozen times or more during the last million years. These sheets were up to 2500 metres thick and spread over two-thirds of the continent when the climate was at its coldest.

Questions

Figure 7 and Figure 5

1. *a*) (*i*) Where did the main ice sheets originate? (*ii*) Name two ice sources in the United States.
   b) Suggest why ice gathered in two different types of locality.
2. *a*) In what part of the continent did ice extend the farthest south?
   b) How do you account for this?

Figure 7, Figure 5 and general

3. *a*) Which regions show features of glacial erosion? What specific landforms would you expect to see?
   b) Briefly explain how the ice created the landforms.

4. *a*) What do you understand by the term 'tundra'?
   b) Where can you find tundra in North America at present?

5. 'In the glacial equation Canada's loss has been the United States' gain'. Elaborate on this statement.

Figure 7   *The Great Ice Age*

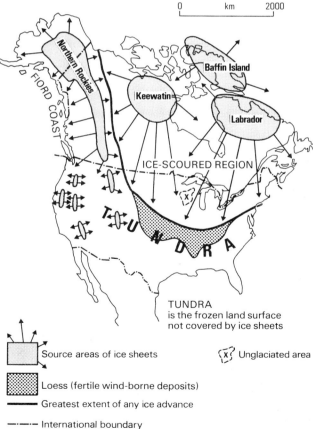

TUNDRA is the frozen land surface not covered by ice sheets

Source areas of ice sheets

Loess (fertile wind-borne deposits)

——— Greatest extent of any ice advance

—·—·— International boundary

⦃x⦄ Unglaciated area

13

Climatic features

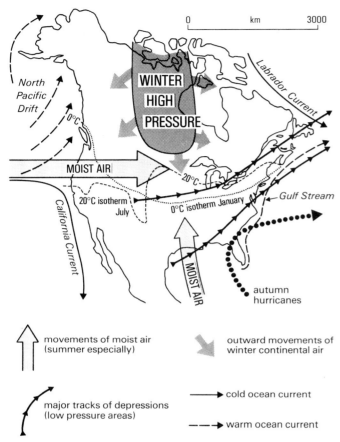

Figure 8 *Selected climatic features*

movements of moist air (summer especially)

outward movements of winter continental air

major tracks of depressions (low pressure areas)

cold ocean current

warm ocean current

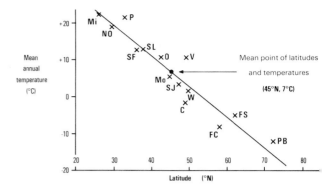

Figure 9 *Temperature/latitude graph*

Mean point of latitudes and temperatures (45°N, 7°C)

Table 2   Latitude and mean annual temperature

Climatic Station	Position Lat. °N	Position Long. °W	Mean Annual Temp. °C
Miami	26	81	23
New Orleans	30	90	20
Phoenix	33	112	22
San Francisco	36	123	13
St Louis	38	91	13
Omaha	42	96	11
Montreal	45	74	6
St John's	47	53	4
Vancouver	49	123	11
Cochrane	49	82	−1
Winnipeg	50	97	+2
Fort Chimo	58	68	−8
Fort Smith	60	113	−5
Point Barrow	72	156	−12
Mean Point	45		+7

(Average of latitudes and temperatures)

TEMPERATURE RELATIONSHIPS

A well known relationship is the decrease in temperature with altitude: on average, for every 100 m climbed the temperature falls 0·6°C.

In the following exercises scattergraphs and 'best fit' lines are used to examine relationships between temperature and (*i*) latitude, (*ii*) distance from the sea, (*iii*) ocean currents.

1. *Temperature is affected by latitude.* Information from Table 2 is first plotted (Figure 9) with all 14 points marked. The mean point is next shown and the 'best fit' or regression line drawn *by eye* to pass through it. Most points lie quite close to this 'best fit' line: thus the statement is correct. It is possible to quote an approximate rate of decrease in temperature as the latitude increases: about 8°C for every 10° of latitude. However,

there are three points—Vancouver, Cochrane and Fort Chimo—that do not lie too close to the regression line. As temperature in these three cases seems to be affected by other factors a further explanation must be looked for. Vancouver and Fort Chimo are coastal stations, which leads to 2.

2. *Temperature range is affected by distance from the ocean.* Compared with land surfaces, oceans have a slower summer rise of temperature, because the sun's rays penetrate deeply into water, while currents allow deep mixing. However, the oceans also cool slowly; heat remains well into the winter season.

le 3   Annual temperature range and distance from the sea

matic ion	Position Lat. °N	Long. °W	Distance from sea (km)	Annual temperature range °C
cago	42	88	1000	28
onton	54	114	900	31
ouis	38	91	900	27
nipeg	50	97	800	38
Smith	60	113	800	41
ahoma	37	97	700	24
e	44	116	600	24
onto	44	80	600	27
treal	45	74	500	31
on	50	118	400	23
ningham	31	87	300	25
enix	33	112	300	20
arane	49	82	250	36
amento	38	122	100	15
Orleans	30	90	50	16
n point			500	27

Exercise 1

From Table 3 make your own graph. Through the mean point draw in the regression line 'by eye' (*hint:* it should rise 2°C for every 100 km moved inland).
a) Do the points lie close to this line?
b) Suggest a reason why the temperature range is 'off line' at (*i*) Chicago (*hint:* Lake Michigan), (*ii*) Cochrane (*hint:* lowest temperature of nearest sea inlet).
c) Does statement 2 appear to be acceptable? Why?

3. *Temperatures at coastal stations are affected by ocean currents.*

Table 4   Latitude and ocean currents

Climatic Station	Position Lat. °N	Long. °W	Mean annual temperature
Cold currents			
St John's	47	53	4
Fort Chimo	58	68	−8
Frobisher Bay	64	68	−12
San Francisco	36	123	13
San Diego	33	117	16
Mean point	48		3
Warm currents			
Point Barrow	72	156	−12
Boston	43	71	10
Miami	26	81	23
Juneau	57	134	6
Vancouver	49	123	11
New Orleans	30	90	20
Mean point	46		10

Exercise 2

Draw the five 'cold current' stations on a graph like Figure 9. Put in the regression line 'by eye'.
a) Does the line form a close fit with the points? On the same graph, using a different colour, plot the six 'warm current stations'. Draw in another regression line 'by eye'.
b) Is it a close fit with the points?
c) From Figure 8 name two currents with which each regression line is associated.
d) Do you think that statement 3 is acceptable? Explain why.

Question

Figure 8 and the account

1. Write a short account of temperature variations in North America.

PRECIPITATION AND ITS CAUSES

Regional variations in precipitation (rain, snow, sleet, hail, etc.) are just as marked as those in temperature. Since the ranges of the Western Cordillera lie across the path of moisture-laden air coming from the Pacific Ocean, heavy relief precipitation occurs on the westward facing slopes, reaching well over 200 cm annually on northern parts of the coastline. On descending the eastern slopes of each mountain range the moving air tends to warm up, absorbing moisture and giving comparatively dry conditions (rain shadow effect).

Many depressions or 'lows' seem to be formed where upper-airstreams swirl down on to the eastern foothills of the Rockies. Once formed, the depressions increase in strength and cross to the Atlantic side of the continent, often via the St Lawrence Valley. In winter another depression track runs from the Gulf of Mexico north-eastwards to affect the whole eastern coastal region. Heavy precipitation occurs, often in the form of snow, in the north-eastern USA and eastern Canada.

In summer, warm, moist air persistently flows from

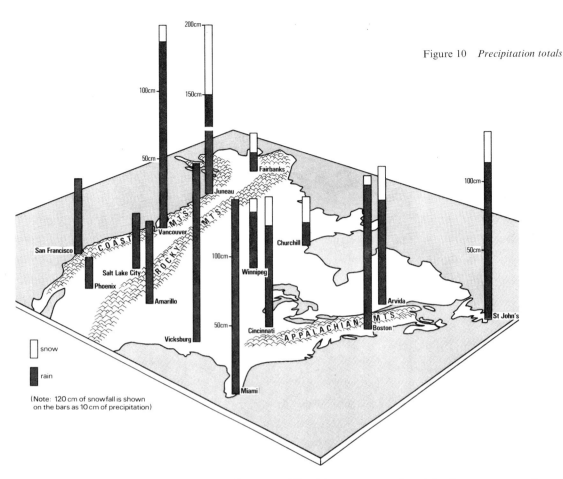

Figure 10 *Precipitation totals*

(Note: 120 cm of snowfall is shown on the bars as 10 cm of precipitation)

snow

rain

the Gulf of Mexico to the Central Lowlands, creating unpleasantly 'sticky' conditions sometimes as far north as Canada. The lower layers of this humid air mass are heated by contact with the land surface and rise upwards in strong convection currents. As cooling takes place, clouds build up, thunder and lightning develop and heavy downpours result. While the moist air continues to move in, convectional rainfall occurs each day. An extreme type of convectional storm is the short-lived, but extremely destructive tornado.

The driest areas are found in the extreme north and south-west of the continent. Over much of the Arctic region the long winter season is dominated by a high pressure system of cold subsiding air, which edges southwards over much of the Central Lowlands. Moist air from the Pacific is pushed away by the high pressure system and snowfall amounts are small. Much further south a settling mass of tropical air similarly keeps out low pressure systems, helping to form the extensive deserts and semi-arid areas that characterise the valleys and plateaus of the south-western USA.

Questions

The account and general

1. Draw simple diagrams to illustrate the causes of:
   a) relief rainfall in western Canada;
   b) convection rainfall in south-eastern USA.

Figure 10 and the account

2. *a)* Trace the outline of the continent from the map.
   b) (*i*) Mark with X all those towns which have at least 90 cm total precipitation. (*ii*) Draw a line to enclose the places marked X in the eastern part of the continent. Do the same for the western coast.

c) Attempt to explain why the western area marked is smaller that the eastern.

3. *a)* On an outline of the continent mark with an *S* all those towns which record 10 cm or more of precipitation falling as snow.
   b) Using the information on Figure 10, work out how deep the snow will lie on the ground (assuming none melts) at: (*i*) Winnipeg, (*ii*) St John's and (*iii*) Juneau.
   c) Explain why the highest snowfall totals occur near the edges of the continent: (*i*) in the coastal mountains of Alaska, and (*ii*) on high ground in eastern Canada.

Natural vegetation

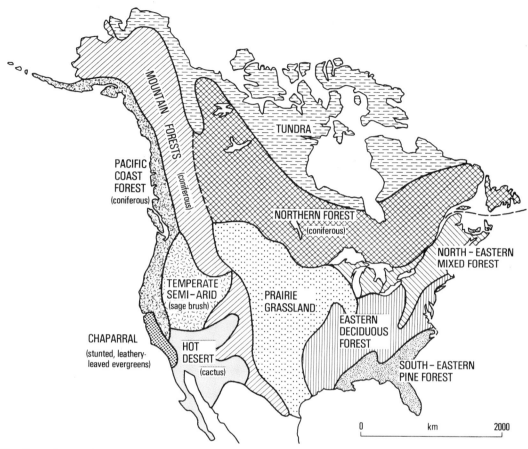

Figure 11 *Natural vegetation*

SOME NATURAL SYSTEMS OF PLANTS, SOILS AND CLIMATE (ECOSYSTEMS)

Very few areas of North America have not been affected in some way by human occupation and little 'natural' vegetation remains. However, in the more rugged north and west the imprint of people is less marked and areas of wilderness or wildscape may still be seen, often set aside as National Parks.

FORESTS

Forests still cover a greater area than any other kind of vegetation in North America, but there are many types of trees according to the different natural factors at work.

The Northern Forest consists of small-sized pines, spruces and firs. It stretches in a virtually continuous belt across the whole width of Canada. During the long winters the frozen ground creates 'drought' conditions which the evergreen conifers survive by becoming dormant. Melting snow washes nutrients downwards from the top layers, resulting in poor soils known as *podsols*. However, the trees are undemanding and resume their slow growth as soon as the temperature rises above 5°C.

Along the Pacific coast, imposing stands of coniferous trees, reaching over 65 metres in height, grow in the warm, moist climate. In California several remaining stands of redwoods are protected because of their great age and beauty. The Sierra redwood (*Sequoia gigantea*) is found in the Sierra Nevada at heights varying from 900 to 2700 metres. Some of these trees are known to be over

17

Plate 5 *Coast redwoods, Muir Woods, California*

3000 years old, their diameters at the base measure up to 11 metres and they are as much as 90 metres high. The more slender Coast redwood (*Sequoia sempervirens*) survives a mere 2000 years but is even loftier than its relative; the tallest specimen now known is 112 metres in height.

Questions

The account and general

1. *a*) Make a short comparison of tree size, speed of growth and visual attractiveness of the Northern and Pacific Coast forests.
   b) Attempt an explanation of the differences noted.

The account and Plate 5

2. Why was the redwood so commercially attractive to the early lumbermen?

The account and general

3. *a*) How can the great age of the redwoods be determined?
   b) Approximately how old were today's mature Sierra redwoods when, (*i*) Jesus Christ was born, and (*ii*) the Battle of Hastings was fought?

Plate 6

4. *a*) Identify the small tree in front of the man (*hint:* it is common in Britain).
   b) List some of the characteristics of the maple tree.
   c) Comment on the general nature of the woodland.

Plate 7

5. *a*) Draw a simple annotated sketch of the view shown to include the following features: (*i*) coniferous trees on the valley floor; (*ii*) forested slopes of poorer trees up to the tree line; (*iii*) the unforested higher slopes.
   b) Attempt to explain the distribution of the trees (*hint:* position, temperature, soil).

Figure 12 *Comparitive heights of Nelson's Column and Coast redwood*

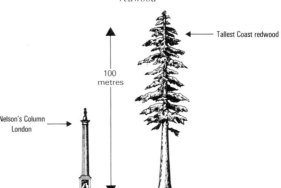

Plate 6 *A maple forest*

Plate 7 *Montana Rockies*

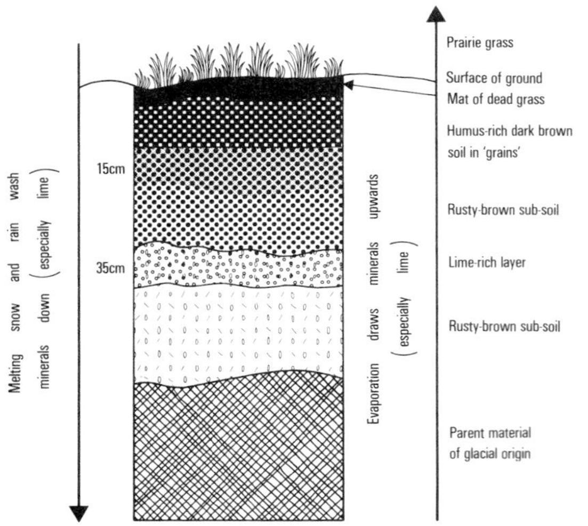
Prairie grass
Surface of ground
Mat of dead grass
Humus-rich dark brown soil in 'grains'
Rusty-brown sub-soil
Lime-rich layer
Rusty-brown sub-soil
Parent material of glacial origin
15cm
35cm
Melting snow and rain wash minerals down (especially lime)
Evaporation draws minerals upwards (especially lime)

Figure 13 *Prairie soil profile*

OTHER ECOSYSTEMS

The lowland heart of the continent was once a huge prairie grassland. The natural balance of climate, soil and plant growth have made it ideal for arable farming (Fig. 13).

The cold tundra region which stretches across the whole of the north of the continent has a growing season of just a few weeks, allowing only mosses, lichens and stunted trees to grow. There is hardly any true soil and the surface is much disturbed by frost action and becomes waterlogged in the summer. For most of the year the ground is snow-covered and, below a shallow surface layer, is permanently frozen (permafrost).

In the south-western United States there are many very warm or even hot regions with little rainfall. However, some plants, especially cacti, are well adapted to this severe desert environment. A spectacular example of such an adjustment is the Saguaro cactus. Following a soaking rain, often in the form of thunderstorms, the Saguaro's shallow, wide-spread root system draws up immense quantities of water, which are absorbed by sponge-like tissues. A mature plant, weighing from 6 to 10 tonnes, may take up as much as a tonne of water. During extended droughts, the Saguaro gradually uses its stored water, shrinking in girth and decreasing in weight. The Saguaro is so successful that it may live for 200 years.

Questions

Figure 13 and the account

1. *a*) Explain briefly how the prairie soil is formed.
   b) Why is this soil so valuable for crop growing?

Figure 13 and the account

2. *a*) Suggest why the tundra soil contains few fragments of humus.
   b) (*i*) Why is melting snow unable to drain freely through the ground? (*ii*) Describe the resulting surface conditions during the brief summer season.
   c) How is the settling mass of air (high pressure) assisted by the cold ground surface in winter?

Plate 8, the account and general

3. *a*) (*i*) Estimate the height of the cactus shown. (*ii*) Suggest why the cactus has spines instead of leaves.
   b) Smaller cacti are often kept as house plants. In your home, how closely would the conditions resemble the plant's natural environment?

General

4. Why have some ecosystems in North America been far more affected by people than others?

Plate 8 *A Saguaro cactus, Arizona desert*

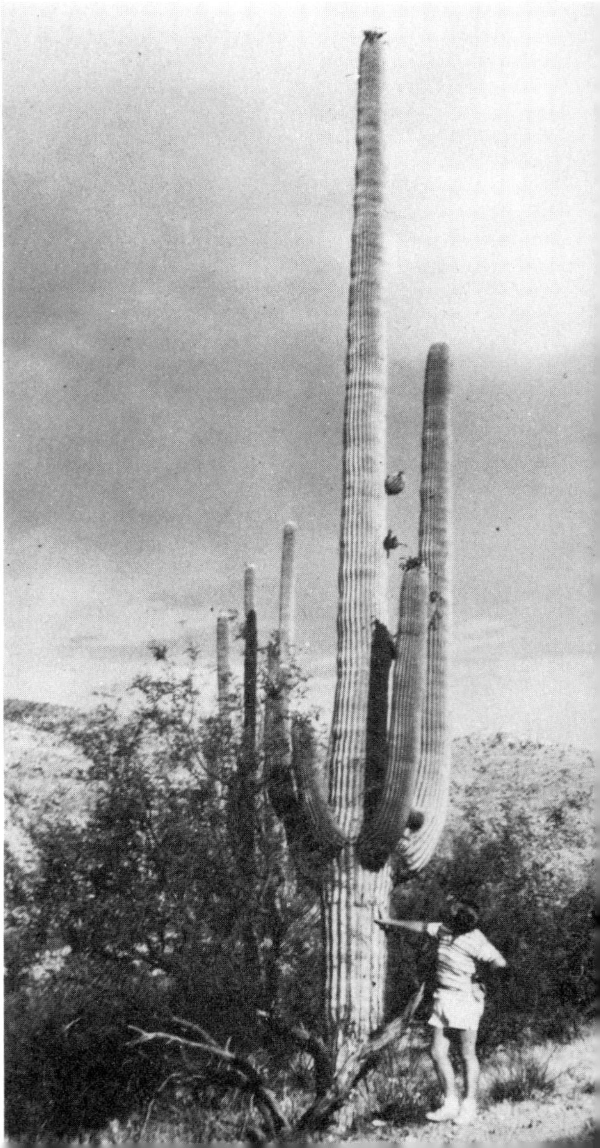

The Continental Framework 2: Settlement and Population

Discovery and colonisation

North America was first settled by groups of Mongolian nomads who, about 30 000 years ago, crossed from Asia to Alaska by land bridge before the Bering Strait was formed. These people filtered eastward and southward across the continent and eventually spread to Central and South America, where certain tribes developed impressive civilisations. Their only likely visitors were a group of Norsemen, who in the tenth century established a short-lived colony which they called 'Vinland', probably in present-day Newfoundland.

In 1492 the continent was 'discovered' by Christopher Columbus, an Italian navigator in the service of Spain. Sailing westward in search of a new trade route to Asia, he made landfall in the Bahamas and encountered the native people, who he called 'Indians' in the mistaken belief that he had come ashore in the East Indies. After Columbus other European explorers reached the mainland; one of these, Amerigo Vespucci, gave his name to the whole of the New World.

During the next 200 years many different European groups established settlements in North America, but three nations dominated the colonisation of the continent—Spain, France and Britain.

THE SPANISH were first on the scene, but after their explorations of the area between Texas and California failed to yield the hoped-for plunder they concentrated their interests on the wealthier lands to the south. However, Spain's territorial claims in North America were maintained by a thin scattering of mission and farming settlements.

THE FRENCH explored the St Lawrence River in 1535 and encountered the Algonquin Indians, whose word *kanata*, meaning 'settlement of huts', was mistaken for the name of the country. The French founded Quebec in 1608 and established this part of Canada—New France—as their main area of settlement. From this base they explored through the Great Lakes region then down the entire length of the Mississippi River, laying claim to a huge

Plate 9   *Mayan pyramid, Yucatan Peninsula*

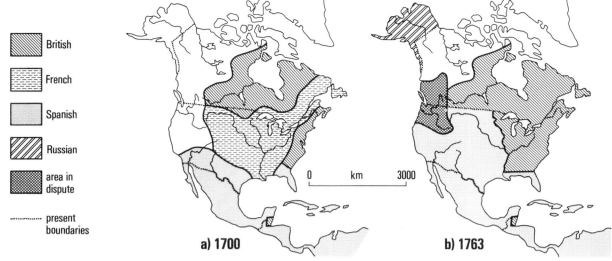

British

French

Spanish

Russian

area in dispute

present boundaries

a) 1700

b) 1763

0 km 3000

Figure 14 *European claims to North America*

territory which they called 'Louisiana'. The present-day Louisiana State is only a small part of that territory.

THE BRITISH were the last to arrive, settling along the Atlantic coast. Hemmed in by the Appalachian mountain range, they were less thinly spread than the Spanish and French. From small beginnings at Jamestown, Virginia (1607) and Plymouth, Massachusetts (1620) the settlements grew in number, size and strength. By the middle of the eighteenth century there were thirteen thriving colonies in America. British influence in Canada was first established by the Hudson's Bay Company (formed in 1670) whose fur-trading territories lay to the north of the area settled by the French. In addition, small British

settlements had taken root along Canada's Atlantic coastline.

The rivalries amongst the three colonial powers were intense. In particular, the British colonists were in continual conflict with the French and their Indian allies. After a series of wars culminating in the British capture of Quebec, the French empire in North America collapsed. In 1763 Canada and all French territory east of the Mississippi passed to Britain while French claims west of the river were ceded to Britain's ally, Spain. It was from this expanded British sphere of influence that two new nations, the United States and Canada, were to emerge, although in very different ways.

Questions

Plate 9, an atlas, the account and general

1. *a*) (*i*) In which country is the Yucatan Peninsula? (*ii*) Name another group of Indian people who established a civilisation in South America.
   b) Why were the Spanish more interested in other parts of the New World rather than in North America?

The account and general

2. Why were the following places given these names: (*i*) Louisiana, (*ii*) Jamestown, (*ii*) Plymouth (Massachusetts)?

Figure 14 and an atlas

3. List the names of major US cities (three in each case) which show:
   (*i*) British influence east of the Appalachians;
   (*ii*) French influence west of the Appalachians;
   (*iii*) Spanish influence in the south-west.

Figure 14 and general

4. Name two North American colonies established by other European nations after 1492 (*hints:* (*i*) the Czar sold it to the USA in 1867; (*ii*) it was re-named New York).

Figure 14, the account and an atlas

5. *a*) Which European nation lost most territory in North America between 1700 and 1763?
   b) Name the small islands which are the last vestiges of that nation's North American possessions (*hint:* south coast of Newfoundland).

The emergence of two nations

THE GROWTH OF THE UNITED STATES AND ITS CAPITAL CITY

On 4 July 1776 the leaders of the thirteen existing American colonies met in Philadelphia to sign the 'Declaration of Independence' from British rule. These colonies thus became the first 'United States of America'. A federal republic was established, in which the individual states kept many of their powers but surrendered others to a national government (Congress) and a president, both elected by all the American people.

In the nineteenth century the United States believed it was the nation's 'Manifest Destiny' to expand westward, acquiring and settling new territories. When the population of a territory reached 60 000 it was normally granted statehood, and by 1912 all such areas on the US mainland had become fully-fledged states. Alaska was purchased from Russia in 1867, and the Hawaiian Islands became an American possession in 1898. With the granting of

Figure 15   *Territorial growth of the USA and Canada*

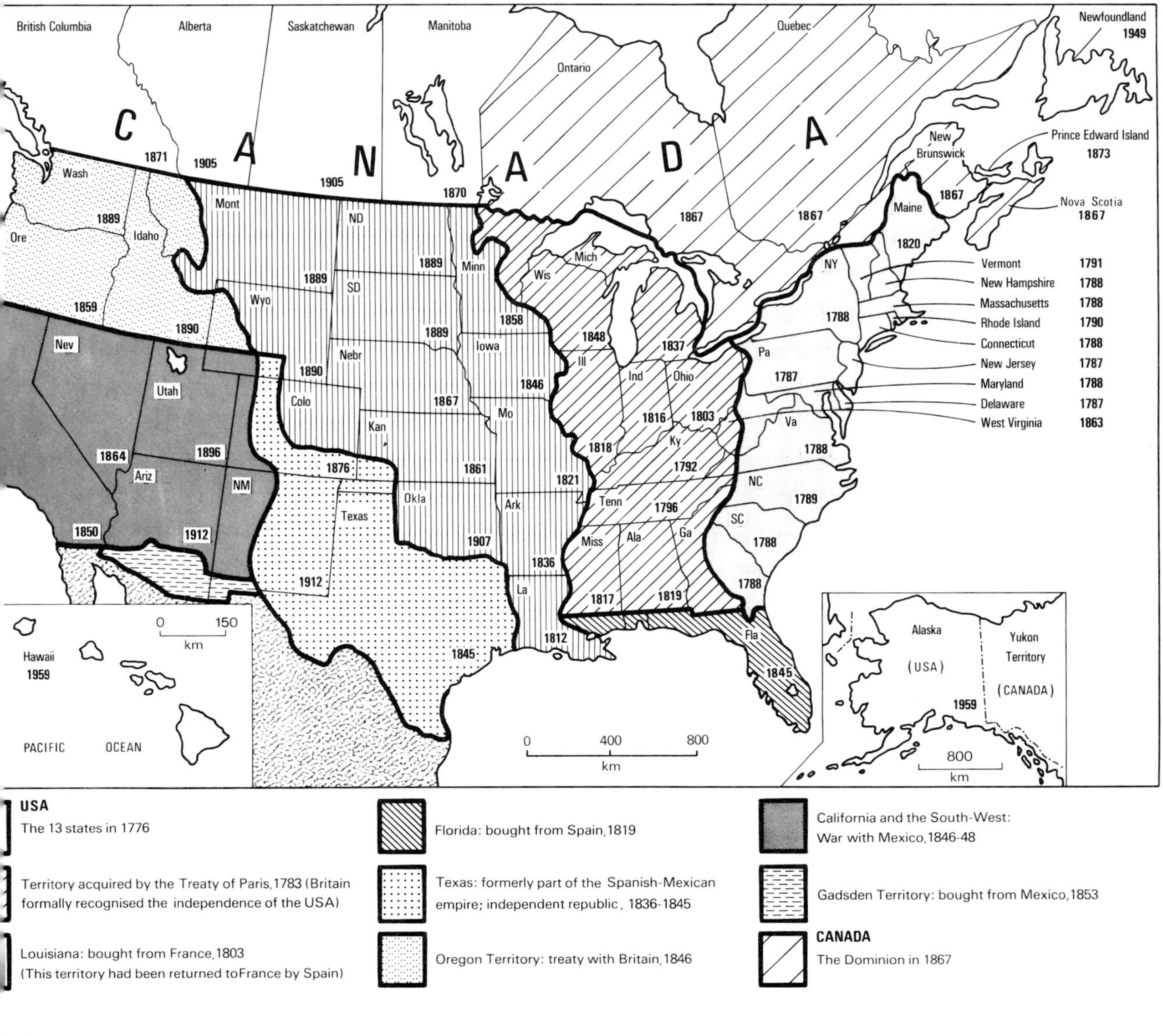

USA
The 13 states in 1776

Territory acquired by the Treaty of Paris, 1783 (Britain formally recognised the independence of the USA)

Louisiana: bought from France, 1803
(This territory had been returned to France by Spain)

Florida: bought from Spain, 1819

Texas: formerly part of the Spanish-Mexican empire; independent republic, 1836-1845

Oregon Territory: treaty with Britain, 1846

California and the South-West:
War with Mexico, 1846-48

Gadsden Territory: bought from Mexico, 1853

CANADA
The Dominion in 1867

statehood to these two territories the number of states rose to 50 and the present national area was complete.

In general the federal system has worked to the advantage of all Americans, but sometimes the policies of federal and state governments have been in serious conflict. In 1860, for example, the Southern states left the Union over the issue of slavery. In the Civil War that followed, more than 600 000 Americans died. The North won the war and the Union was re-established. However, each of the 50 states continued to control many of its own affairs.

WASHINGTON DC

The federal capital was established in 1800 in a specially designated area, the District of Columbia (DC). Careful consideration was given to the exact location of the new capital and to the planning of its streets and public buildings. Up to 1974 the whole of Washington DC was controlled by the federal government but it is now run by an elected mayor and council like other American cities. However, the federal government has retained control over the National Capital Service Area, the historic city centre which attracts some 20 million tourists every year (more than anywhere else in the USA).

Questions

General knowledge

1. *a*) What events led up to the Declaration of Independence?
   b) (*i*) What action did Britain take after the Declaration of Independence, and (*ii*) what was the outcome?
2. *a*) (*i*) How many stars and stripes appeared on the first American national flag? (*ii*) What did they represent?
   b) Which part of the flag's design was continually changing until 1959, and why?

The account and general

3. The United States is a federal republic.
   a) Explain briefly what this means.
   b) Name one other federal republic elsewhere in the world.
4. *E pluribus unum* is the national motto of the USA.
   a) What does it mean?
   b) Explain why the motto is appropriate.
5. *a*) Why was the American capital named Washington?
   b) Why is the District of Columbia not part of any state?
   c) Name the two states which originally gave up land for the District of Columbia.
6. Explain why:
   a) Washington was originally chosen as the site of the federal capital;
   b) Washington is poorly situated to serve as the nation's capital nowadays.

Plate 10   *Aerial view of Washington*

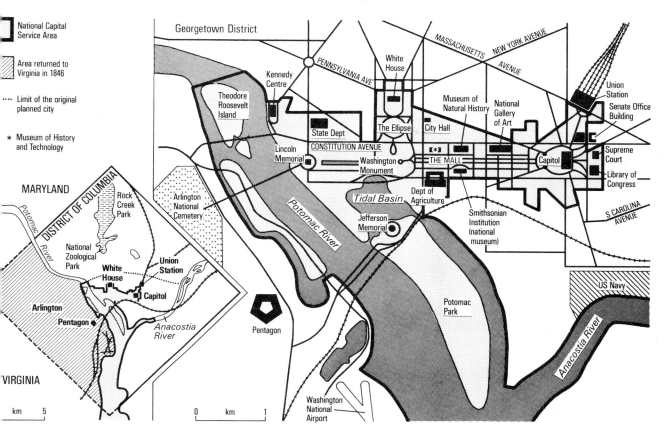

Figure 16   *Washington, DC, capital of the USA*

Plate 10, Figure 16 and the account

7. *a)* From where was the photograph taken?
   b) Identify the buildings labelled A, B and C.
8. *a)* Name the buildings which house (*i*) the President,
   (*ii*) Congress, (*iii*) the Department of Defence.

b) List the names of five presidents commemorated in Washington.
9. *a)* Describe the layout of Washington.
   b) How, and why, does it contrast with most other capital cities?

THE GROWTH OF CANADA AND ITS CAPITAL CITY

In contrast to the American colonies, Canada remained under British control until 1867 when the first four provinces joined together to become the self-governing Dominion of Canada. The new nation adopted the federal system of government but retained links with Britain through the Crown. Thus present-day Canada is both a monarchy and a senior member of the Commonwealth.

Canada's territorial growth followed the American pattern of pushing westward. Indeed, remote British Columbia agreed to unite with the eastern provinces only on the understanding that a railway (the Canadian Pacific) would be built to link the two areas. By 1905 the present union of all the provinces was complete, except for Newfoundland which for some time remained a separate, self-governing dominion. The extensive territories of northern Canada, however, have not yet attained full province status and are controlled directly by the federal government.

Although there are sometimes tensions between the federal government and the various provinces (especially French-speaking Quebec), the advantages of belonging to a unified Canada seem to outweigh the drawbacks.

OTTAWA

Like Washington, the site of Canada's capital city had to be chosen carefully. Ottawa was an obscure pioneer settlement when it was selected as capital by Queen Victoria in 1867, despite the rival claims of the much larger Kingston and Toronto (Ontario province), and Quebec City and Montreal (Quebec province). Today, Ottawa is the centre of an attractive National Capital Region.

Plate 11   *Stamp featuring the Parliament Building, Ottawa*

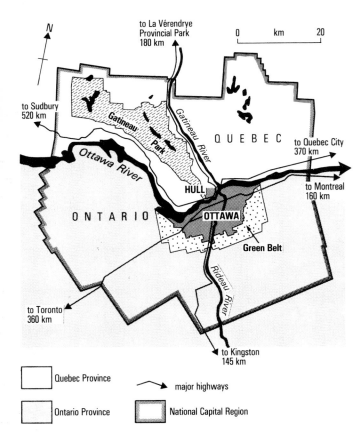

Figure 17   *Ottawa, capital of Canada*

Questions

Figure 17, an atlas and general

1. *a*) Name the four founder provinces of the Dominion of Canada.
   b) In what ways did the expansion of Canada: (*i*) imitate, and (*ii*) differ from that of the USA?
2. *a*) In what year did Newfoundland become a province of Canada?
   b) Suggest why Newfoundland joined so much later than the other provinces (*hint:* position).
   c) Name the mainland area which forms part of Newfoundland province.
3. *A mari usque ad mare* is Canada's national motto.
   a) What does it mean?
   b) Why is it appropriate?
4. *a*) Why do you think that little-known Ottawa was chosen as the federal capital in 1867?
   b) (*i*) What advantages were there in Ottawa's position in 1867? (*ii*) Is this still advantageous? Why?

Figure 17

5. *a*) Name the provinces in which the National Capital Region lies.
   b) Name: (*i*) the principal river on which Ottawa stands and (*ii*) the town on the opposite bank.

Plate 11

6. Identify: (*i*) three features which indicate British, French and American influences in Canada; (*ii*) the emblem that is distinctively Canadian.

Atlas and general

7. *a*) List some of the advantages and disadvantages of having the 49th parallel as the boundary between the United States and Canada.
   b) Why are the disadvantages less important than those of similar boundaries elsewhere?

The United States : a nation of immigrants

One definition of an American is 'someone who came from somewhere else'—even the Indians and Eskimos were originally immigrants. In 1776 the population of the thirteen colonies totalled about 2·5 million. The great majority were descendants of settlers from the British Isles—although from early colonial times people brought from Africa as slaves had formed a significant element in the population.

The chances of a present-day American being of wholly British origin are no more than twelve per cent. The American population began to lose its British basis as long ago as the 1840s, when a trickle of immigration from continental Europe swelled to a tidal wave between 1880 and the First World War. By 1924, when the 'open door' entry policy ended, about a third of the total US population were first and second generation European immigrants. Like the British, these immigrants brought with them their names, languages, religions, national customs and, not least, their food and drink. Although some groups were more easily integrated than others, they all contributed to the cultural diversity of the present-day United States.

Table 5   The American people

	Estimated number	Percentage of the total population
Whites	186 225 000	86·81
Blacks	24 763 000	11·51
Others	3 661 000	1·7
Total	214 649 000	100·0

(US Abstract of Statistics, 1977)

Plate 12   Billboard of Pledge of Allegiance

Questions

Figure 18 and general

1. In what year did the USA population pass: (*i*) the 50 million mark, (*ii*) the 100 million mark?
2. *a*) Approximately how many immigrants entered the United States between 1820 and 1970?
   b) Why is the USA often described as a 'melting pot' of peoples?
3. Which countries supplied most immigrants: (*i*) in the nineteenth century, (*ii*) in the twentieth century? Name two countries in each case.

Plate 13   *Russian immigrant ship approaching New York, 1892*

4. *a*) Which two factors have constantly encouraged migration from Europe to the USA?
   b) Name two special factors which attracted people to the USA.

Plate 12 and the account

5. *a*) Why do you think the daily Pledge of Allegiance takes the place of a religious assembly in American schools?

b) Why did immigrant children overcome the language problem more quickly than their parents?

Table 5

6. *a*) Suggest what peoples are included in 'Others'.
   b) Construct a bar graph to show the population figures.
   c) Comment on the general population structure.

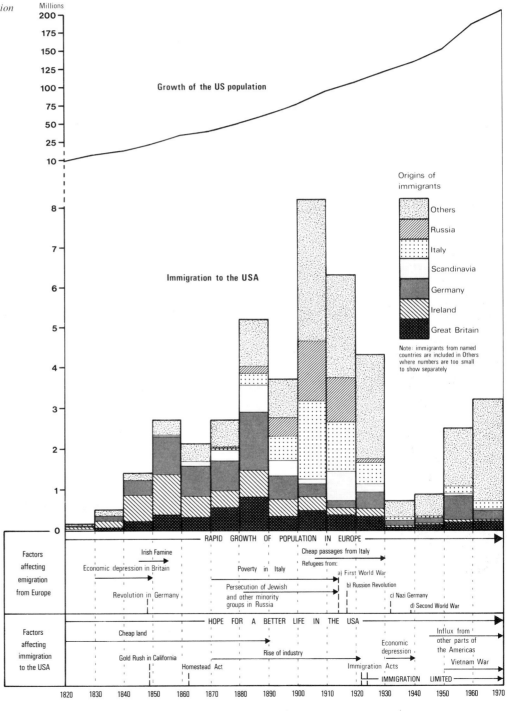

Figure 18 *Immigration and the growth of population in the USA, 1820–1970*

Wealth and poverty in the USA

The United States is the richest nation in the world. With impressive drive, efficiency and inventiveness the American people have successfully exploited their country's generous endowment of natural resources. As a result, by almost any measure of national or personal wealth, the United States comes top or near the top of the world 'league table'.

The majority of Americans enjoy a high standard of living and much of the nation's manufacturing industry is geared to the demands of a great 'consumer society'. Indeed, many Americans buy as 'necessities' goods which would be regarded as luxuries in almost any other part of the world. The emphasis is on comfort, convenience and labour-saving devices, especially in the home. Some idea of the affluent American life-style can be gained from Table 7.

Unfortunately, the great wealth of the United States is unevenly distributed by race and by region. Indeed millions of US citizens are officially classified as 'poor' and receive social security payments from the government.

Table 6 World wealth and poverty: some contrasts

Position in 'League Table'	Country	*GNP per head (£s)	Population (millions)
1	Kuwait	8440	1
2	Switzerland	4670	6
3	Sweden	4530	8
4	USA	3960	214
5	Canada	3850	23
10	France	3310	53
21	UK	2100	56
26	USSR	1420	254
47	Mexico	580	60
80	China	210	823
94	Kenya	120	13
107	India	80	608
122	Bangladesh	50	79

*The total annual value of a country's goods and services, divided by its total population.

(*World Bank Atlas*, 1977)

Table 7 Ownership of consumer durable goods
(Figures are percentages of American households possessing the items listed.)

Cars		Television sets		Washing machine	Hot-air clothes dryer	Refrigerator	Freezer	Dish-washer	Air-conditioner
one	two or more	black & white	colour						
50	34	99·9	78	73	59	99·8	44	40	54

(US Abstract of Statistics, 1977)

While poverty in the USA is usually not comparable with the kind of poverty found in many Third World countries (see Table 6), it is important enough to receive a great deal of official action. Much progress has recently been made, but poverty continues to be a major problem in the ghettos of northern cities and in the rural South. In both areas it is usually the black person who fares worst.

Table 8 Poverty* in the United States (millions of people)

	1959		1976	
	Total	Below the poverty line	Total	Below the poverty line
Whites	158·8	28·5	186·2	16·7
Non-whites	20·5	11·0	28·4	8·3
Totals	179·3	39·5	214·6	25·0

*In 1976 the official 'poverty line' was set at an income of approximately £3400 for a family of four.
(US Abstract of Statistics, 1977)

Questions

Table 6 and general

1. 'The United States is the richest country in the world.' Explain why this statement is correct despite the USA's position in the league table. (*hint*: population figures)

2. Elaborate the statement that 'poverty in the USA is usually not comparable with the kind of poverty found in many Third World countries'.

Table 7

3. a) Name one item, often regarded as a necessity in many parts of the USA, for which there is never likely to be much demand in British homes. Explain why not. (*hint*: climate)

   b) Try to compile similar information about ownership of consumer goods in Britain. Compare your findings with Table 7.

Table 8

3. a) Construct bar graphs to illustrate the statistics.

   b) Comment on the trends revealed.

   c) Would the American definition of poverty be regarded as valid in Britain? Give your reasons.

Canada's population: a summary

Because of the many similarities with its neighbour, the population of Canada is presented in diagrammatic form.

Questions

Figure 19

1. *a)* Copy the layout of Figure 19, making equal widths of columns. Then draw accurately the height of each of the four 'boxes', using the statistics provided.
   b) Discuss the population changes shown in the diagram.

Figure 20 an atlas and general

2. *a)* What was the total Canadian population in 1971?
   b) (*i*) What common origins are shared by the first eight listed peoples? (*ii*) Commonwealth countries in the Caribbean area have recently become an important source of immigrants in 'Others'. Name three such countries.
3. *a)* Name (*i*) two languages which are spoken by the largest numbers of Canadians, and (*ii*) two which have existed longest in Canada.
   b) The phrase 'two founding peoples' is often applied to Canada. Is it appropriate? Give your reasons.

Figure 20, Figure 21 and general

4. *a)* In which region is the population mainly of French origin?
   b) (*i*) Which parts of Canada are omitted from Figure 21? (*ii*) What group of people, named in Figure 20, is mostly found in this area?

Figure 21 and an atlas

5. Briefly describe the distribution of Canada's: (*i*) total population, and (*ii*) urban population.

Figure 21   *Distribution of Canada's population*

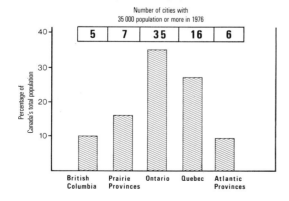

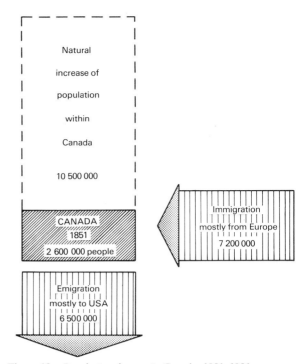

Figure 19   *Population changes in Canada, 1851–1951*

Figure 20   *Origins of Canada's population (1971 Census)*

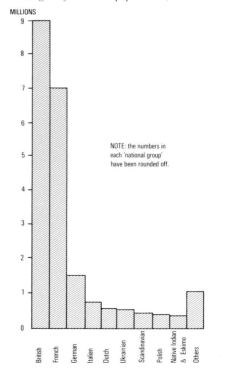

NOTE: the numbers in each 'national group' have been rounded off.

New England

Introduction

Despite its generally unpromising environment, New England offered a fresh start to the Pilgrim Fathers and other pioneer settlers from 'Old England'. These colonists built close-knit, self-sufficient communities, held together by a strong religious faith and a remarkable capacity to make the best use of the limited resources of the forests, streams and sea.

By 1776 the people of New England had become the political, economic and cultural leaders of the American colonies, a position challenged only by Virginians. Indeed, the influence of New Englanders in shaping the nation has been out of all proportion to their numbers. As the United States expanded westward many 'Yankees', a term originally applied to New Englanders, left their home region in

Figure 22 *New England: physical background and products*

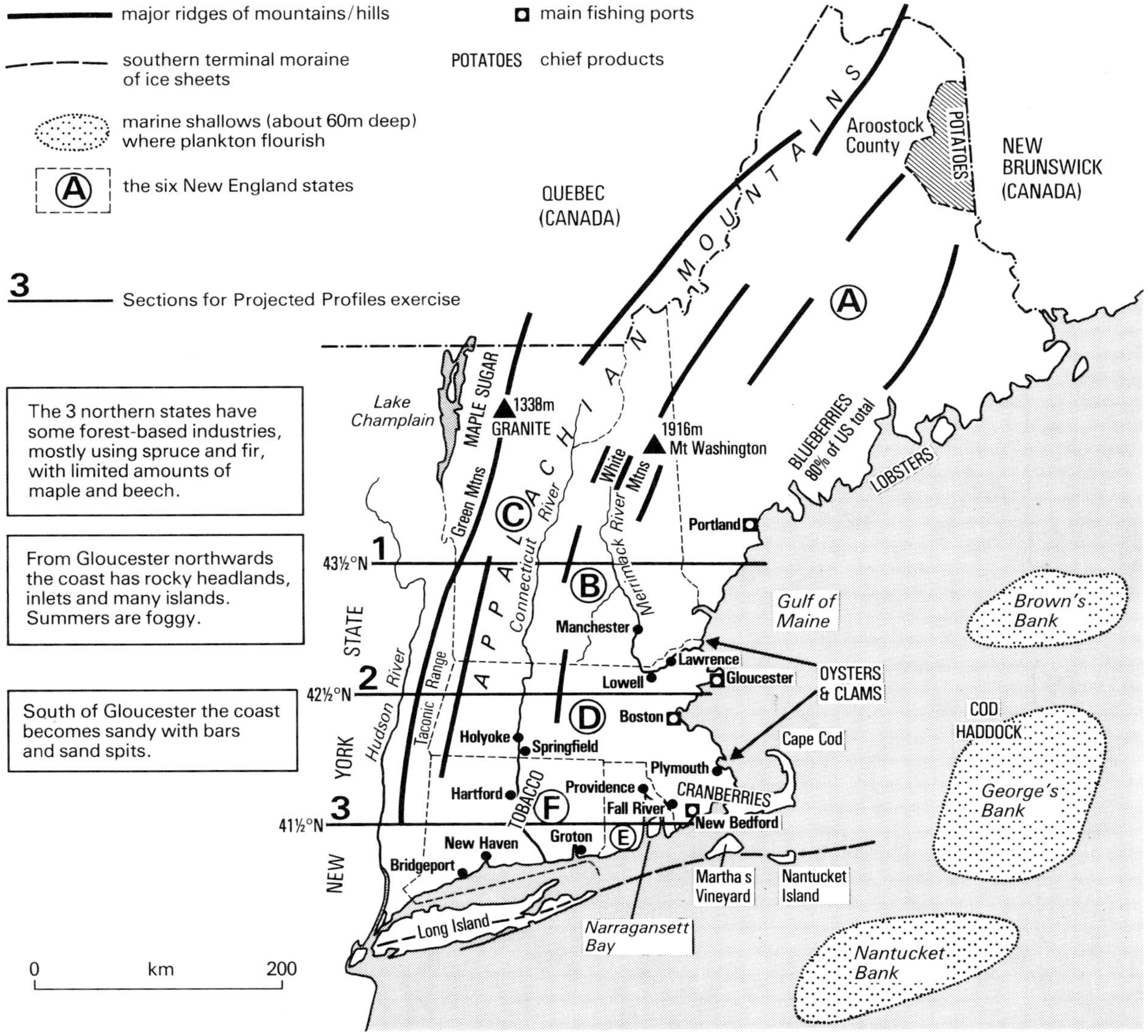

Key:
- ▬▬▬ major ridges of mountains/hills
- ▬ ▬ ▬ southern terminal moraine of ice sheets
- marine shallows (about 60m deep) where plankton flourish
- (A) the six New England states
- □ main fishing ports
- POTATOES chief products
- **3** ▬▬ Sections for Projected Profiles exercise

The 3 northern states have some forest-based industries, mostly using spruce and fir, with limited amounts of maple and beech.

From Gloucester northwards the coast has rocky headlands, inlets and many islands. Summers are foggy.

South of Gloucester the coast becomes sandy with bars and sand spits.

QUEBEC (CANADA)

Aroostock County — POTATOES

NEW BRUNSWICK (CANADA)

APPALACHIAN MOUNTAINS

Lake Champlain

MAPLE SUGAR

Green Mtns

▲1338m GRANITE

White River Mtns

▲1916m Mt Washington

Connecticut River

Merrimack River

BLUEBERRIES 80% of US total

LOBSTERS

(A)

(C)

Portland □

43½°N **1**

(B)

Manchester

Gulf of Maine

Brown's Bank

NEW YORK STATE

Hudson River

Taconic Range

Lawrence

Lowell

Gloucester □

OYSTERS & CLAMS

42½°N **2**

(D) Boston □

Holyoke ● Springfield

COD HADDOCK

Cape Cod

Hartford ●

TOBACCO

Providence ●

(F)

Fall River ●

CRANBERRIES

New Bedford

George's Bank

41½°N **3**

New Haven ●

Groton ●

(E)

Bridgeport ●

Martha's Vineyard

Nantucket Island

Long Island

Narragansett Bay

Nantucket Bank

0   km   200

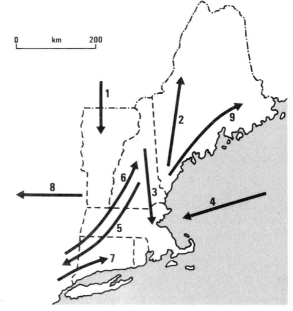

search of better agricultural land and wider opportunities. They carried with them the names of their original towns, and there are now 15 Portlands, 16 Plymouths and 23 Salems scattered across the nation. At the same time, Europeans, as well as Canadians from regions immediately to the north, continued to be attracted to New England.

By 1900 New England's early economic lead had been lost as the region's factories and products became obsolete, causing acute unemployment in some areas. Fortunately the second half of the twentieth century has seen a revival of New England's fortunes, due mainly to the rise of technology-based industries in the south of the region and the development of leisure areas in the north. Special attractions include the rugged coastline of Maine in summer, the mountains for winter skiing, and the deciduous woodlands during the fall (autumn) when they become a spectacular blaze of orange, scarlet and crimson.

Figure 23   *New England: people on the move*

Questions

Figure 22 and an atlas

1. Describe in some detail the location of New England.
2. *a*) Identify the New England states, numbered A to F on the map.
   b) Which state (*i*) has no coastline, and (*ii*) is the smallest in the USA?

Table 9   New England States: area and population

State	Area (km^2)	Population (1976)
Connecticut	12 973	3 117 000
Maine	86 027	1 070 000
Massachusetts	21 386	5 809 000
New Hampshire	24 097	822 000
Rhode Island	3 144	927 000
Vermond	24 887	476 000
England	130 360	46 450 000

Table 9

3. *a*) What is New England's total (*i*) area, and (*ii*) population?
   b) How does each compare with the corresponding figure for 'Old England'?
   c) Name the state which is the most populous.
   d) What is remarkable about the populations of the largest and smallest states (by area)?

Figure 23, the account and general

4. Match up the following movements with the numbered arrows shown on Figure 23:
   a) out-migration westwards;
   b) influx of French-Canadians;
   c) visitors (from urban centres) to vacation homes;
   d) employment attraction of (*i*) Boston, (*ii*) New York, to rural New Englanders;
   e) spread of urbanisation from New York;
   f) immigration from Europe.

Physical background

New England has few coastal plains or major river valleys and those that do exist are often littered with glacial boulders and sands. Much of the region lies between 100 and 300 metres above sea level and has quite a rugged landscape. In the west and north the ridges and peaks of the Appalachians form a mountainous area, with Mt Washington rising to almost 2000 metres. The upstanding portions are all that now remain of an ancient fold mountain system, whose granite, marble and slate provide landforms that are highly resistant to erosion and weathering. However, ice sheets of the last million years affected the region considerably; hilltops were planed off while coastal areas were covered with organic material and sediment carried by meltwater streams.

Climatically New England is fairly uniform. Winters are long and severe, summers short and warm. Low pressure systems cross the region at all seasons, normally originating in the Central Lowlands of the USA. Total annual precipitation is between 90 and 115 cm, the main feature of

Table 10   New England: some climatic averages

	Average temp °C		Frost-free days per year	Snow depth (cm)
	January	July		
Aroostook County (Maine)	−12	19	117	255
Hartford (Connecticut)	−3	23	176	101

which is heavy winter snowfalls. Precipitation is dramatically increased as the depressions cross the higher ground of the Appalachians. In the early months of 1977 and 1978, intensive low pressure systems brought the worst blizzard conditions this century.

Naturally, steep hillsides and large glacial boulders have interfered with soil development. Even districts with thicker soils suffer because the heavy precipitation leaches (washes out) soil nutrients.

Questions

Figure 24 and the account

1. *a)* Make a tracing of the profiles, then complete the foreground section 3 using the given heights.
   b) Identify the features labelled (*i*) to (*ii*).
   c) If you were asked to draw a further profile of 1° of latitude north of section 1, state two reasons why the sectional frame would be inadequate.
   d) How do the projected profiles help to explain (*i*) the relative isolation of New England, and (*ii*) the lack of economic development of the three northern states?

Figure 22 and the account

2. *a)* How far south did the ice sheets reach?
   b) What effects did the ice have on the surface of New England?

Figure 24 and the account

3. Explain why the depth of snow on the Green Mountains exceeds that of any other area shown on Figure 24.

Figure 24   *Projected profile graph of New England's surface*

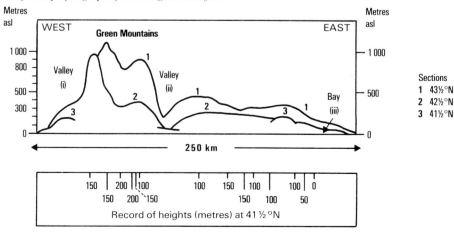

Farming in New England

Farming is severely limited by the combination of poor soils and short growing season, especially in the three northern states. As might be expected, the number of farms has fallen continuously during the twentieth century and the area of cultivated land in the entire region is little more than one-third of what it was a hundred years ago. The decline has been particularly marked in recent years; in New England the cultivated area shrank from 3·1 million to 1·9 million hectares between 1964 and 1974.

The majority of New England farmers now concentrate on milk production, poultry raising and market gardening (truck farming), choices which are greatly influenced by the plentiful growth of grass in the warm season, and by the nearby cities of the Atlantic Coast.

Table 11   Vermont dairy farming
Annual Balance Sheet (£) for a medium-sized farm, with 57 cows

Expenses		Receipts	
Hired labour	40 000	Milk sales	48 300
Concentrated feed	157 000	Calf sales	3 200
Fertiliser and lime	21 000	Miscellaneous	1 800
Petrol, oil, vehicles	19 000		
Repairs	21 000		
Buying of cattle	14 000		
Transport of goods	16 000		
Interest payments on equipment	24 000		
Miscellaneous	70 000		

Certain districts also specialise in particular products such as tobacco, cranberries and potatoes.

TOBACCO

Under the shade of many kilometres of cheese-cloth (to control temperature and humidity) high value 'cigar-wrapper' tobacco is grown on moderately fertile loams in the Connecticut Valley. Although production has been halved since the 1960s the total value still reaches £20 million a year.

CRANBERRIES

Cranberries are cultivated in marshy and peaty areas in south-east New England. The fruit is in special demand as a sauce for turkey. The Pilgrim Fathers celebrated the first 'Thanksgiving' with a wild-turkey dinner, an event commemorated by an annual holiday throughout the United States.

POTATOES

In districts near the Canadian border potatoes are a special crop which dominate the farming landscape. They are often sold as seed potatoes in the rest of the USA.

Questions

Table 11 and general

1. *a)* Total the expenses and the receipts. How much is left for the family to live on?
   b) What is the biggest expense? Discuss whether or not this could be reduced.
   c) Explain why the farmer is buying some cattle yet selling calves.
   d) What major item for cattle is not directly included because it is normally neither bought nor sold?

Plate 14 and general

2. Why does the farm specialise in dairying rather than crop production?

Figure 22, Table 11, the account and an atlas

3. On what grounds can New England be divided into distinctive northern and southern areas? (*hint:* Take the northern boundary of Massachusetts as the dividing line.)

Plate 14   *A Vermont dairy farm*

Industrial growth, decline—and recovery

The region's limited farming potential forced many New Englanders to look to the sea for a living, and a strong maritime tradition developed. Fishing and whaling became major activities and trade was established with the West Indies, where dried fish and meat were exchanged for tobacco and sugar. This trade in turn led to the building of sailing ships to carry cargo. Money gradually accumulated in the small ports and was often used to set up manufacturing activities in the home, producing clothing and household wares.

When the techniques for harnessing water power developed, small industries were established next to any stream which could be diverted to drive the machinery. However, only those places with a reliable flow of water could operate efficiently. This, combined with the increasing scale of production, meant that river locations with rapids were sought after. The best known are Holyoke on the Connecticut River, and Manchester, Lawrence and Lowell on the Merrimack.

About one hundred years ago the advent of steam power generated by burning coal ended the era of water power. New England felt the full impact of the Industrial Revolution. Some large mills were adapted to the new form of energy, but the most important development was the construction of factories on coastal inlets where imported coal and raw materials could be handled; for example, at Fall River and New Bedford. Most of the industrial processing was based on imported raw materials, so that traditional local products such as fleeces (woollen industry), cattle hides (shoe making and leather) and timber accounted for only a few factories. Intricate and lengthy processes involving relatively small amounts of raw material became the main feature of industrial growth. The products made ranged from watches, jewellery, firearms, brassware and hardware to cotton textiles and rubber. For many decades southern New England completely dominated American production of woollen textiles, shoes and leather and a whole range of cotton goods.

However, as power demands increased in the twentieth century, New England could not compete with energy-rich regions elsewhere in the USA. Outdated machinery and premises, and high wage rates, also placed New England at a disadvantage compared with its competitors. In particular, cotton growing areas around the southern edge of the Appalachians took advantage of hydro-electric power (HEP), local coal and lower wage rates to expand, until by the 1920s the new areas had taken the lead in the production of cheap cotton goods. Such developments forced New England to specialise further in fine quality products.

Despite attempts to keep pace with new trends in artificial fibres and changing clothing styles, New England's textile industry has not prospered. Since 1939 over three-quarters of all textile jobs have disappeared, first affecting cotton textiles and later woollens. Although New England still retains a 70 per cent share of the total US production of wool textiles, the overall decline was little short of a disaster. The consequences were particularly serious in the Greater Boston area, Rhode Island and south-east Massachusetts, but isolated towns in northern New England were even more drastically affected.

Plate 15   *Former textile factory, New Hampshire*

One traditional industry which has survived all the up-heavals of the twentieth century is the manufacture of firearms. From small beginnings in tinkers' ware the industry now produces 70 per cent of all the handguns and sporting and military rifles in the USA. Famous companies such as Colt, Remington and Winchester are located at Hartford, Springfield, Bridgeport and New Haven. American citizens have traditionally had the right to own weapons on a much freer basis than almost anywhere else in the world. However, so many guns have fallen into criminal hands that laws may soon be passed to exert more control on the sale of firearms. But until this happens—and there is considerable opposition to such a move—the gun makers of south-west New England will continue to enjoy a buoyant market for their products.

Shipbuilding is another traditional industry which has taken on a new importance in the twentieth century. Quincy (near Boston) and Bath (near Portland) specialise in constructing tankers and bulk carriers, but New England's major centre is Groton, Connecticut, which produced the world's first nuclear submarine.

Table 12   A century of change in New England manu-facturing industries

	Number of jobs	Percentage of US total
1870	559 000	21·5
1970	1 467 000	7·6

Figure 25   *Changing industrial locations and ring roads (Boston area)*

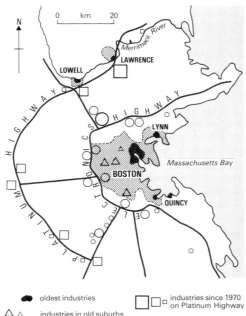

- ⬤ oldest industries
- △ △ industries in old suburbs
- ◯ ◯ ◌ industries on first ring road
- ☐ ☐ ◌ industries since 1970 on Platinum Highway
- ⬗ 1975 boundaries of cities

Questions

Plate 15

1. *a*) How can you tell that this is an old factory?
   b) For what purpose is it now being used?

The account and general

2. *a*) Comment on the changes shown in Table 12.
   b) To what extent is the description 'in decline' applicable to New England's industries?
3. In what ways did New England's industrial development up to the Second World War (*i*) differ from, and (*ii*) remain similar to that of Britain?
4. *a*) Why did so many ordinary Americans want to own firearms in the nineteenth century?
   b) Argue the case for and against the proposed law to control the sale of firearms. (*Note:* 30 million Americans own handguns and each year another two million guns are sold. Every year 23 000 Americans are killed by firearms.)

Fortunately the decline in textile employment has been offset by a remarkable expansion in electronics and similar types of industry, including the manufacture of television sets, communications equipment, computers, optical goods, sophisticated engines and other apparatus used in the field of aerospace. In the Boston area alone, well over 100 000 people are employed in these modern industries, long-established skills being used to manufacture high value finished products. However, success is also due to the research carried out by industrial firms and local universities such as the Massachusetts Institute of Technology, which has strong links with engineering. Finally, the location of modern industry depends on a large market nearby and good transport systems. In the densely settled southern part of New England, with its expanding population and motorway network, these conditions are fully met.

Changes of industrial location in the Boston area are shown in Figure 25. In the twentieth century, sites in the Merrimack Valley and in Boston became too cramped and out-dated, both inside and outside the factories. Attractive industrial estates were eventually set up in open areas between suburban housing development. But as more houses, shopping areas and office blocks filled in the remaining spaces, the movement of people and goods to and from the factory became more and more congested. After 1950, construction of a motorway around Boston encouraged industrialists and others to establish modern buildings along the new 'Electronics Highway'.

Table 13   Developments along Electronics Highway

Year	Number of companies	Number of workers	Average workforce
1958	209	25 131	122
1962	396	44 748	113
1967	729	65 616	90
1973	1212	83 649	69

Although there are still open spaces near the first ring road, an outer ring highway has been built, 25 km beyond the first, in a mainly rural area. To give it an attractive image the name 'Platinum Highway' is used and the advantages of motorway links and pleasant surroundings receive much publicity. Almost 200 factories and warehouses, eighteen shopping centres and a great deal of new housing have been constructed. An increased population of 650 000 now occupies a broad zone along the Platinum Highway.

Table 14   Types of development along Electronics Highway

	Number of firms	Percentage of total	Area needed	Work-force
Manufacturing industry	329	19·2	Large	Small
Research and development	150	8·7	Small	Large
Warehouse and distribution	400	23·4	Medium	Medium
Business offices	836	48·7	Small	Medium

Questions

Plate 16 and the account

1. Describe how large areas of land are used for at least three separate enterprises.

Table 13 and general

2. *a)* Construct a graph with 'companies' on the vertical axis and 'workers' on the horizontal axis. Indicate years at appropriate points on the graph.
b) Is the result of joining the points a straight line or not? Why? Could this trend be related to the availability of land? What do you think?

Table 14 and general

3. Explain why a motorway link is an advantage to:
   a) each of the four categories of firms listed;
   b) the supermarkets of the new shopping centres.

Tables 13, 14 and the account

4. Is it likely that the rate of growth along the Platinum Highway will match that of the first ring road? Explain your answer.

Plate 16   *Industrial development, Platinum Highway, Boston*

Megalopolis

A first look

Megalopolis means 'very large city' and describes the huge chain of towns, cities, suburbs and satellite areas extending along the USA's north-eastern seaboard. This is the world's largest, wealthiest and most productive urbanised region where about 43 million people, approximately one-fifth of the total US population, occupy less than 2 per cent of the nation's land area.

Despite the general intensity of urbanisation Megalo-polis is far from being one continuous sprawl of concrete, brick and steel. Its major centres are separated by extensive rural and semi-rural areas, and the overall population density is less than that of Britain. What binds this region together as one 'super-city' is the network of industrial and commercial links and the overlap of its suburban dormitory areas. In this respect it is difficult to tell where one city ends and another begins.

Figure 26 *Megalopolis: position and extent*

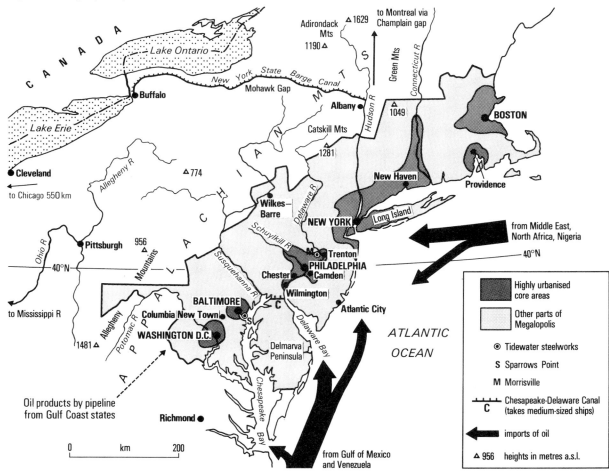

The astounding development of Megalopolis can hardly be ascribed to any special natural resources. Its soils, for example, are of generally poor quality and there are few mineral deposits of any great value. Instead the region's rise to pre-eminence is best explained in terms of its history and geographical position. It was here that the early colonies flourished, and where the United States first emerged as a nation—giving the region's cities a head start which proved a key factor in their subsequent growth.

Facing Europe and situated in middle latitudes, Megalopolis is ideally located for shipping and trade. Wide valleys flooded at the end of the Ice Age now form great estuaries which allow sea-going vessels to penetrate deep inland at all seasons. With the exception of Washington, the tidewater cities all developed into great ports, competing for trade and industry since colonial times. They also served as entry points for millions of immigrants and as gateways to the rich hinterlands beyond the Appalachians.

Apart from its industrial and commercial importance, Megalopolis contains the seat of the federal government and is a major cultural centre which continues to influence many aspects of American life. In short, Megalopolis can be described as 'Main Street, USA'.

Such is the impetus of growth that no end is yet in sight. In terms of overall population increase Megalopolis still leads the nation. Nowadays, however, it is the suburban areas which are proving more attractive than the core cities. Most of the latter are either growing very slowly or are actually losing population.

Table 15   The major urban centres of Megalopolis

| | Population (1970) | | Characteristics of Metropolitan Area (city plus suburbs) | | | |
	Metropolitan Area	Core city	Rank in USA	% increase 1960–75	% living in core city	% of workers in manufacturing*
New York	9 561 000	7 482 000	1st	0·2	78·3	24·6
Philadelphia	4 807 000	1 816 000	4th	10·7	37·8	30·8
Washington DC	3 022 000	712 000	7th	44·1	23·6	6·5
Boston	2 890 000	637 000	8th	7·5	22·0	22·4
Baltimore	2 148 000	852 000	14th	19·1	39·7	25·2

National average increase in population, 1960–75: 19·1%   *National average 26%

Questions

Figure 26

1. *a)* Approximately how far, in kilometres, does Megalopolis extend (*i*) north-south (Boston—Washington), and (*ii*) east-west (New York—Wilkes-Barre)?
   b) Megalopolis is sometimes known as 'Boswash' or 'Bosnywash'. Why?

Figure 26 and an atlas

2. Name five states which lie entirely within Megalopolis.

Table 15 and the account

3. Name the only metropolitan area where population is growing faster than the US population as a whole.

4. *a)* What is remarkable about the number of people now living in the suburbs compared with the core cities?
   b) What general trend does your answer suggest?
5. *a)* How important are manufacturing activities in the major metropolitan areas?
   b) Are there any exceptions? Why?

General

6. Parts of Long Island, New Jersey ('The Garden State') and the Delmarva Peninsula concentrate on truck farming (the intensive cultivation of crops such as tomatoes, peas, beans, melons and strawberries).
   a) (*i*) What is the origin of the term 'truck farming', and (*ii*) what is it usually called in Britain?
   b) Why is truck farming important in Megalopolis?

Philadelphia and Baltimore : two great ports

PHILADELPHIA

The 'City of Brotherly Love' was founded in 1681 by the Quaker William Penn. It was the first place in America to benefit from town planning, and its geometric grid of straight streets was repeated in almost every North American city. Scene of the Declaration of Independence, the city was the USA's capital from 1790 to 1800

Philadelphia is now the centre of a vast complex of heavy industry spreading along the banks of the Delaware and Schuylkill rivers. Particularly important is the new integrated iron and steel works at Morrisville which enjoys the advantages of cheap water transport and proximity to the large eastern market. The Philadelphia area is also the largest oil-refining centre on the Atlantic coast and the greatest shipbuilding centre in the United States. Chester and Camden have particularly important shipyards.

Other leading industries include chemicals and motor vehicles at Wilmington; aircraft, spacecraft, and missiles in Philadelphia itself; food canning at Camden; carpets and woollen goods, paper and rubber products, leather tanning and sugar refining. In fact the Philadelphia district is the most diversified industrial area in the USA.

Table 16   Philadelphia's foreign trade (million tonnes)

	Imports	Exports
Mineral fuels	39·2	1·1
Raw materials	11·5	0·6
Machinery and manufactured goods	1·9	0·8
Food and drink products	1·5	1·1
Chemicals	0·2	0·2
Total tonnage:	54·3	3·8
Total value: (£M.)	£1091	£343

BALTIMORE

Founded in 1729 on the Patapsco estuary, Baltimore is nearer to the farmlands and coalfields of the interior USA than any other Atlantic port, although its seaward connections to the north and east are hampered by the Delmarva Peninsula. Baltimore's largest single industry is the huge iron and steel works at Sparrows Point but it is also important for shipbuilding, food canning, car and aircraft assembly, chemicals, fertilisers and oil, and copper and sugar refining.

Questions

Table 16, Figure 26 and the account

1. *a)* Name two mineral fuels, and two raw materials imported by Philadelphia.
   b) Explain the list of imports in relation to Philadelphia's industries.
2. Calculate the average value of (*i*) a tonne of imports, and (*ii*) a tonne of exports. Account for the difference.

The account and general

3. Name the industries which are likely to need a riverbank location. Explain why they need this.

Figure 26 and an atlas

4. Why is the Delmarva Peninsula so called? (*hint:* names of states).
5. How has Baltimore's accessibility to shipping been improved?

SPARROWS POINT: A TIDEWATER IRON AND STEEL WORKS

The Sparrows Point plant was founded in 1887 and purchased by the Bethlehem Steel Company in 1916. Since the 1950s the company has created one of the world's largest integrated iron and steel works, with a capacity of about 9 million tonnes of steel a year—a remarkable achievement in an area which lacks both coal and iron ore.

Sparrows Point produces a wide variety of steel goods, but the emphasis is on flat rolled steel (sheets and tin-plate), pipe and wire products. Among the local steel-using industries are the Company's own shipyards along the Patapsco River, but the numerous structural, building and manufacturing concerns of Megalopolis consume much greater quantities. Further afield, the expanding oil and gas industries of states in the south and south-west are also important customers, as well as companies specialising in the canning of food and drink products.

Plate 17 *Sparrows Point iron and steel works*

Key

1 Coal storage areas (coal from West Virginia via Norfolk (Va.) by coastal colliers)
2 Ore yards
3 Scrap yard
4 Coke ovens
5 Blast furnaces
6 Basic oxygen and open-hearth furnaces
7 Plate, slabbing and flanging mills
8 Rod, wire and pipe mills
9 Rolled sheet and tinplate mills
10 Shipyards

Questions

Plate 17 and general

1. *a*) Where is Sparrows Point? Describe its location in some detail.
   b) How does the plant (*i*) overcome the lack of local raw materials, and (*ii*) manage to sell its products competitively?
2. *a*) What is an *integrated* iron and steel works?
   b) What influenced the siting of (*i*) the coke ovens, and (*ii*) the ore yards?
   c) How were the open storage areas in the foreground made available?

3. Compile a linear flow diagram to illustrate the production of Sparrows Point iron and steel.
4. *a*) What type of product from Sparrows Point will be used by (*i*) local shipyards, (*ii*) the construction trade, (*iii*) the oil and gas industry, and (*iv*) food and drink canneries?
5. The Bethlehem Steel Company maintains a financial interest in all the foreign mines supplying ore to Sparrows Point. Why?

New York City

HISTORICAL NOTES

The area's first inhabitants were the Algonquin Indians who called it *Man-a-ha-ta*, 'heavenly place'.

1524: The site of New York was visited by Verrazano, an Italian navigator.

1609: Henry Hudson, an English navigator working for the Dutch, sailed up the Hudson River as far as Albany and claimed the territory for The Netherlands.

1626: The Dutch purchased Manhattan Island from the Indians for 24 dollars' worth of beads, buttons and other trinkets. The Dutch built a fortified settlement on the southern tip of the island and called it New Amsterdam.

1653: New Amsterdam's population numbered 800.

1664: The Dutch colony was seized by the English and renamed New York.

1785–90: New York served as the capital of the United States.

1818: First regular shipping service between New York and Liverpool.
Influx of European immigrants began.

Figure 27 *Greater New York*

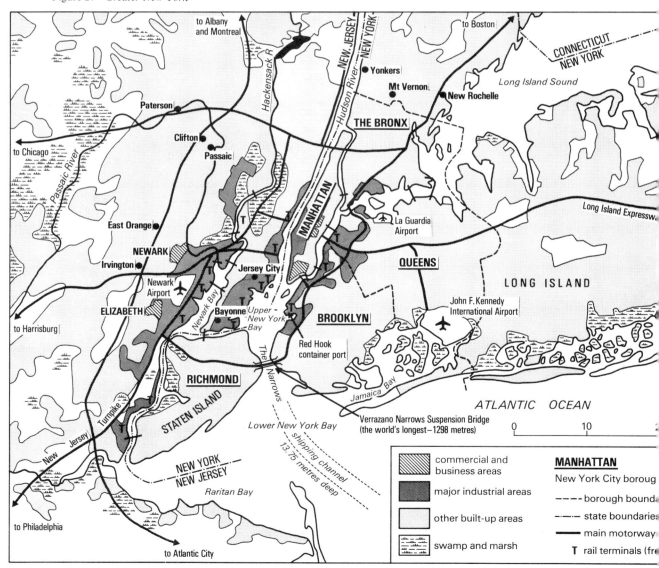

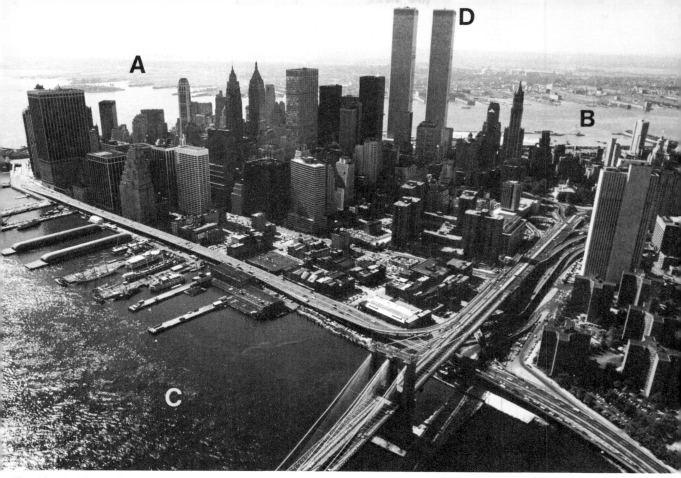

Plate 18 *Aerial view of Manhattan island*

1825:	Erie Canal opened (enlarged in 1918 and re-named New York State Barge Canal).
1914–18:	Influx of black Americans from the Southern states began.
1918–present:	New York continues to attract both foreigners and Americans from other parts of the USA. (In 1970, 42 per cent of the city's population were either foreign-born or had foreign-born parents.)

At the very heart of Megalopolis lies bustling, cosmo-politan New York, since 1790 the largest city in North America. New York grew more rapidly than other east coast ports because of its advantageous trading position at the seaward end of the Hudson-Mohawk valley. This easy route into the interior has been followed succes-sively by canal, rail and motorway links. Many other roads and railways from all over the continent have also focused on New York, making it one of the world's great route centres and giving access to some 140 million people who live within a 1100 km radius. This is beyond question the world's biggest and richest market.

THE PORT OF NEW YORK

New York's landward connections are more than matched by its superb natural harbour. It is ice-free, seldom affected by fog, needs no dredging and has a tidal range of only 1·5 metres, allowing ships to arrive and depart at all times. The port has nearly 300 deep-water berths and over 1200 km of waterfront (740 km in New York, the re-mainder in New Jersey). A large fleet of tugs, barges and lighters speeds the turn-round of ships, and excellent ware-houses and storage facilities are available for all kinds of cargo. Specialised handling equipment, such as that at the Red Hook container terminal, makes New York North America's leading container port. In addition, Man-hattan's huge World Trade Centre houses hundreds of shipping companies, marine insurance firms and govern-ment agencies, all of which specialise in the administration of international cargo movements.

With these advantages it is small wonder that the port of New York is the busiest in the world, clearing over 25 000 ship movements a year and handling approxi-mately 15 per cent of the total US foreign trade by tonnage

43

and 40 per cent by value. More than half the latter is dealt with along the short stretch of Hudson River frontage shown in Figure 28. Most bulk cargoes such as oil, ores and chemicals are handled by specialised terminals at Staten Island, Newark and Bayonne, where large-scale refining and processing takes place. In all, port activities provide a livelihood for about 10 per cent of New York's population.

Questions

Figure 26, the account and an atlas

1. Explain in detail how the existence of the Hudson-Mohawk gap has assisted the growth of New York.
2. Only one-third of New York's total water-borne commerce (200 million tonnes per annum) is with foreign countries.
   a) From what area of the USA is New York's main bulk-cargo commodity imported?
   b) Over what distance is this cargo carried?

Figure 27

3. a) Name (*i*) the three main islands of New York City, and (*ii*) the three main rivers.
   b) Which two of the five named bays form the heart of the port? How can you tell?

Figure 28

4. a) Which section of the port handles the passenger liner *Queen Elizabeth II*?
   b) Why has this type of transatlantic traffic declined steeply since the Second World War?

Figure 27 and the account

5. Only two railway terminals (Grand Central and Pennsylvania passenger stations) are located on Manhattan. Describe and account for the location of the other terminals.
6. a) Why is the Verrazano-Narrows Bridge so named? (*hint:* Historical Notes)
   b) How did the opening of the bridge in 1964 (*i*) influence the decision to locate the new container port at Red Hook, and (*ii*) benefit through-traffic travelling between Boston and Philadelphia?

MANHATTAN: THE HEART OF NEW YORK CITY

Although the world-famous skyscrapers are synonymous with New York in popular imagination, they occupy only two relatively small areas of Manhattan, which itself is only one of five boroughs constituting New York City. Moreover, the city now forms one part of a much larger metropolitan region (population 16 662 000) extending into three states.

Despite Manhattan's comparatively insignificant size (59 km²), most of the activities which make New York the USA's financial, commercial, entertainment, cultural and fashion capital are crowded on to this small island. Amidst the ceaseless hustle and bustle, Manhattan offers the New Yorker a wide range of renowned museums and art galleries, together with dozens of theatres and cinemas along and 'off' Broadway, the 'Great White Way'. For the shopper, fashionable Fifth Avenue and the huge department stores of the Midtown area are irresistible attractions.

Even more important are the commercial and financial interests. As New Yorkers are fond of saying, 'Manhattan's business is business'; in fact no less than one-third of all the office space in the USA is located there. The Downtown area dominates the world of American finance, while in the skyscrapers of Midtown most big American corporations have main or branch offices. In several specialised services Manhattan is virtually unchallenged. For example, its publishers account for 75 per cent of all American books, and 70 per cent of all US advertising agencies have Manhattan addresses.

Competition for Manhattan's limited space has made the land the most expensive in the world. Nevertheless approximately half of New York's 850 000 manufacturing employees work in Manhattan. The industries are characterised by a large number of small-scale factories employing an average of only 25 workers. They specialise in small, high-value products such as jewellery, electronic components and scientific instruments, and in 'consumer non-durables' (short-life goods bought by the general public).

More people are employed in the clothing industry than in any other. The Midtown 'Garment District' covers only 80 hectares but contains some 4000 workshops which produce 35 per cent of all the clothing made in the United States. During working hours this district is one of the busiest parts of the city. Workers can be seen pushing racks of clothes through the streets and transporting batches of cloth from one factory to another.

Taking into account the whole metropolitan area, New York is the world's greatest manufacturing centre (measured by the value of goods produced). Its 26 000 factories cover almost the complete range of industries listed by the US government.

Questions

Figure 27

1. a) Name (*i*) New York City's five boroughs, and (*ii*) the three states into which the metropolitan region has spread.
   b) What physical factor has limited the westward sprawl of the built-up area?

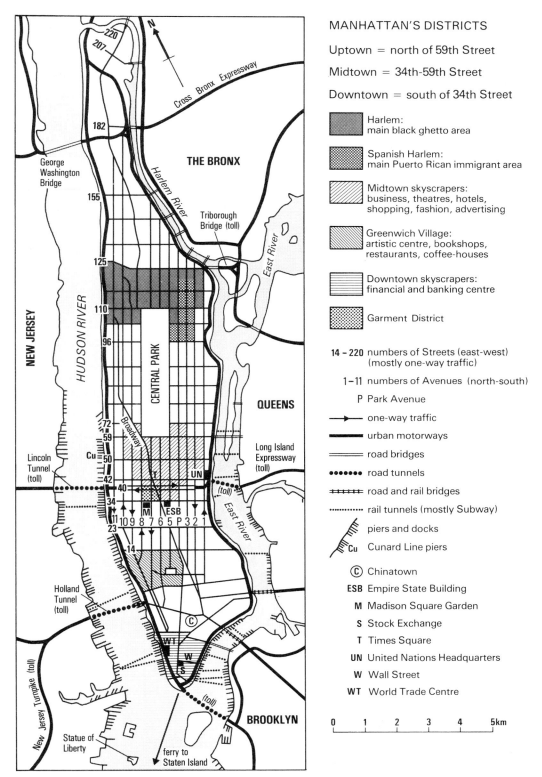

Harlem:
main black ghetto area

Spanish Harlem:
main Puerto Rican immigrant area

Midtown skyscrapers:
business, theatres, hotels,
shopping, fashion, advertising

Greenwich Village:
artistic centre, bookshops,
restaurants, coffee-houses

Downtown skyscrapers:
financial and banking centre

Garment District

14 – 220 numbers of Streets (east-west)
(mostly one-way traffic)

1–11 numbers of Avenues (north-south)

P Park Avenue

one-way traffic

urban motorways

road bridges

road tunnels

road and rail bridges

rail tunnels (mostly Subway)

piers and docks

Cu Cunard Line piers

Ⓒ Chinatown

ESB Empire State Building

M Madison Square Garden

S Stock Exchange

T Times Square

UN United Nations Headquarters

W Wall Street

WT World Trade Centre

0   1   2   3   4   5km

Figure 28 *Manhattan*

Plate 18 and Figure 28

2. a) (i) Which district of Manhattan is shown in the photograph, and (ii) what are the district's main functions?
b) Identify the features indicated by letters A–D on the photograph: A state; B river; C strait; D twin sky-scrapers.

Figure 28

3. Most US cities have only one skyscraper cluster, usually called 'downtown' or the 'central business district' (CBD), incorporating offices, shops, entertainment, etc. Does the layout in New York conform to this pattern, or not? List the city's characteristics in detail.

The account and general

4. a) What does the existence of the skyscrapers suggest about Manhattan's geology?
b) In what ways have other physical characteristics of the locality encouraged the construction of skyscrapers?
5. The twin towers of the World Trade Centre are the highest buildings in New York (110 storeys, 411 m). About 350 000 people work in the Centre and another 80 000 visit it daily.
a) What are the advantages of concentrating all the offices dealing with the same business (international shipping) in the one centre?
b) What daily problem does the large number of employees and visitors cause for Manhattan?

Figure 28, the account and general

6. a) Describe the precise location of the Garment District. (*hint:* use the New Yorkers' method of referring to avenue and street numbers, e.g. '9th and 42nd' means the corner of 9th Avenue and 42nd Street.)
b) How can the average workshop afford to be sited there?
c) List the advantages and disadvantages of this location for the clothing industry.
7. Manhattan is an important tourist centre. List some of its attractions

Table 17   Manhattan as a residential area, 1790–2000

Year	Population of Manhattan	Manhattan's population as a percentage of New York City's	Population density
1790	33 000	67·1	560
1830	203 000	83·9	3 440
1870	942 000	63·7	15 970
1910	2 331 000	48·9	39 510
1950	1 930 000	24·8	32 710
1970	1 539 000	19·5	26 080
1980 (*estimate*)	1 457 000	18·4	24 690
2000 (*estimate*)	1 408 000	18·0	23 860

8. Comment on the trends shown in Table 17. What do they indicate about Manhattan as a residential centre?

NEW YORK: CITY IN CRISIS

In common with most other American cities New York is currently experiencing a variety of problems which together have created an urban crisis. Because New York is the USA's largest city the scale of the crisis is greater than elsewhere; the stresses of urban living have become more difficult to deal with, and solutions to the problems are harder to find. Of these problems three of the most important are traffic congestion, poverty and crime.

Nowadays most US cities are heavily dependent on the motor car, but New York still enjoys the advantages of a highly developed public transport system. Of the estimated four million people who enter Manhattan on a typical working day approximately 75 per cent rely on some form of 'mass transit', especially the subway (underground railway). Even so, New York has crippling traffic problems caused by more than 800 000 motorists who still creep, bumper to bumper, into Manhattan every day.

To speed the flow of traffic into the city many kilometres of limited access, extra-wide motorways (called 'freeways' and 'expressways') have been constructed. Despite the high costs of building these roads, and the environmental damage they cause, they have simply created even worse congestion on the city's streets. In the days of horse-drawn vehicles the average speed in Manhattan was 18 km/h; today's motorist can manage only 11 km/h.

Over the years New York has received many thousands of immigrants from abroad and from other parts of the USA, a constant stream of new people who gave the city its rich diversity and dynamism. Since 1950 most of the new arrivals have been black Americans from the southern states and Spanish-speaking Puerto Ricans, who are generally poor, unskilled and have large families. Consequently they pay much lower taxes to the city council than did the numerous better-off white people who have moved out of New York as the newcomers have moved in.

At the same time, the poorer groups are a much greater burden on the city's resources and increasing numbers have qualified for 'welfare'—social security payments to cover basic items like food and rent. In fact over one million people, about one in seven of New York's entire population, now receive such benefits. As a result the city no longer has enough money to pay for other important public services, and the quality of life in New York has deteriorated rapidly. To improve the situation would mean imposing still higher demands on the remaining tax-payers, even more of whom would leave the city.

The great majority of blacks and Puerto Ricans occupy decaying and derelict tenements and other slum housing, much of which was condemned at the turn of the century.

Plate 19   *Harlem ghetto scene*

Such overcrowded districts, hemmed in by invisible walls of prejudice, are known as 'ghettos'. There are several of them around the city centre but the largest is Harlem, only a short distance from the glittering skyscrapers of Midtown Manhattan. It is a very different world indeed. The ghetto's low standards of housing and education are matched by high rates of unemployment, while the general poverty and despair breed violence, vandalism and lawlessness.

Not surprisingly, the problems of Harlem and similar areas have spilled over into other parts of the city. Nowadays ghetto youths are responsible for more than half of all the crime in New York, which is high in the rankings of 'unsafe' American cities. For example, tens of thousands of burglaries and 'muggings' (street robberies) are reported every month while, on average, one murder takes place every five hours. Indeed, the total crime committed in a single Manhattan police precinct (only 2 km^2) exceeds that of the entire London region (an area of 2200 km^2).

BIG BUSINESS IN NEW YORK—IS THERE A FUTURE?

Faced with the immensity of these problems, many business corporations are following the lead of ordinary people and moving out of the city and into the suburbs. In 1966, 198 of the leading industrial companies had their headquarters in Manhattan, in 1975 only 120 remained. For many firms the prestige of a Manhattan address is now outweighed by the cost, insecurity and sheer inconvenience of working in the city centre. For the New York authorities the continuing exodus of the big companies is a financial disaster. Without the substantial taxes contributed by these firms the city's hopes of finding effective solutions for its deepening problems seem very slight indeed. Although the very existence of its glittering skyscrapers makes it difficult to believe, New York is virtually bankrupt. In the long term, funds supplied by the state and federal governments may prove to be the only remedy for the city's chronic financial difficulties.

Figure 29   *Diagrammatic section through a typical US city*

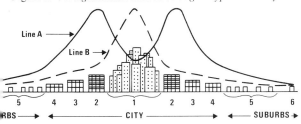

Skyscrapers of the CBD	**4** Terraced houses
Tenement blocks of inner city ghettos	**5** Detached houses (suburban)
Apartment blocks (flats)	**6** Detached houses (exurban)

Lines **A** and **B** See questions

47

Questions

The account

1. The level of car ownership in New York City (1 car to 5 people) is the lowest in the USA. Why?

Figure 28, the account and general

2. *a*) List the problems and expenses faced by the motorist who commutes to Manhattan.
   b) How does Manhattan's 'grid-iron' street plan help to reduce traffic congestion?

The account and general

3. Explain how urban motorways can damage the environment.

An atlas

4. Where is Puerto Rico, and to which country does it belong?

Plate 19 and the account

5. *a*) List the characteristics of a ghetto.
   b) How do ghetto conditions contribute to the problem of crime in New York?

Table 18

6. *a*) Describe the main trends shown in the table.
   b) To what extent are problems similar to those of New York's ghetto-dwellers likely to be found in the other cities?

The account and general

7. 'Nearly all New York's problems could be solved by money'. Discuss the truth of this suggestion.

Figure 29

8. *a*) Look at lines A and B. One of the lines indicates the density of residential population, the other indicates land values. Which is which?
   b) What is the general relationship between the height of buildings and (*i*) population density, (*ii*) land value?

Table 18   Black population in the main cities of Megalopolis

	1960	1970	Percentage of total city population 1960	1970
New York	1 088 000	1 667 000	14·0	21·2
Philadelphia	529 000	654 000	26·4	33·6
Washington DC	412 000	538 000	53·9	71·1
Baltimore	326 000	420 000	34·7	46·4
Newark	138 000	207 000	34·1	54·2
Boston	63 000	105 000	9·1	16·3

(US Abstract of Statistics, 1977)

Megalopolis : alternatives for a better future

There may never be a complete answer to the enormous problems of New York and the other big cities of Megalopolis, but two current schemes offer some alternatives to the congestion and tensions that characterise much of the region. In their different ways both Columbia New Town and Amtrak's new trains indicate that the future of Megalopolis is not entirely bleak.

COLUMBIA NEW TOWN

Columbia in Maryland (see Figure 26) is the first major New Town to be built in the United States. It is a specially planned attempt to solve some of the problems of living in Megalopolis. Started in 1963 by a private development company, the town will eventually house a socially balanced community of 110 000 people grouped in spacious village-type neighbourhoods.

The main objective is to make Columbia completely self-contained by creating industrial and commercial employment within its own boundaries. With this in mind, the New Town's location was carefully chosen for the easy distribution of consumer products throughout the huge market of Megalopolis. Already many major companies have set up factories in Columbia and the target of 40 000 jobs should easily be reached. Residents thus have a short journey to work and, unlike millions of others in the region, they are spared the stress and expense of commuting long distances to established urban centres. At the same time they enjoy all the advantages of good housing in an attractive and virtually problem-free environment. Small wonder that Columbia is regarded by many as the blueprint for future developments in Megalopolis.

AMTRAK: THE REVIVAL OF PASSENGER RAIL TRAFFIC?

Megalopolis is the busiest route corridor in the USA, the great majority of traffic being carried by road and air. By the 1960s motorways were reaching saturation point, while air space was so crowded that the major airports were 'rationing' flights. By contrast, a mere 1 per cent of inter-city passengers were travelling by train—a reflection of the steep decline in rail services since the Second World War. Railway companies were going bankrupt and it began to look as though there would soon be no long-distance passenger trains anywhere in the United States. Faced with this prospect, in 1971 the federal government created Amtrak an official corporation which pays railway companies to retain and improve the few surviving inter-city services.

In Megalopolis the most important Amtrak trains are the all-electric Metroliners which run between Washington and New York. These ultra-modern expresses offer a greatly improved rail service between the region's major urban centres. Their comfort and punctuality have proved especially popular with business people, many of whom have been attracted away from the more expensive airlines. Also, because the new trains operate directly from city centre to city centre, passengers avoid most of the delays and other difficulties associated with alternative means of travel.

Like most other passenger rail systems throughout the world, Amtrak runs at a loss and some of its services are threatened with closure. Even so, as one oil crisis follows another, the logic of travelling by rail should eventually register with increasing numbers of Americans. Whatever the ultimate fate of Amtrak services elsewhere, in Megalopolis successful trains like the Metroliner have already proved their vital role in shaping the region's transport future.

Table 19   Comparative passenger journey times: Washington–New York

Mode of transport	Total journey time*
Metroliner train	2 hr 30 min.
Airliner	2 hr 45 min.
Car (via motorways)	5 hr 30 min.

*City centre to city centre.

Questions

The account and general

1. *a)* Name the New Town nearest to your home area.
   b) What is the main difference between Columbia and New Towns in Britain?
2. List the advantages of living in Columbia compared with (*i*) a big city, and (*ii*) a residential suburb in Megalopolis.

Table 19, the account and general

3. Calculate the average speed of each form of transport. (*hints:* (*i*) distance is 350 km (approximately); (*ii*) airliner's actual flight time is only 50 min.)
4. *a)* Why is the Metroliner's total journey time less than that of (*i*) the car, and (*ii*) the airliner?
   b) What other advantages do the train's passengers enjoy?

Plate 20   *An Amtrak express*

The Agricultural Heartlands

Introduction

Extending across the north-central part of the United States is the country's most important food-producing area. It contains some of the most efficient farms in the world and includes the whole of the Middle West and most of the Great Plains. The Middle West is roughly that part of the Central Lowlands lying south of the Great Lakes and between the Missouri and Ohio Rivers. Further west the Great Plains rise from the Central Lowlands, usually almost imperceptibly but sometimes in the form of a pronounced escarpment—the Break of the Plains.

Most of this huge region has excellent soils and wide,

relatively level expanses of land which have favoured the efficient use of machinery. However, considerable climatic variations led to the emergence of several specialised farming regions, traditionally described as 'crop belts'. There is still a good degree of specialisation within the different areas shown on Figure 30 but it is important to note that in reality they overlap quite considerably and that the boundary lines are only generalisations. Also, in recent years there has been much diversification within each area, and the entire region now approximates much more closely to 'mixed farming' than it did a few decades ago.

Figure 30 *The Agricultural Heartland: specialised farming regions*

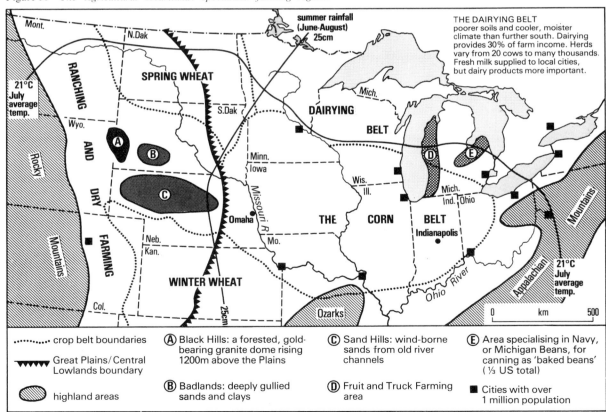

THE DAIRYING BELT
poorer soils and cooler, moister climate than further south. Dairying provides 30% of farm income. Herds vary from 20 cows to many thousands. Fresh milk supplied to local cities, but dairy products more important.

········· crop belt boundaries

ⓐ Black Hills: a forested, gold-bearing granite dome rising 1200m above the Plains

ⓒ Sand Hills: wind-borne sands from old river channels

ⓔ Area specialising in Navy, or Michigan Beans, for canning as 'baked beans' (⅓ US total)

Great Plains/Central Lowlands boundary

ⓑ Badlands: deeply gullied sands and clays

ⓓ Fruit and Truck Farming area

highland areas

■ Cities with over 1 million population

In the mid-nineteenth century, when pioneer farmers first settled in the Middle West, the land was divided into 'sections' of 1 square mile ($1·6 km^2$). Each farm occupied a quarter-section, hence the standard farm size was 160 acres (64·75 hectares). As the frontier of settlement moved west the government at first applied the same system to the Great Plains, but eventually it was realised that half-sections or even whole sections were necessary to support the average family. Over the years many changes have taken place but the distinctive chequerboard landscape remains and today's farms are often family-run businesses handed down from the early pioneers.

Questions

Figure 30, the account and an atlas

1. *a*) Which states lie (*i*) wholly, and (*ii*) partly within the Middle West?
   b) Account for the origin of the term 'Middle West'. How appropriate is it nowadays?

Figure 30 and general

2. *a*) Account for the specialisation of farming in (*i*) the Dairy Belt, and (*ii*) the area marked D.

b) Name Michigan's specialist crop, much of which is exported to Britain.

Figure 30 and the account

3. Why was more land necessary to support a pioneer family on the Great Plains than elsewhere in the 'heartland'?

The Great Plains

A CLIMATE OF EXTREMES

Shut off from the rainfall and moderating influences of the Pacific, the Great Plains are completely open to air masses originating in the Arctic and the Gulf of Mexico. In winter most of the region is snowbound; in summer, cloudless skies create an inferno of heat. The conflict between fronts of warm and cold air produces tornadoes and devastating hailstorms. Windless days are the exception. In summer, strong winds cause rapid evaporation, dust storms and soil erosion; in winter, blizzards pile up deep snowdrifts—sometimes rapidly transformed into disastrous floods by warm Chinook winds from the Rockies.

In this region of climatic hazard, averages of temperature and rainfall are practically meaningless. In North Dakota temperatures may range between $-40°C$ and $+40°C$ in the same year! There is also extreme variability of first and last frosts, and the length of the growing season cannot be accurately predicted. Even worse, rainfall is completely unreliable, with annual variations of 25 per cent or more. This means that places along the 50 cm isohyet may have 35 cm one year, 65 cm the next and a 'killer drought' the year after.

Table 20   The Great Plains: climatic statistics

Bismarck (510 masl) (N. Dakota)	J	F	M	A	M	J	J	A	S	O	N	D	
Temp °C	−13	−13	−4	6	12	18	21	20	14	7	−2	−9	Range 34
Precip. cm	1	1	3	4	6	8	6	5	3	3	2	1	Total 43

Abilene (530 masl) (Texas)	J	F	M	A	M	J	J	A	S	O	N	D	
Temp °C	7	9	12	16	19	25	27	29	27	21	17	11	Range 22
Precip. cm	2	2	3	6	10	7	5	6	6	6	3	3	Total 59

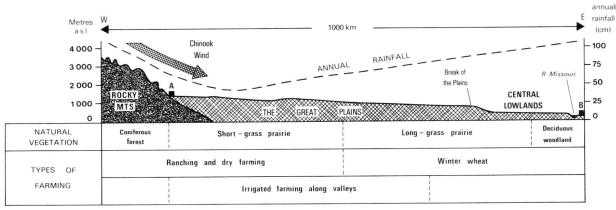

Figure 31 *Diagrammatic section through the Great Plains*

Questions

Figure 31

1. The term 'Great *Plains*' is really a misnomer. Comment on this statement.
2. Describe the relationship between rainfall, natural vegetation and agriculture.

Table 20

3. Draw two climatic graphs using the information in the table.
4. a) Compare the two areas, using the headings: (*i*) temperature range; (*ii*) number of months below freezing point; (*iii*) length of growing season (i.e. months above 5°C); (*iv*) total rainfall; (*v*) rainfall regime (i.e. distribution through the year).
   b) Account for (*i*) the major similarities, and (*ii*) the major differences.

EARLY RANCHING: THE WILD WEST

Until about 1860 there was little attempt to settle the Great Plains, mainly because it was wrongly assumed that land with no trees would not support crops. In addition, the lack of timber for housing, fuel and fencing, and the difficulty of finding water away from the river valleys, deterred settlement in what was described as 'The Great American Desert'. This left the way open for ranching, which was the only profitable type of agriculture in the early days.

The great expanses of the Plains became open ranges for hundreds of thousands of stock owned by 'cattle barons' and tended by 'cowboys'. Initially the herds consisted of Texas Longhorns, which were extremely hardy but carried relatively little meat, a situation subsequently improved by the importation of British breeds, especially the black Aberdeen Angus and the white-faced Hereford.

Without fences an annual round-up was necessary to check the herds and to brand calves for identification. An equally important job was that of driving the cattle to the nearest railhead town. From there they were transported eastward to cities such as St Louis, Kansas City and Chicago, bringing prices for meat and hides ten times higher than in the west. Such traffic became big business; 1·5 million cattle were railed through Abilene between 1868 and 1871.

The vast 'cattle kingdom' on the Great Plains lasted a mere 20 years or so, but long enough for the creation of the Wild West legend. By 1880, newly invented, cattle-proof barbed wire spelled the end of the open range, and as railways, crop farmers and proper law enforcement spread westward the brief but colourful era of 'wide-open' cattle towns such as Dodge City was brought to a close.

Meanwhile, however, the senseless slaughter of millions of buffalo by white hunters and the removal of the Plains Indians to reservations had opened up new areas of grassland nearer the Rockies. The cattle drives then headed west for the different purpose of stocking these fresh ranges, and new 'cow-towns' such as Cheyenne and Laramie sprang up. These never acquired quite the same lawless reputations as the earlier ones, and some remain important centres of the cattle industry today.

Questions

Figure 32 and an atlas

1. a) Name the rivers marked 1–3.
   b) Of which great river system are they tributaries?

Figure 32 and the account

2. a) Why did the major cattle trails originate in Texas?
   b) (*i*) In which states were the early 'cow towns' located?
   (*ii*) Account for the establishment of new cow towns and cattle trails after 1872.

The account and general knowledge

3. 'It was not the Colt and Winchester that tamed the West but barbed wire'. Elaborate this statement.

Figure 32 and general

4. The sheep and goats are raised mainly for wool. In what type of natural environment are they more important than cattle?

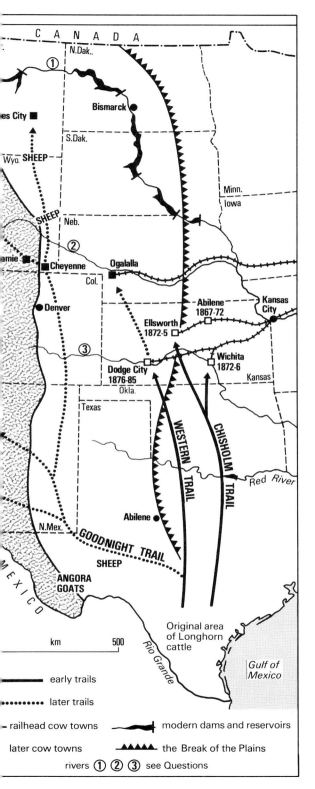

THE MODERN CATTLE INDUSTRY: AN ACCOUNT BY A SOUTH DAKOTA CATTLEMAN

'Today's cattle-owner is a business executive who uses many of the same techniques as any other executive. This may even include commuting—driving from the office in town to the range or feedlot where the cattle are.

Cattle people are of two basic types: producers and feeders. The vast range country in the western two-thirds of South Dakota is a producer's area. Even in good fertile country where grass grows thick and high a minimum of half a hectare of land is required to support one cow and calf—an 'animal unit' in cattle language. In some parts of western South Dakota, 20 hectares are required to support one animal unit. Obviously, a producer must have a tremendous investment in land, sometimes thousands and thousands of hectares.

The producer sells his or her 230 kg calves to a feeder, who doubles their weight before they are slaughtered by the meat packer. The feeder, incidentally, is the person who has introduced most of the scientific efficiency into the cattle business. The producer can't do too much with Nature. It still takes a cow nine months to have a calf and she usually has only one at a time. There isn't a great deal to be done about the nutritional value of grass either. So the producer can't make the calves get fatter faster.

The feeder is a blend of cattle-owner, chemist and dietician. Feeding is a highly automated operation with more vitamins, nutrients and special food additives than ever go into a human diet. In some cases, the operation is computerised, too. With little increase in the number of cows out on the range, the feeder has enabled the average American to consume about 55 kg of beef a year, compared with only 40 kg ten years ago.

Some feeder operations are huge, but most of them keep 500 animals or less, while the average South Dakota producer has only 125 cows and calves. In all, there are roughly 40 000 cattle businesses in the state.

Although the business is highly competitive, most cattle people would not quit under any circumstances. Producing or feeding cattle is a way of life—cowboys on horseback or in pickup trucks, round-ups, chuck wagons and branding irons. Time-clocks, office politics, promotions and smog are not part of this life. Finally, cattle people are proud of being their own bosses, and of being responsible for their own success.'

(From an article by J. McCulloch in *South Dakota*, vol. 7, no. 2, 1975)

Figure 32 *Great Plains cattle country*

53

Questions

The account

1. How does the life of modern cattle owners compare with that of:
    a) their nineteenth century counterpart;
    b) a city business executive.
2. Why does the 'animal unit:area' ratio change in western South Dakota?
3. Explain why, if demand for beef increases, it is the 'feeder' rather than the 'producer' who is better able to increase supply.

Figure 32

4. The large dams in South Dakota were completed by the federal government in the 1960s. How have they helped to develop the feedlot system?

Figure 33 and general

5. *a*) Explain how the feedlot operates.
    b) What are the advantages of this system?

The account and general

6. Many tonnes of high-protein foodstuffs are used to produce one 450 kg steer, from which comes 210 kg of meat for eating, and of which only 16 kg is high-grade steak. Argue the case for and against this apparently wasteful method of food production, mentioning any possible alternatives.

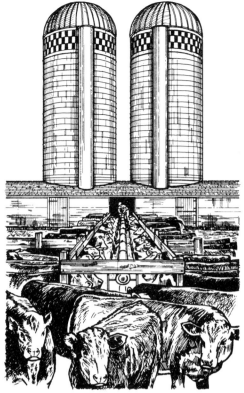

Figure 33   *A feedlot on a modern cattle farm*

The great American granary

The major wheat-producing regions of the United States overlap both the western margins of the Central Lowlands and the eastern Great Plains. The huge expanses of level land favour large-scale mechanised farming, and the rich black 'chernozem' soils provide remarkably high yields for extensive methods—although much depends on the weather.

Winter wheat is sown in autumn to make an early start. It survives the winter and resumes active growth in the spring. Further north, as in the Canadian prairies, the severe winter and shorter growing season allow only spring wheat to be grown. Throughout the wheatlands summer rain and high temperatures promote rapid growth, while the dry, sunny autumn assists ripening and harvesting.

THE DUST BOWL AND DRY FARMING TECHNIQUES

Since the Great Plains were first cultivated, the western boundary of the wheatlands has frequently changed. During wet spells the grassland far to the west was ploughed up, often to make a quick profit. In 1934 the worst drought on record occurred, after years of continuous wheat-cropping had exhausted the ability of humus to bind the soil. The result was that huge quantities of soil were blown away, creating the Dust Bowl, mainly in Kansas, Oklahoma and northern Texas, but affecting every other Plains state as well.

After the Dust Bowl tragedy, much of the land was returned to grass and has never been ploughed since. Elsewhere 'dry farming' techniques help the soil to absorb and retain moisture, and prevent exhaustion by continuous cropping.

In the drier areas a crop is produced every other year, the seeds being deep-planted to ensure access to moisture. On the fallow land, mechanical cultivators are used to undercut the soil and kill moisture-taking weeds without breaking up the surface too much. This has the

Plate 21 *Buried machinery on a Dust Bowl farm, 1936*

remarkable result of producing, on average, more wheat than by continuous cropping. After harvesting, the stubble is left in the ground to trap the winter snow, which boosts the soil's water content in spring; soil-ridging produces the same effect.

Crop rotations are now the rule rather than the exception. The different crops are grown in strips across the direction of the prevailing wind. In the spring wheat area, oats and barley are well adapted to the short growing season, while sorghum (a cereal rather like millet) is important further south. Significantly, fodder is the major use of all these alternative crops. Some of the feed is sold to neighbouring cattle-owners but many wheat farmers now keep their own livestock to vary the use of the land and restore its fertility. On sloping ground, other conservation methods include terracing and ploughing along contours to prevent the run-off of surface water.

MODERN TRENDS

A great deal of scientific research has gone into maintaining soil fertility by applying artificial fertilisers, and into controlling the voracious grasshopper swarms and other insect pests. Experiments have also produced drought-resistant and fast-growing strains of wheat, so that cultivating the Great Plains is now much less a matter of chance than it used to be. Even so, it is likely that more of the marginal wheat lands will be devoted to grazing and mixed farming. Similarly, the increasing number of irrigation schemes, both large and small, mean an expansion in the production of fodder and more specialised crops.

Wheat growing is now so efficient that the area cultivated will continue to shrink—but with no fall in production. At the same time, small family farmers are

Figure 34 *The western Great Plains: annual rainfall variations, 1878–1946*

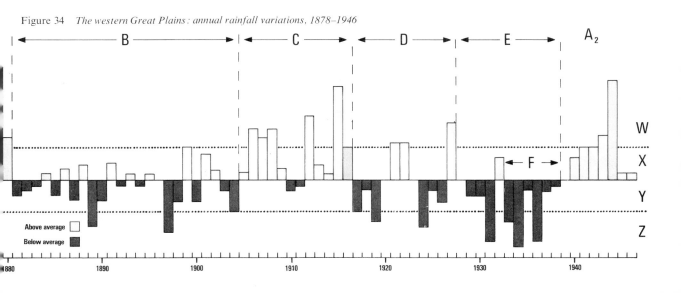

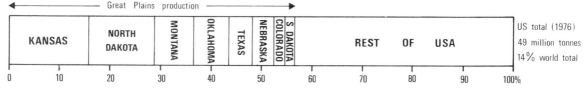

Figure 35 *US wheat production*

selling out to more mechanised concerns, and the largest farms now run into thousands of hectares. Even the harvesting has become a specialised job. Teams of men with combine harvesters begin the assault in Texas in May and gradually 'chew' their way north to the Canadian prairies. The journey takes five months, working eighteen hours a day and seven days a week. In one hour each of the giant ten-tonne machines can cut enough wheat to keep the average British family in bread for forty years!

Quite apart from general rural depopulation, there is another trend—abandoning the farm during the long snowbound winter months. 'Sidewalk farmers' live in the towns and commute to their land only when it needs attention. Others, the more prosperous 'suitcase farmers', spend five months of spring and summer raising and harvesting the crop, and then pack up and head for the winter sunshine of Florida or California. Small wonder that many rural communities, especially in the northern Plains, have all but vanished.

Questions

Figure 34

1. *a*) In your note book, match up the letters on the graph with the following descriptions:
   Blocks of years (A–E)   Harvest obtained (W–Z)
   Wet, Predominantly   None, Poor, Fair, Good.
   Wet, Widely Variable,
   Comparatively Dry, Dry,
   Dust bowl.
   b) How many of the 68 years had (*i*) 'average' rainfall, (*ii*) a good harvest, and (*iii*) no harvest?

Figure 35

2. Approximately what proportion of the USA's total wheat crop comes from the Great Plains?

Figures 30, 35 and the account

3. *a*) Approximately what proportion of the Great Plains' total production is (*i*) spring wheat, and (*ii*) winter wheat?
   b) Why are the two types of wheat grown in different areas?
   c) What physical features separate the two wheat areas?

The account

4. What is dry farming, and why is it necessary?

5. The Dakotas were two of the three states whose population actually decreased between 1960 and 1970. List some of the reasons why people are leaving this area.

Plate 22 and the account

6. *a*) Describe the landscape as fully as possible.
   b) Account for the alternating strips of cropland and fallow.

Plate 22   *A Wheat Belt landscape*

The Corn Belt : the richest farms on earth

Corn originated as a small wild plant in Central America and became the cultivated cereal which nourished the brilliant Inca, Aztec and Maya civilisations. The North American Indians adopted it from their southern relatives and were growing it on some 20 000 hectares when Columbus discovered the New World. It soon became the mainstay of the pioneer white settlers who, over the centuries, greatly improved the original strain. Significantly, the Indian word for corn was 'maize', which also means 'mother'. Outside the USA the cereal is still generally known by its Indian name.

In the United States today a greater area is devoted to corn than to any other crop. It is grown in practically every state but nowhere is it so important as in the Corn Belt of the Middle West. In this part of the Central Lowlands the ice sheets levelled off most of the low hills and filled the valleys with glacial drift. Over much of the area deep, stoneless, moisture-retaining soils were deposited, while the western part is covered by fertile loess. Climatic conditions are ideal for growing corn, which needs a minimum of 140 frost-free days. Between June and August night temperatures rarely fall below 10°C and rise to the high 20s by midday. Since most rain also falls in the growing season—often in the form of thunderstorms—the corn rapidly develops into tall, sturdy plants, each with 200 times more grains than its primitive ancestors.

Although corn occupies up to 40 per cent of the cultivated area it takes so much fertility from the soil that rotations are widely used. Of the rotation crops soyabeans (soybeans) have become very important. They are an excellent soil-restorer and make a good hay and grazing crop, but some of the soyabean harvest is sold as a cash crop for conversion into edible oil and flour, soap, paint and varnish. The high protein content of the crop has long been valued in concentrated feed for animals, but more recently soya products have been processed for human consumption, particularly as 'textured' meat substitutes.

Table 21   The Corn Belt : climatic statistics

Indianapolis (251 masl) (Indiana)	J	F	M	A	M	J	J	A	S	O	N	D	
Temp °C	−2	−1	4	11	17	22	24	23	19	13	5	0	Range 26
Precip. cm	7	7	10	9	10	9	8	8	9	7	9	8	Total 101

Omaha (336 masl) (Nebraska)	J	F	M	A	M	J	J	A	S	O	N	D	
Temp °C	−6	−4	3	11	17	22	25	24	19	12	4	−2	Range 31
Precip. cm	2	2	3	7	10	12	10	8	8	6	3	2	Total 73

Plate 23   *Typical Corn Belt farm*

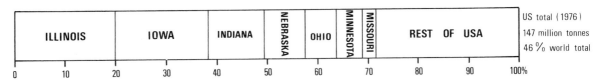

Figure 36 *US corn production*

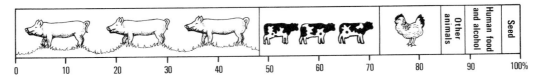

Figure 37 *How corn is used*

Some Corn Belt farmers specialise almost entirely in crop production while others run feedlots like those in South Dakota, since cattle raised on the Great Plains are brought east for fattening. However, the majority of farms grow corn and soyabeans for feeding to their own stock. Large silos and lofty barns are necessary for storing the feed and for housing the animals in winter.

In fact, the Corn Belt is the USA's leading livestock region, producing over half the pigs and approximately one-third of the other livestock. The farms in Iowa, for example, are so efficient that from little more than 100 hectares of land the average farmer produces enough beef each year to feed 295 Americans and enough pork to feed 524. The whole system is clearly geared to supplying large urban populations living at a high standard and consequently eating more meat than cereals. The system may be criticised as wasteful but the farms themselves are the most productive in the world.

Questions

Figure 30

1. To the south the Corn Belt is limited by poorer, non-glacial soils and by the Ozark uplands. List the factors which form the boundaries: (*i*) to the north; (*ii*) to the west; (*iii*) to the east.

Table 21 and the account

2. *a*) Make a comparison of the two areas. (*hint:* use the same headings as for Abilene and Bismarck [see question 4 in the Great Plains section])
   b) What climatic features make both the Omaha and Indianapolis areas suitable for corn growing?

Figures 30 and 36

3. *a*) Name the three states which lie entirely, or almost entirely, within the Corn Belt.
   b) Approximately what proportion of the US corn total is produced by (*i*) these three states, and (*ii*) the seven named on the diagram?

Typical corn belt crop rotations

(A)	(B)	(C)
Corn	Corn	Corn
Oats	Corn or	Soyabeans
Pasture	Soyabeans	Oats
(Grass, clover or	Oats	Pasture
alfalfa)	Pasture	Pasture

4. Which rotation is likely to be used on soils that are (*i*) of average fertility, (*ii*) poorer than average, and (*iii*) better than average? Explain your answer.

Figure 37 and general

5. *a*) How much of the corn is (*i*) marketed 'on the hoof', and (*ii*) fed to animals (of all types)?
   b) What kinds of human food are produced from corn?

Service centres in the Middle West

Although the Middle West contains several giant in-dustrial cities, most of the larger settlements are of only moderate size and exist essentially to meet the special needs of the region's farming communities. These medium-sized centres usually have a variety of factories, often of considerable local importance. Many of these buy up the produce of Middle West farms and then process it into food ready for the table. For example, Battle Creek (Figure 38) is the original home of Kellogg break-fast cereals. Other factories specialise in manufacturing fertilisers, agricultural machinery and other equipment that the farmer needs. A drive to the large town also gives the farmer's family an opportunity to visit bigger stores and brighter places of entertainment than are usually avail-able nearer home.

For most farm families, however, day-to-day require-ments are met by the much smaller country towns where the population usually numbers hundreds rather than thousands. In these centres, whose tree-lined streets are nearly always laid out on a grid pattern, most of the buildings are constructed of timber, although the church, town hall, fire station, bank and school may be of brick or stone. Other services usually include a garage, a farm machinery repair shop and perhaps a co-operative creamery or grain elevator, together with a limited range of shops and offices.

Connected to the surrounding farms by a grid of minor roads, these small service centres are as characteristic of the Middle West as the farms themselves. However, for many of these once-prosperous small towns the future seems very bleak. As increasing numbers of farm folk leave the countryside for the city, and as the network of modern motorways extends across the region, so the small centres can expect only a steady decline in their local importance.

Figure 38   *Service centres and communications in part of southern Michigan*

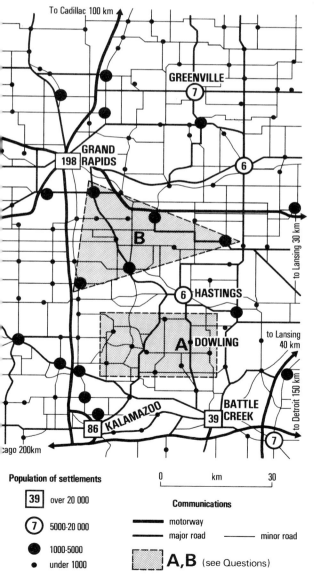

Questions

Figure 38

1. a) In the rectangle marked A, what is the average distance between each centre with less than 1000 pop-ulation and its 'nearest neighbour' of similar size?
   b) Make similar calculations for (*i*) the centres with populations of 1000–5000 in the triangle marked B; and (*ii*) the centres with populations of more than 20 000.
   c) What general relationship is there between size and distance apart?

Figure 38 and the account

2. a) If you were living on a farm at A on Figure 38 which centre would you probably visit for each of the following purposes: (*i*) to buy weekly groceries; (*ii*) to have a tractor serviced; (*iii*) to have dental treatment; (*iv*) to see a film; (*v*) to buy a new harvester; (*vi*) to select an engagement ring; (*vii*) to see a top-class baseball game?
   b) What general relationship exists between a town's size and: (*i*) the range of services it offers; (*ii*) the extent of its 'sphere of influence' over the surrounding countryside?
   c) Why does the area have so many small service centres but only a few large ones?

Figure 38 and general

3. Describe, and account for, the dominant pattern of the road network. (*hint:* original survey)

Figure 38

4. a) Compare the importance of the following as route centres, or 'nodal points': Grand Rapids, Kalamazoo, Battle Creek, Hastings and Dowling. Use this scoring system to establish a 'nodality index' for each town:
   Motorway–5 points; *Major road*–3 points; *Minor road*–1 point. *Example:* Greenville, 4 major roads (4×3=12); 2 minor roads (2×1=2) Nodality index=14.
   b) What is the general relationship between a town's nodality index and its population size?

The Middle West: Industrial Heartland

Introduction

In addition to its phenomenal agricultural wealth the Middle West also contains the most important section of the 'Manufacturing Belt' (see Figure 39). The dominance of the Manufacturing Belt has diminished in the twentieth century as newer industrial centres in the south and west (especially California) have developed, but it still retains a major share of the USA's leading industries, most of which have above-average growth prospects. Moreover, with the decline of some long-established industries in New England and other parts of Megalopolis, the advantage has moved to the Middle West, which has emerged as the nation's undisputed economic heartland.

In the nineteenth century the Middle West's rich endowment of natural resources, particularly iron ore and coal, provided an unparalleled basis for industrial expansion. With the development of railways, canals and natural waterways, especially those of the Great Lakes, a great urban-industrial complex rapidly grew up.

About 40 per cent of the USA's industrial production now takes place within an 800 km radius of Chicago, the region's main city. The various manufacturing centres are so extensive, and the links between them so strong, that another megalopolis can now be recognised—that of 'Chipitts' (Figure 39) which contains five of the USA's

Figure 39   *The Middle West and the Manufacturing Belt*

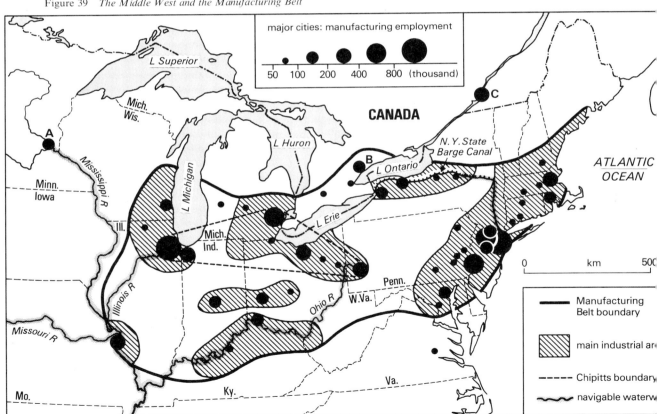

largest cities. Like the original Megalopolis, Chipitts is not a continuous urban-industrial sprawl; its manufacturing towns and cities, although economically interdependent, are physically separated by much farmland, forest and open space.

Table 22   The Manufacturing Belt: a century of change

| Year | Manufacturing Belt's share of US total | | |
	Manufacturing employment (%)	Population (%)	25 largest cities
1870	77	56	18
1970	56	44	13

Table 23   The present-day importance of the Manufacturing Belt

Jobs in the five leading industries	Percentage share of US total
Primary metals	73
Fabricated metals	66
Machinery	69
Electrical equipment	65
Transport equipment	55
Jobs in all 'growth industries'	60
Industrial investment	
New plant and equipment	50
Research and development	50

Since about 1950 the industrial cities of the Middle West, in common with those of Megalopolis, have attracted millions of black Americans from the Southern states. In cities like Chicago and Detroit the problems of black poverty and ghetto-living are as acute as anywhere in the United States.

Questions

Figure 39 and an atlas

1. Name (*i*) the main city (or cities) within each industrial region, and (*ii*) the industrial centres marked A, B and C.
2. *a*) Which states have shorelines on both the Great Lakes and the Atlantic?
   b) Identify the only industrial region which does not have direct access to navigable water.

Tables 22 and 23

3. *a*) The decline of the Manufacturing Belt is only relative. Explain this statement.
   b) What are the Belt's future prospects?
4. *a*) In what ways are the industries dependent on each other?
   b) Why is there a continuing concentration of such industries in the Manufacturing Belt?

Figure 39 and general

5. *a*) Why is 'Chipitts' so called?
   b) Some geographers consider that most of the region shown on Figure 39 (including that in Canada) is really one gigantic 'Great Lakes Megalopolis'. What is the evidence for this?

Plate 24   *Sault Sainte Marie locks*

Iron mining in the Lake Superior district

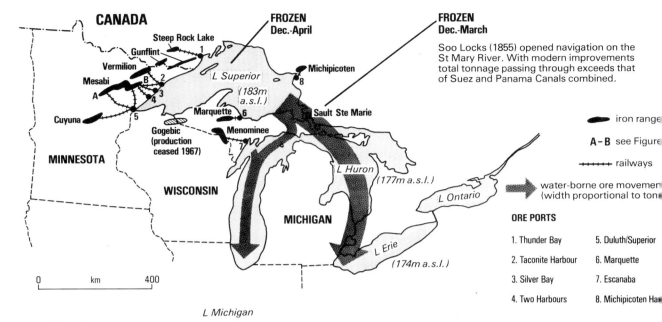

Figure 40   *Lake Superior iron ranges and ore movements*

Around western Lake Superior the Canadian Shield penetrates into the USA, providing the country with its richest deposits of iron ore. There are now five 'iron ranges' of which those in Minnesota are the most important, particularly the Mesabi Range which produces nearly 60 per cent of all usable iron ore from US mines. In nearly a century of mining the Lake Superior deposits have yielded over 4000 million tonnes of high-grade 'haematite' ore. However, the iron content of the ore currently being extracted is only 45 per cent (compared with 70 per cent in the nineteenth century) and remaining haematite reserves have diminished to an estimated 500 million tonnes.

Since the Second World War the threat of rapid exhaustion of the main source of US steel production has led to conservation of home reserves and an increase in imports from reliable foreign suppliers. In addition, methods have been found of using some of the abundant low-grade ores in the Lake Superior iron ranges. Rocks such as 'taconite' exist in reserves of up to 100 000 million tonnes and have a 20–30 per cent iron content dispersed in fine grains throughout the ore. After crushing, the grains are concentrated magnetically and then formed into pellets with a 63 per cent iron content. Unfortunately, however, about two-thirds of all known taconite formations are nonmagnetic and are thus impossible to concentrate economic-

Figure 41   *The Mesabi Range: mining and beneficiation centres*

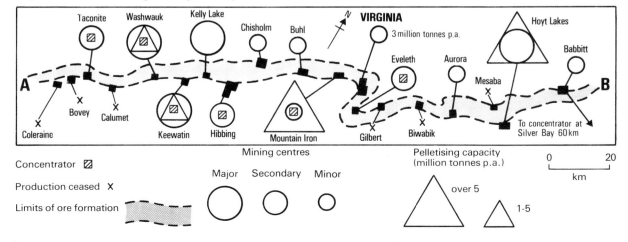

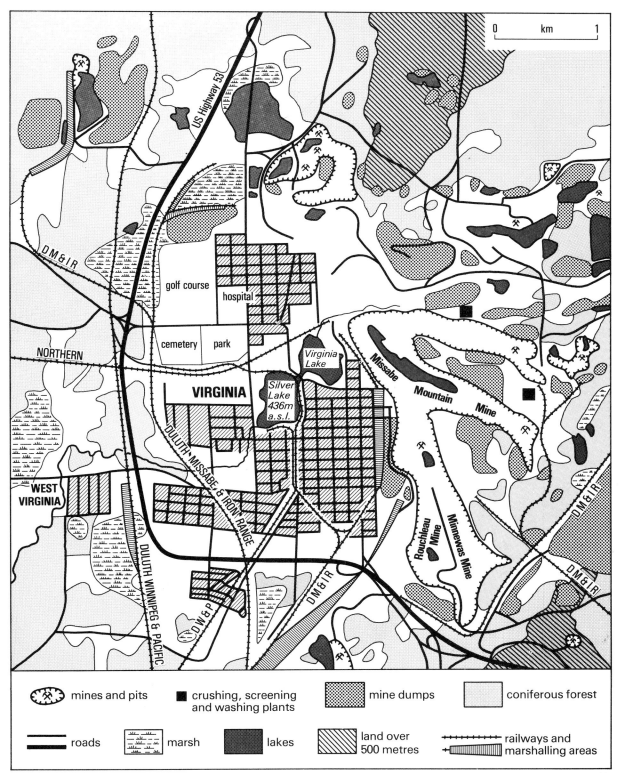

Figure 42 *Virginia, a mining town in Minnesota*

ally by any method yet devised. Nowadays most other types of iron ore are also up-graded or 'beneficiated' before shipment.

The enormous costs of mining and treating the new lower-grade ores have necessitated large-scale operations, conditions which can only be met by surface mines working on a year-round basis. A few dozen surface operations now account for 90 per cent of the USA's production of usable iron ore. Economies of scale are obtained by such devices as mechanical shovels with 200 cubic-metre capacities and huge trucks which can carry more than 200 tonnes of ore to the beneficiation plants. The iron ore occurs mainly in thick beds which are exploited in open, terraced pits as much as 400 metres deep. The pits have a long life, and large quantities of ore are thus produced with minimum damage to the surface area. Even so, a recent government report has predicted that the entire Mesabi Range could eventually become one immense lake.

Table 24   Lake Superior iron ore production

	1945	1955	1975
Lake Superior production (million tonnes)	75	83	64
Lake Superior production as a percentage: of US total of all iron ore	84	80	71
used in USA	83	65	46

Questions

Table 24 and the account

1. Describe and account for the trends shown.

The account and general

2. *a)* List the advantages and disadvantages of taconite.
   b) Why does beneficiation take place before shipment?

Figure 41

3. *a)* What evidence is there that the ore now being mined is low-grade?
   b) In each case, name four mining centres that are (*i*) currently most important, and (*ii*) in danger of becoming 'ghost towns'.
   c) How does Virginia (Minnesota) currently rank as a mining town?

Figure 42 and general

4. *a)* Describe the natural environment of the area before mining commenced.
   b) Discuss in detail the full impact of mining activities on (*i*) the natural environment, and (*ii*) the lives of the townsfolk.
   c) (*i*) What measures could the mine owners (the major US steel companies) take to restore the affected land? (*ii*) Why are they usually reluctant to do so?

Figure 40 and general

5. How is iron ore moved from the mines to the ports of the southern Great Lakes? Write a detailed account, mentioning any special problems involved.

The coalfields of Appalachia and the Middle West

American coal reserves are sufficient to last 300 years, the richest deposits lying in the eastern states (Figure 43). The reserves stretching south from Iowa to eastern Oklahoma

Table 25   Sources of energy used in the USA (percentage figures)

	1900	1960	1980 (est.)
Coal	90	23	36
Oil	4	42	31*
Natural gas	2	31	18
Hydro-electric power (HEP)	4	3	6
Nuclear	0	1	9
Totals	100	100	100
Index of total energy used:	100	420	890

*About 40 per cent of this is imported.

are still virtually untouched but the Appalachian field, which still contains 30 per cent of remaining US reserves, has long produced high-quality industrial coals for conversion into low-sulphur coke for blast-furnaces. Now much depleted, the extensive 2·5-metre thick Pittsburgh Seam was especially important in the early growth of that city's iron and steel industry.

RECENT TRENDS AND PROBLEMS

Since the mid-1950s spectacular gains have been made in productivity, which dwarfs that of other countries (Table 26). Uneconomic pits have been closed down and practically all underground operations are now highly mechanised. Even more impressive are developments on the surface, where opencast mining employs methods and

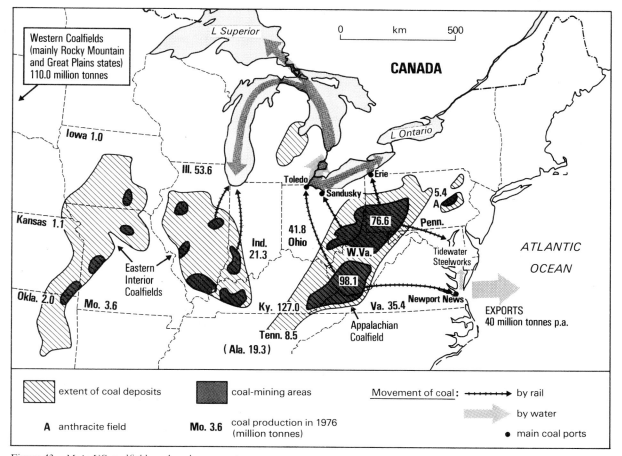

Figure 43   *Main US coalfields and coal movements*

Table 26   How American coal is won

Type of mining	Approximate percentage of total production*	Productivity (tonnes per man day†)
Underground	40	15
Opencast	55	35
Augering	5	45
All types	100	20 (UK: 8·5)

*665 million tonnes in 1977 (UK: 119 million tonnes)
†Total work force: 125 000

equipment similar to those in the Lake Superior iron ranges. The proportion of coal produced by surface mining varies from 90 per cent in Indiana and 70 per cent in Ohio to about 10 per cent in West Virginia where the physical conditions are less favourable. In rugged country opencast mining is known as 'contouring' which leaves a cliff face where further cutting into the hillside becomes uneconomic (Figure 44). At this point a giant 'cork-screw' auger, over 2 metres in diameter, is then bored into the seam, extracting the coal at very low cost. Both auger-ing and opencast mining are increasing; new lands are being dug up at the rate of 60 000 hectares a year.

Figure 44   *Diagrammatic cross-sectioning of coalmining in Appalachia*

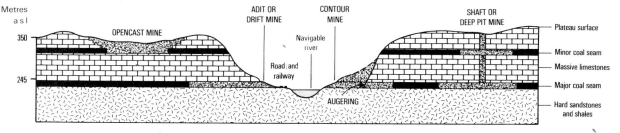

Table 27   Land disturbed by opencast coal-mining

The three 'leading' states	Hectares
Pennsylvania	150 000
Ohio	112 000
West Virginia	79 000
USA total	1 000 000

(Note: For comparison, the total area of the Isle of Wight is 38 000 hectares.)

(*Ohio Division of Geological Survey,* Bulletin 65, *1975*)

In Appalachia, the area worst affected, opencast mining has become a major environmental problem. Apart from disfiguring the landscape, surface mining removes vegetation, causes soil erosion and disrupts drainage. In addition toxic wastes can pollute streams and lakes over a wide area, endangering wildlife, farm animals and human populations. New laws require the restoration of currently mined areas but abandoned workings remain as permanent scars.

Generally speaking, opencast mines produce lower-cost, lower-quality coal mainly for burning in power stations. To cut costs even further, special 'unit trains' carry coal directly between the producing areas and the power plants. Essentially, unit trains are a set of locomotives and freight wagons that remain coupled at all times and carry one single commodity over long distances. Operating on a shuttle basis, each train may be 1·5 km long and carry 10 000 tonnes of coal to a power plant 1500 km away. At the terminals, rail loops enable the trains to be loaded and unloaded while still in motion, thus minimising delays. So successful have these trains become that hundreds more are planned for the 1980s. By then they may pose a serious threat to the traditional Great Lakes coal traffic, much of which is also destined for power plants in the Lakes states and Canada.

For the moment, the main drawback is that the low-grade coal used by the power stations has a high sulphur content and contributes heavily to air pollution. As this situation has recently been outlawed by the US government, effective devices to filter dangerous sulphur fumes from chimney gases are being developed as a matter of urgency. Despite the environmental problems created by its production and use, the likelihood is that American coal will continue to regain some of its former importance—mainly as a result of the world-wide energy crisis.

Questions

Table 25

1. *a)* Draw a bar graph from the statistics (*hint:* make each bar proportional in length to the index of total energy used).
   b) With particular reference to coal, comment on the main trends shown by the statistics.

Figure 44 and the account

2. List the various methods of mining. In what circumstances would each be used?

Plate 25 and Figure 44

3. How do geological conditions in the Appalachian field favour the use of underground machinery?

Table 26 and the account

4. *a)* What is the difference between 'production' and 'productivity'?
   b) How have modern techniques affected (*i*) productivity, and (*ii*) the environment?

Figure 43

5. *a)* Name the three major coal producing states.
   b) Approximately what proportion of the US total is their combined output?

Figures 43, 44 and the account

6. *a)* List (*i*) the various markets for coal, and (*ii*) the means of transporting coal.
   b) How might unit trains affect the trade of (*i*) the Great Lakes coal ports, and (*ii*) Newport News?

Plate 25   *A continuous miner in a Kentucky underground coalmine*

The Middle West's iron and steel industry

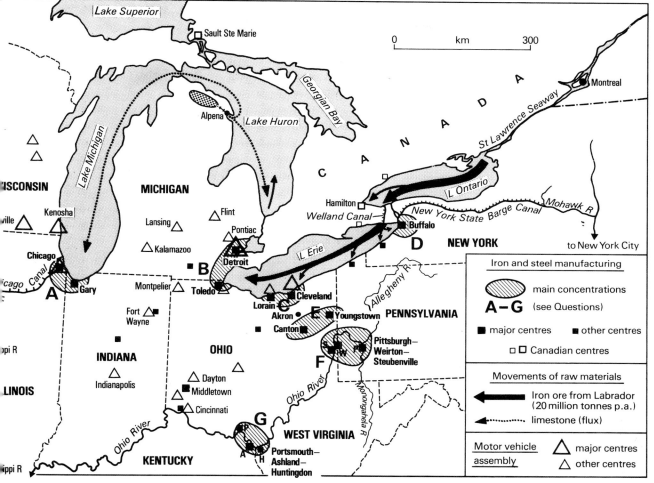

Figure 45   *The Middle West's main industries: iron and steel and motor vehicles*

Questions

Figure 45 and general

1. Five of the main iron and steel areas (marked A–G on Figure 45) are described below. Identify each of the five areas.

i) In the 1840s this area's major city became the first iron and steel centre west of the Appalachians. Initially, local iron ore was smelted using charcoal as fuel, but in 1859 the industry switched to coke and soon afterwards began importing Lake Superior haematite, railed 'up-gradient' from Lake Erie ports (nowadays additional supplies come from Labrador). The industry benefited from proximity to excellent coking coals and quickly expanded to become the USA's leading steel producer, a position it held until the 1920s.

However, steelwork sites were restricted to the narrow valley floors of deeply incised rivers, e.g. where tributaries unite to form the Ohio River. No completely new plant has been located here since 1911, and the area's contribution to national production (once 43 per cent) has fallen to around 10 per cent.

ii) Located around a Great Lakes shore, this outlying area's industry began in the 1880s near the Middle West's largest city where agricultural and general engineering provided a large market for steel. Massive expansion began in 1906 when the world's largest integrated steelworks was opened at a specially created satellite town in the adjacent state.

The area uses iron ore mainly from Lake Superior and coal from fields to the south and south-east. The market-oriented location has proved highly successful; eight major plants now contribute nearly 30 per cent of the USA's total steel output.

iii) Developed in the twentieth century and located on the southern shore of one of the Great Lakes, this area has the advantage of large level sites, more modern works and, in waterfront locations, direct access to ore supplies from both Lake Superior and Labrador. Coal is railed down-gradient from Appalachia at cheap return-cargo freight rates. A further advantage is cheap water transport for finished products.

iv) This area receives both Lake Superior and Labrador iron ore at lakeshore and riverside locations. Coal is railed down-gradient from West Virginia, to which there is some return ore traffic. The area contains several individual steelworks owned and operated by major car manufacturers. The steel is used directly in their own factories.

v) Occupying a position midway between one of the Great Lakes and a major coalfield, this area is equidistant from supplies of ore and coal, both of which are transported by rail.

Table 28   Steel production in the USA

US producing areas	Million tonnes	Percentage of	
		US total	World
Chicago-Gary (Area A on Figure 45)	33	28·2	4·5
Cleveland-Youngstown-Pittsburgh (C, E, F)	27	23·4	3·7
Other centres on Figure 45	25	21·0	3·3
Rest of USA	32	27·4	4·5
Totals:	117	100·0	16·0

Table 28 and Figure 45

2. Combining all the US centres on Figure 45, what percentage do they contribute to the total steel production of (i) the USA, and (ii) the world?

Table 29 and general

3. a) 'Cleveland is primarily a bulk cargo port'. Explain this statement.
   b) Explain the general pattern of Cleveland's trade.

Plate 26   *Ford Motor Company's iron and steel works, River Rouge, Dearborn, Mich.*

Table 29   Commodities handled by the Port of Cleveland

Imports	Million tonnes	Exports	Million tonnes
Iron Ore from Lake Superior	22	Semi-finished iron and steel products	2
Iron Ore from Labrador	3*	All other commodities (including coal and coke, oil and oil products, animal oils and other bulk materials)	2
Limestone	2		
All other commodities (including paper, board, wood pulp, sand, gravel and other bulk materials)	6		
Total	33	Total	4

*Includes small quantities from Liberia and Chile.
(*Ohio Division of Geological Survey*, Bulletin 65, *1975*)

Plate 26 and the information in Question 1

4. List the economic advantages of such waterfront locations compared with iron and steel centres inland.

Figures 40, 43, 45, an atlas and general

5. Draw or trace an atlas map of the Great Lakes—Middle West industrial region. On the map show:
   a) the main concentrations of the iron and steel industry;
   b) the major sources of iron ore, coal and limestone;
   c) the main movements of these commodities.
(*hints:* (*i*) Ensure that the map encompasses all the relevant areas of mining, etc., and that the scale is large enough for all the necessary details. (*ii*) Make use of colour to distinguish the movements of different commodities. (*iii*) Give the map an appropriate title, key and scale.)

Detroit : Automobile capital of the world

In 1908 Detroit's two centuries of placid existence was shattered when Henry Ford introduced two revolutionary new ideas—the assembly line and the mass-produced car. The famous Model T Ford rolled from the production lines in ever-increasing numbers. By 1927, when a completely new model was introduced, over 17 million 'Tin-Lizzies' had taken to the road. Ford's success attracted many other manufacturers to Detroit, quickly establishing it as the world's 'car capital' and a major industrial city (population 1·5 million, metropolitan area 4·2 million).

In the early days there were dozens of American car firms but the numbers rapidly dwindled, mainly because of the huge amounts of capital needed to ensure success in a highly competitive business with large automated factories and expensive research programmes. Since the 1930s the 'Big Three' (Figure 46) have controlled some 90 per cent of US production, which in 1973, a record year, amounted to 11·2 million cars, well over one-third of the world's total output. General Motors is the largest company in the world, having financial assets which dwarf those of most independent nations. Indeed, the Big Three are all important multi-national companies with subsidiary plants in many countries, including Canada and Britain. Thus decisions made in Detroit may have repercussions far beyond the boundaries of the United States.

Within the USA, the automobile industry has grown to

Plate 27 *Stamp, commemorating the French founding of Detroit, 1701*

dominate the national economy. More than 10 per cent of the wealth produced each year is spent on buying, maintaining and insuring a total of over 100 million private cars (there are also 26 million other vehicles). In all, one American worker in every six is dependent directly or indirectly on the motor vehicle industry. The assembly plants alone employ 1·5 million people, but the fortunes of many other industries are tied to the demands of the motor manufacturers. For example, the motor industry is the biggest single user of steel (16 per cent), malleable iron (41 per cent), rubber (73 per cent) and glass (36 per cent).

Figure 46 *Detroit: Motor City*

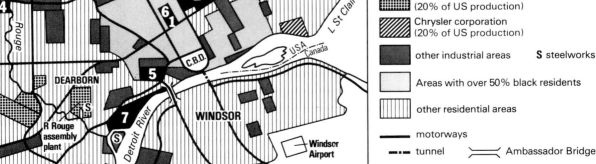

Plate 28 *Ford assembly line, River Rouge works*

Small wonder that the production and sales of cars are often used as indicators of the nation's general economic health.

The car assembly plants were once nearly all located in Detroit itself, but since the Second World War there has been considerable decentralisation. Factories have been established in several areas with big markets for cars (e.g. California) although the vehicles are constructed mainly from parts made in Detroit. Even so, the greatest concentration of car factories remains in Detroit and in a ring of neighbouring towns in Michigan and adjacent parts of Ohio and Indiana (Figure 45). Detroit alone still accounts for about one-third of all vehicle assembly, while most of the 50 000 firms supplying the mass of equipment and myriad components that make up a modern car are located in numerous centres throughout the surrounding region. Akron, which specialises in the production of tyres, is particularly important, and so is Toledo for its glass.

Judged in terms of the percentage of workers in manufacturing (35 per cent compared with the national average of 26 per cent) the Detroit region is the most highly industrialised area in the United States. One-third of the manufacturing workers are employed in the vehicle assembly and related industries. The city's other industries include pharmaceuticals, office equipment, TV components, salt and meat products.

CURRENT PROBLEMS OF THE CAR MAKERS

Detroit's car makers first came under attack in the 1960s when their products were described as 'unsafe at any speed'. Since then the law has required all new cars made in the United States to incorporate a wide range of safety features, many of which have since been adopted in Britain and other countries.

Many US cities, including Detroit, suffer awesome problems of air pollution caused mainly by thousands of slow-moving cars. Government regulations required that by 1978 pollution from car exhausts had to be cut to only 10 per cent of the 1971 levels. To try to comply with the new rules the automobile engineers devised combustion and filtering devices which are now fitted to all new American cars. By 1975, however, little improvement had been achieved; motor vehicles still pumped nearly 90 million tonnes of carbon monoxide and other pollutants into the atmosphere.

A third major problem began in 1973 when the OPEC nations forced a four-fold rise in the world price of oil. The 'energy crisis' severely affected the USA where motor vehicles were consuming over 1000 million litres of fuel every day. Because public transport has all but withered away, most Americans have no practical alterna-

71

tive but to continue using their cars, which account for over 90 per cent of all passenger transport. Consequently, the government have given the car makers ten years to achieve dramatic fuel economies (Table 30), and drivers of 'gas-guzzlers' are threatened with tax penalties.) But unless Detroit's engineers can design engines of unprecedented efficiency the *average* weight of new cars will have to be reduced, thus ending the era of the large American automobile.

Table 30   Average US and British saloon cars: a comparison of size and economy

	Year	Weight	Litres per 100 km
US car	1964	1400	18
	1974	1800	22
	1977	1400	14
British car (Morris Marina 1·8)	1977	900	9
Targets set by US Government	1980	—	11
	1985	—	8

Questions

Plate 27, Figure 46 and general

1. *a*) What is the meaning of the French name 'Detroit', and why is it appropriate?
   b) How is the city's founder commemorated in the modern car industry?

The account and general

2. In 1908 Ford built 6000 Model Ts, each selling at $950. In 1921 the equivalent figures were 1 250 000 and $325. Why did the car become cheaper?

Figure 46

3. What evidence is there that black Americans form a large percentage of Detroit's car workers?
4. 'For each of the following districts of Detroit name the car company which has major works located there: (*i*) Dearborn, (*ii*) Hamtramck, (*iii*) Highland Park.

Figure 46 and Plate 26

5. In what ways does the River Rouge assembly plant enjoy a better location than most others?

The account and general

6. What are the main advantages and disadvantages of having:
   a) thousands of suppliers of components and equipment, and
   b) decentralised assembly plants?

Table 31

7. *a*) Draw a pie-graph from the statistics.
   b) What percentage of the car is composed of (*i*) metals, (*ii*) other minerals, and (*iii*) vegetable products?
   c) What is the economic significance of the footnote?

Table 32

8. Graph the statistics, using a framework of two vertical lines (for 1950 and 1974) drawn 10 cm long and 10 cm apart.

Table 31   What goes into a typical American car? (1978 model)

	Weight (kg)	Percentage of total
Steel	847	60·5
Iron	223	15·9
Rubber	78	5·6
Oil and other fluids	63	4·5
Aluminium	36	2·6
Glass	32	2·3
Plastics	30	2·1
Soft trim, paper, cardboard	30	2·1
Copper	11	0·8
Zinc	11	0·8
Paint and protective dip	10	0·7
Lead	8	0·6
Miscellaneous	21	1·5
Total	1400	100·0

(Note: About 7 million cars are scrapped every year!)

Table 32   Changing levels of car ownership in the USA and selected countries.

	Cars per thousand population	
	1950	1974
USA	265	495
Canada	130	455
UK	50	255
France	40	290
Sweden	40	320
West Germany	25	275
Italy	10	265
Japan	2	145

Chicago : industrial metropolis

Chicago was created mainly by the railways, which focused on the city just as the Middle West was being opened up to settlers. Chicago processed and marketed the grain and livestock of the new farmlands and became the major commercial and financial centre for the growing rural and urban population throughout the region. It also developed as a great manufacturing centre, producing agricultural machinery and supplying all the varied needs of its vast hinterland. With the added advantages of cheap water transport, by 1890 Chicago had become the USA's second largest city, a position it still holds (population 3 099 000, metropolitan area 7 015 000).

The city's first industrial areas were located along the banks of the Chicago River (Figure 47) but the developing rail network attracted many of the newer industries, especially those dependent on rapid transport. After 1870 large industrial plants requiring huge expanses of land moved to the southern edge of the city and beyond. Here, steel mills, cement plans, electrical machinery, railway rolling stock and car factories created a zone of heavy industry later intensified by the addition of power stations, oil refineries and petrochemical works. In all, Chicago has approximately 14 000 factories representing 95 per cent of the complete range of industries listed by the US government. At present one-third of the city's work force is employed in manufacturing industries, and Chicago is second only to New York as an industrial centre.

Figure 47 *The Chicago Metropolitan Region*

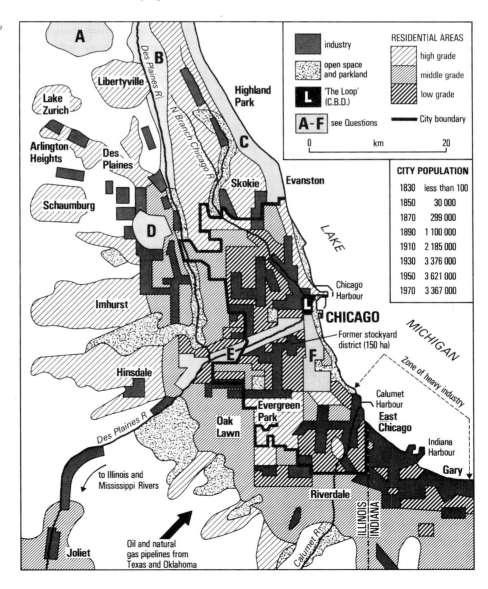

Legend:
- industry
- open space and parkland
- **L** 'The Loop' (C.B.D.)
- **A–F** see Questions
- 0 km 20

RESIDENTIAL AREAS
- high grade
- middle grade
- low grade
- City boundary

CITY POPULATION
Year	Population
1830	less than 100
1850	30 000
1870	299 000
1890	1 100 000
1910	2 185 000
1930	3 376 000
1950	3 621 000
1970	3 367 000

Map labels: A, B, Des Plaines R, Libertyville, Lake Zurich, Highland Park, N Branch Chicago R, C, Arlington Heights, Des Plaines, Skokie, Evanston, LAKE, Schaumburg, D, Imhurst, Chicago Harbour, L CHICAGO, Former stockyard district (150 ha), MICHIGAN, E, F, Hinsdale, Zone of heavy industry, Calumet Harbour, Evergreen Park, East Chicago, Oak Lawn, Indiana Harbour, Des Plaines R, Gary, to Illinois and Mississippi Rivers, Riverdale, ILLINOIS, INDIANA, Joliet, Oil and natural gas pipelines from Texas and Oklahoma, Calumet R

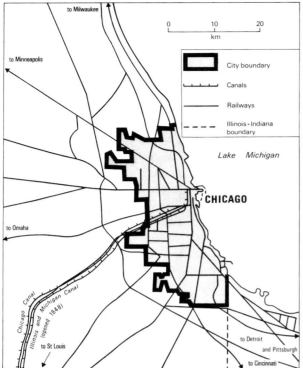

Figure 48 *Chicago: canals and railways*

Figure 49 *Chicago: modern motorways*

Figure 50 *Chicago: residential patterns, 1920*

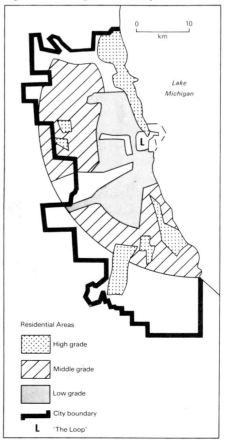

Traditional forms of transport remain important as carriers of freight, while newer forms have reinforced Chicago's role as the major city of the US interior. The modern motorway system focuses on Chicago, which has become a leading centre of road transport. Chicago annually despatches nearly 60 million tonnes of goods by road or rail, double the amount of New York or Los Angeles. In addition, 85 per cent of the maritime commerce of the Great Lakes is transacted in Chicago's offices. To underline the city's continuing business and commercial pre-eminence, O'Hare International is the busiest airport in North America.

During the 1960s half a million, mostly white, Chicagoans left to take up residence in the pleasanter environment of the suburbs. At the same time, the city gained a third of a million black people. By 1970 black residents numbered 1 103 000—almost a third of Chicago's total population. Most of the black population lives in sub-standard housing near the city centre, overcrowded ghetto areas which have several times erupted in serious rioting. This particular movement of population, producing a poor (black) central city, surrounded by affluent (white) suburbia, has become the pattern of metropolitan development throughout the USA.

Questions

An atlas and general

1. *a*) Measure the distance (*i*) between Chicago and the agricultural producing areas (e.g. Nebraska), and (*ii*) between Chicago and the main nineteenth century food-consuming areas (the cities of the Atlantic coast).
   b) Using your answers to *a*), explain why Chicago became the main grain-processing and meat-packing centre during the nineteenth century.
   c) Chicago's stockyards and slaughterhouses closed down in the mid-1950s. Why did the large meat-packing companies, such as Armour and Swift, move their plants further west, e.g. to Omaha?

Figures 48 and 49

2. Compare the rail and motorway networks with reference to *a*) their general pattern, and *b*) the type of traffic now carried.

Figures 47, 48, 49 and general

3. With reference to the location of *a*) industry and *b*) residential areas, comment on the role played by (*i*) waterways, (*ii*) railways and (*iii*) motorways.

DOWNTOWN CHICAGO

At the heart of Chicago lies its central business district, 'The Loop'—so called because it was once encircled by an elevated urban railway. Despite competition from newer satellite centres in the suburban fringe, The Loop retains its traditional role as the business, commercial and financial hub of the entire metropolitan region; its skyscrapers reflect high land values.

Like the CBDs of many other American cities, The Loop has a dual personality. By day, it swarms with both whites and blacks going shopping or to work. By night, however, most whites return to the suburbs leaving the central area almost entirely to the black population.

Questions

Figure 51

1. The Chicago River, which is the city's main sewer, has been reversed to flow inland. Why?
2. What evidence is there that Chicago is a major centre of *a*) transportation, *b*) commerce, and *c*) learning, culture and recreation?
3. The line of Michigan Avenue represents the original lake shore. How has the reclaimed land been put to use?

Figure 51   *Downtown Chicago*

The account

4. In 1974 the city council announced 'Chicago 21', a long-term redevelopment plan which aims to replace 30 km² of central city slums with racially-integrated housing for 120 000 people.
   a) Why is Chicago 21 necessary?
   b) How do you rate its chances of success?

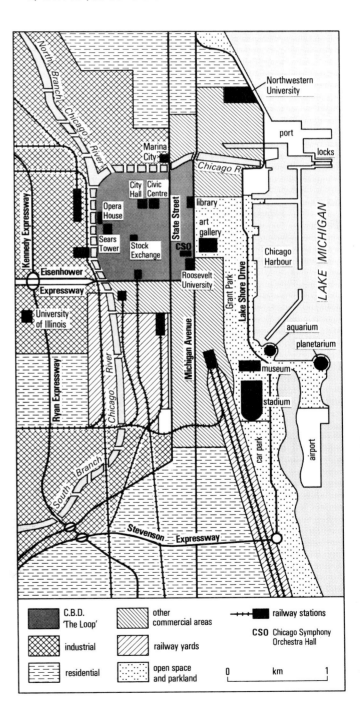

Figure 52

4. *a*) List the advantages of the Sears Tower compared with (*i*) the much smaller building that it replaced, and (*ii*) most conventional skyscrapers.
   b) The Sears Tower has been criticised for adding to the congestion of The Loop. Explain how this might happen.

Plate 29 and Figure 51

5. Marina City includes two 65-storey cylindrical apartment buildings, offices, shopping area, bowling alley, ice rink, multi-storey car parks and a marina for 700 small boats.
   a) In what direction was the photograph taken?
   b) (*i*) To what income group do the residents of Marina City belong? (*ii*) Why did the city council encourage its construction?

Plate 29   *Marina City, Chicago*

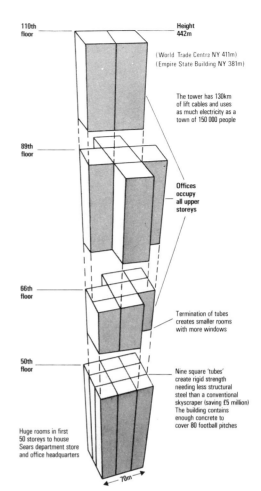

110th floor

Height 442m

(World Trade Centre NY 411m)
(Empire State Building NY 381m)

The tower has 130km of lift cables and uses as much electricity as a town of 150 000 people

89th floor

Offices occupy all upper storeys

66th floor

Termination of tubes creates smaller rooms with more windows

50th floor

Nine square 'tubes' create rigid strength needing less structural steel than a conventional skyscraper (saving £5 million) The building contains enough concrete to cover 80 football pitches

Huge rooms in first 50 storeys to house Sears department store and office headquarters

70m

Figure 52   *The Sears Tower, Chicago: the world's tallest*

ANALYSING CHICAGO'S STRUCTURE

Before fire destroyed much of the city in 1871, Chicago's residents, whether poor or better-off, lived in the same areas near their places of work. The rebuilding of the city coincided with the development of public transport such as trams and suburban railways, which enabled the middle class residents to live farther from the city centre. At the same time Chicago began to receive a massive influx of European immigrants who crowded into the housing vacated by the middle classes. These two trends, combined with the growth of industry, led to the continuous outward expansion of the city, which became divided into several different social and land-use areas.

Similar patterns developed in other cities both in the United States and elsewhere. A number of 'models' have been put forward to generalise about these urban patterns. Two of these will be examined and applied to Chicago.

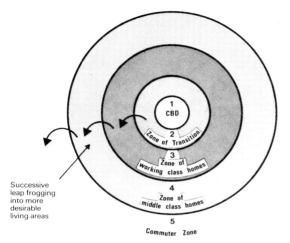

Figure 53   *The Concentric or Zonal Model*

Zone 4. *Middle-class homes.* This area contains newer and more spacious houses occupied by middle-class families with larger incomes, who make a longer journey to work, usually in the Central Business District. This more desirable area is often the goal of people in Zone 3.

Zone 5. *Commuter zone.* This area lies beyond the city's continuous built-up area and is the home of the wealthy. Many residents commute daily to the city centre, one hour's travelling time often marking the zone's outer limit. Much of the area may still be open country although the small settlements within it have often changed their character from local communities to city 'dormitories'. It is often the ambition of status-seeking people in Zone 4 to buy an expensive house in the commuter zone.

2: THE SECTOR MODEL

This model also assumes outward growth from the CBD but suggests that any contrasts in land use around the city centres will be extended as the city expands—even if the contrasts originated by mere chance. Thus distinctive sectors or wedges of land use will radiate outwards from the centre, often along major routeways.

Figure 54   *The Sector Model*

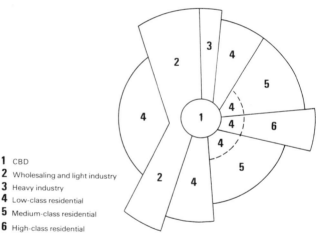

1 CBD
2 Wholesaling and light industry
3 Heavy industry
4 Low-class residential
5 Medium-class residential
6 High-class residential

1: THE CONCENTRIC OR ZONAL MODEL

This model assumes that the city grows outwards from its central area, forming a series of concentric zones.

Zone 1. *Central Business District* (The Loop in Chicago).

Zone 2. *Transitional zone.* An area of older housing, in the process of being taken over for offices and industry, or being subdivided into smaller low-rent housing units. This area attracts most of the first-generation immigrants and is generally characterised by low standards of housing, low incomes and many kinds of social problems. Earlier immigrant groups eventually succeeded in 'leap-frogging' outwards to disperse in other parts of the city, but this pattern has not been repeated by the black Americans who are the zone's present inhabitants.

Zone 3. *Working-class homes.* This area also has older housing but the white working-class families living here are generally more stable with higher living standards and fewer social problems. To live in this area has traditionally been the first objective of people in Zone 2.

Questions

Figure 50 and general

1. Account for the 1920 residential patterns in terms of the two theories. Which seems to be the more relevant?

Figures 47, 50, 53, 54 and general

2. *a*) What major changes have taken place since 1920?
b) To what extent does modern Chicago fit each of the two models?

Figure 47, the account and general

3. Identify from the following list the areas marked A–F on Figure 47: (*i*) a black ghetto, (*ii*) a commuter settlement, (*iii*) a zone of heavy industry, (*iv*) a very desirable residential area, (*v*) open space and parkland, (*vi*) O'Hare International Airport.

General

4. Attempt a simple analysis of your local urban area using the theoretical models. Which seems to be the more relevant?

The Southern States

Introduction

'The South' is historically associated with plantation agriculture, slavery, and the Confederate States which tried to break away from the Union during the Civil War (1861–5). This account will deal mainly with the eleven states comprising the Middle and Deep South (Table 33), an area nearly six times larger than Britain and containing about one-fifth of the USA's total population. While not lacking variety, all these states have heavily wooded landscapes and share a warm humid climate which makes the pace of life generally slower than in the north.

Defeat in the Civil War not only disrupted the South's flourishing economy but created a racial problem too. Many of the region's white population found it impossible to accept ex-slaves as their equals, and for a century Southern blacks endured apartheid in most aspects of

Table 33   States comprising The South

The Middle South (or Hill-land South)	Kentucky, West Virginia, Virginia, Tennessee, North Carolina
The Deep South (or Plainsland South)	Arkansas, Louisiana, Mississippi, Alabama, Georgia, South Carolina

everyday life. Schools and colleges were racially segregated, as were buses, trains and facilities in hotels, theatres and restaurants. Blacks were also denied voting rights and, since they were excluded from many jobs, were prevented from making a full contribution to the South's economic recovery. Indeed, by the 1930s the South had fallen so far behind the rest of the United States that it was officially described as 'the nation's economic problem

Figure 55   *The South: Civil War divisions and main cities*

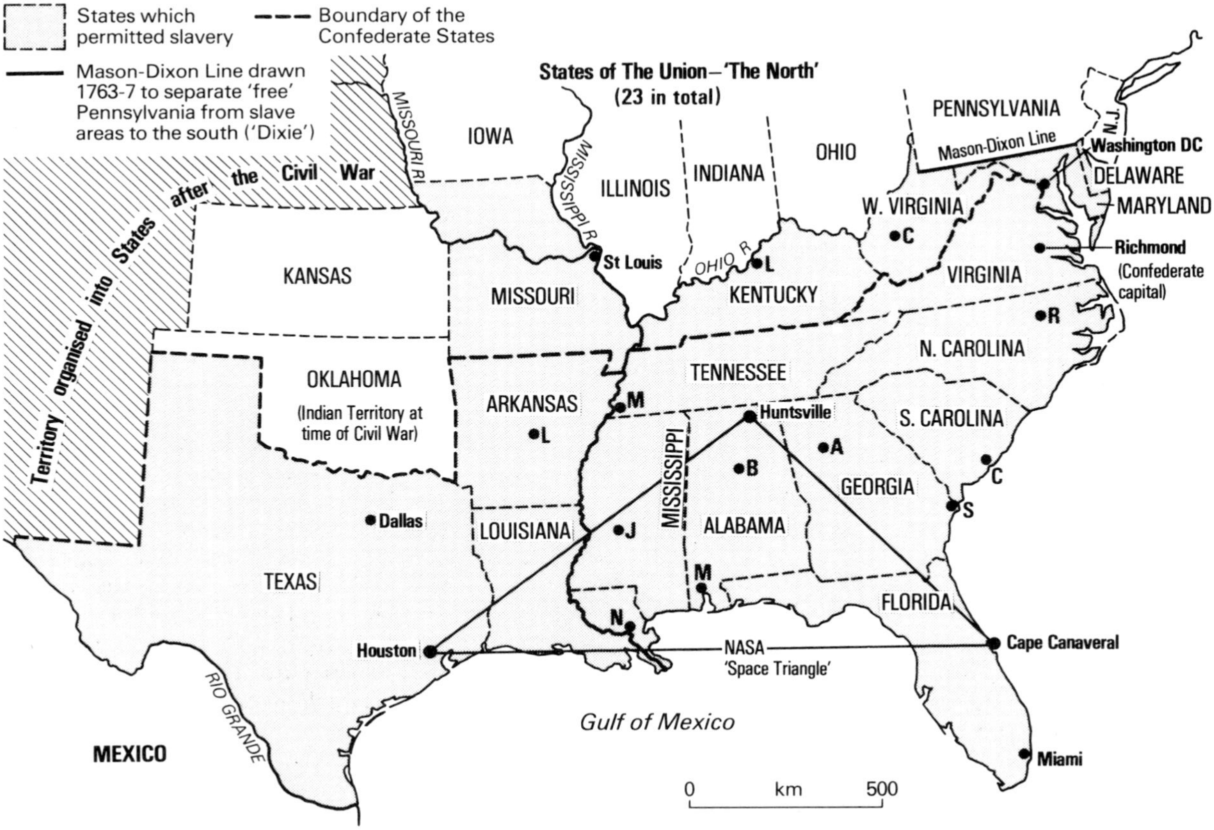

No. 1', an underdeveloped region within the world's most developed country.

The traditional image of the South as sleepy, rural and backward has changed dramatically since then. Federal legislation in the 1960s abolished the worst aspects of segregation, and Southern blacks now enjoy most of the civil rights for which they have campaigned so long. Not that all of the 'Old South' has been swept away; it is still more dependent on agriculture than most other parts of the USA, and it still contains a greater proportion of poor people—both black and white—than any other region.

However, with considerable help from the federal government, a 'New South' is emerging, complete with up-dated agriculture, expanding cities and booming modern industries, e.g. those of the NASA 'Space Triangle'. The New South is now rapidly catching up with the rest of the USA and there are signs that the outflow of people—especially black people—is at last slowed down.

Questions

Table 33 and an atlas

1. *Middle South/Deep South.* What is the geographical basis for this division of the region?

Figure 55 and an atlas

2. *a)* How many Confederate States were there?
   b) Name the cities shown by their initial letters.

The account and general

3. *a)* What is meant by 'apartheid'?
   b) In which country is apartheid official government policy?

Figure 55 and general knowledge

4. *a)* Name the places at the points of the 'Space Triangle'.
   b) What do the initials NASA stand for?

Black Americans : exodus from the South

There have been black Americans ever since 1619 when slaves from Africa were used by the English colonists to tend tobacco fields along the hot, humid Virginia coast. During the next two-and-a-half centuries slavery became widespread as tobacco, sugar and cotton plantations were established throughout the South. The plantation owners built up enormous fortunes and the Southern economy flourished—but at the expense of much human misery. The evil system of slavery was finally abolished following the North's victory in the Civil War, when four million blacks gained their freedom.

The great majority of black Americans remained tied to the rural South until the First World War. At that time northern manufacturers, no longer able to obtain their usual supplies of cheap immigrant labour, began to draw upon the huge reservoir of workers in the South. Since then increasing numbers of blacks have moved to the cities of the industrial north and, since the Second World War, to those of California and other Western states. As a result, several such cities now have a black population larger than that of any Southern state.

Recently black Americans have made significant breakthroughs in gaining equal opportunities in education, jobs and housing, and in raising their general standard of living. But most of these improvements have been made in areas where blacks are relative newcomers. In the South, where blacks remain predominantly rural, the traditional attitudes of the white majority are more deeply entrenched and progress has been much slower.

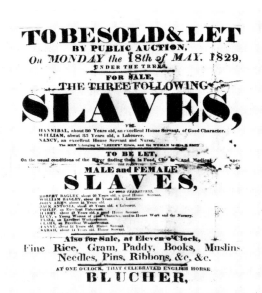

Plate 30   *Slave sale advert*

79

Questions

Table 34   Southern States and their black population (1975)

States of the Middle and Deep South	Black population (thousands)	Blacks as a percentage of total population
Alabama	920	25·4
Arkansas	356	16·9
Georgia	1 288	26·1
Kentucky	244	7·2
Louisiana	1 134	29·8
Mississippi	841	35·9
North Carolina	1 193	21·9
South Carolina	867	30·8
Tennessee	651	15·6
Virginia	931	18·7
West Virginia	64	3·6
Other Southern States		
Florida	1 179	14·2
Oklahoma	191	7·1
Texas	1 530	12·5

(*US Abstract of Statistics, 1977*)

Table 34 and an atlas

1. Draw or trace a map of the South, including the boundaries of the states listed in the table. Name each state and shade or colour it to show black people as a proportion of the total population.

(*i*) Use four percentage categories: 0–9·9; 10–19·9; 20–29·9; 30 and above.

(*ii*) Use light shading or colour to show low percentages and increasingly darker shading or colour for the higher percentages.

(*iii*) On the map add information to show each state's total black population (in millions) and whether it is a larger (+) or smaller (−) percentage than in the USA as a whole (11·5%) e.g. Alabama 25·4 (+).

(*iv*) Give the map an appropriate title, key and scale.

2. *a*) Name the states where black people (*i*) are more than 20 per cent of the total population, and (*ii*) number more than 0·75 million.

b) What geographical pattern do these states form on your map?

3. In 1976 there were 24·8 million black people in the USA.

a) Approximately what proportion of this total still live in the Southern states?

b) Where, in general terms, do the remainder now live?

Table 35, the account and general

4. *a*) Describe, and account for, the differences between the incomes of black families in the South and those living elsewhere in the USA.

b) Since the Second World War black Americans have been leaving the South at a rate of 100 000 a year. List as many reasons as possible for this exodus.

Table 35   Comparison of average family incomes, 1973

	Approximate annual income (£)	Income as a percentage of whites'
Black families in the South	4735	55
Black families outside the South	6045	70
Black families in the USA	5135	60
White families in the USA	8630	100

(*US Abstract of Statistics, 1977*)

Plate 31   *Black poverty in the South*

The Deep South's shrinking Cotton Belt

The so-called Cotton Belt has never been devoted entirely to the cultivation of cotton. A large proportion of the total area has always been heavily wooded; some districts have traditionally specialised in other cash crops (e.g. tobacco) and some land has always been used for food crops (especially corn). Even so, from about 1800 until well into the twentieth century cotton completely dominated Southern agriculture, especially in the six states comprising the 'Deep South' (Table 33).

Although cotton remains an important cash crop throughout the region, the traditional picture has changed dramatically. Whereas in 1900 the Deep South was still growing nearly two-thirds of the USA's total cotton crop, today the proportion has fallen to less than one-third, and the area planted with cotton has shrunk even more drastically. Only in Mississippi does cotton remain the most valuable crop, but even there it does not occupy the most land.

Table 36   The Deep South: climatic statistics

Vicksburg (75 m a.s.l.)

	J	F	M	A	M	J	J	A	S	O	N	D	
Temp °C	9	11	15	19	23	26	28	27	24	19	14	10	Range 19
Rainfall cm	13	13	14	13	11	10	11	9	7	7	10	13	Total 131

New Orleans (15 m a.s.l.)

	J	F	M	A	M	J	J	A	S	O	N	D	
Temp °C	12	14	17	20	24	27	27	27	25	19	16	13	Range 15
Rainfall cm	11	10	11	12	11	14	17	14	12	9	9	12	Total 142

Figure 56   *Agricultural speciality areas of the present-day Cotton Belt*

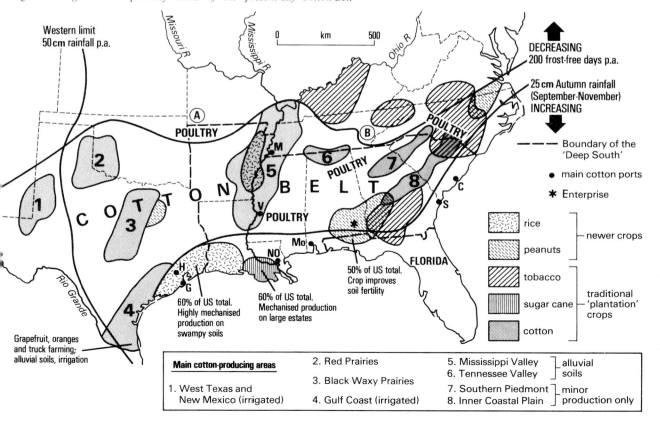

Main cotton-producing areas

1. West Texas and New Mexico (irrigated)
2. Red Prairies
3. Black Waxy Prairies
4. Gulf Coast (irrigated)
5. Mississippi Valley — alluvial soils
6. Tennessee Valley — alluvial soils
7. Southern Piedmont — minor production only
8. Inner Coastal Plain — minor production only

There are several reasons for the decline of cotton's dominance in the Deep South but none more important than the destruction caused by the boll weevil, which first appeared in southern Texas in 1892. The weevil's eggs are laid in the developing cotton boll; after hatching, the larvae destroy the fibre then fly away to lay more eggs. In the warm, moist conditions of the Deep South the insect pest multiplied rapidly and by 1921 an army of boll weevils had invaded the entire Cotton Belt. Eventually insecticides were developed to control the weevils, but in many areas the only certain remedy was either to move out and grow cotton further west (where the insects could not survive the drought and frost) or to stay put and grow a completely different crop. In both cases farmers enjoyed greater prosperity than before, and the boll weevil was soon regarded as a blessing in disguise.

Another factor in the decline of cotton-growing was the condition of the soil. Cotton is an extremely exhausting crop and a century or more of monoculture eventually caused much land to be abandoned. Furthermore cotton was often cultivated in clean-weeded rows on sloping land, and the exposed soil was easily washed away by frequent thunderstorms. The remaining cotton growers have also had to contend with an increasing shortage of labour caused by the exodus of blacks to the northern cities.

In addition, increasing competition now has to be faced from major producing areas both overseas and in the western USA. With more fertile soil, and the benefit of better machinery and irrigation techniques, the newer American producers obtain twice the yields of those in the Deep South and at half the cost. The more efficient areas are also better able to withstand the most recent threat to cotton production—synthetic fibres.

Plate 32   *Boll weevil monument, Enterprise, Alabama*

Plate 33   *Mechanical cotton harvesters, Mississippi Valley*

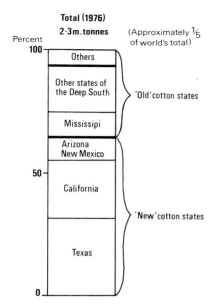

Figure 57 *US cotton production*

duction of conservation techniques, especially new crop rotations (e.g. cotton, soybeans, hay) which are superseding the old monoculture.

Above all, diversification of land use in the Deep South is the most important feature. Many farmers who once grew cotton have been experimenting with new ways of making their land productive. As a result, three important trends have emerged. The first is the production of a variety of speciality crops such as peaches (e.g. in Georgia), peanuts and vegetables. The second is an increased emphasis on livestock. Large-scale poultry farms in the South now produce over half the USA's chickens, while the development of hay and pasture lands has made the rearing of cattle important throughout the region. The third trend is the development of forestry, which has boosted the local pulp and paper industries. The South now has about two-thirds of the USA's pulpmill capacity, the greatest concentration being along the coast between Savannah and Mobile.

Questions

Figure 56 and an atlas

1. *a*) What climatic factors form the boundaries of the Cotton Belt in (*i*) the north, (*ii*) the west, and (*iii*) the south?
b) Account for the southward 'bulges' of the northern boundary at A and B.
2. Which of the ports shown handle the most cotton today? Explain your answer.

The account and general

3. Account for *a*) the decline of cotton production in the Deep South, and *b*) the success of the 'new' cotton states.

Plate 32, Figure 56 and the account

4. Why was the monument erected to an insect pest?

MODERN TRENDS

The cotton farmers of the Deep South now concentrate production on the most fertile areas and on level land where modern machinery can be used. Greater efficiency is also attained by amalgamating small farms into larger estates known as 'neoplantations'. More than two-thirds of the Deep South's cotton is now picked mechanically. Yields are also being increased by using the full range of modern scientific methods. In many cotton districts low-flying aircraft, spraying various chemicals on to the growing crop, are now a common sight. In addition, the ravages of soil erosion are being prevented by the intro-

Questions

Plate 33 and the account

1. *a*) To what extent does the scene illustrate modern trends in cotton farming in the Deep South?
b) List any other factors which are improving efficiency.

Figures 56 and 55

2. Name four states with large tobacco-growing districts.

Figure 56 and Table 36

3. Describe and account for the distribution of rice production.

Figure 58 and the account

4. Write a detailed explanatory account of the information given in the bar graphs.

Figure 58 *Typical modern agricultural patterns in the Deep South (Mississippi)*

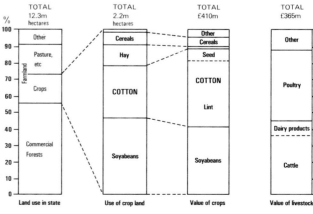

The Tennessee Valley Authority (TVA) : an example of regional planning

Before 1933 the Tennessee Valley was one of the South's most depressed regions. It was essentially an agricultural area where forest clearance and poor farming techniques had caused soil erosion on a massive scale. The irregular flow of the River Tennessee with its huge silt load made it virtually useless for navigation, and created a flood hazard both along its own course and in the lower Ohio and Mississippi valleys.

In 1933 the basin of the Tennessee was selected by the federal government for a comprehensive scheme of planned regional development. The TVA was set up with three main aims: to improve navigation, to control flooding and to generate HEP. These objectives were achieved by building an impressive series of multi-purpose dams and by providing a 2·75-metre deep navigation channel for barges between the Ohio and Knoxville.

The major dams on the Tennessee itself generate most of the HEP, while the principal role of the smaller dams on the tributaries is to store water until needed for power generation or for navigation, and to retain water if floods threaten. The Kentucky Dam is the key to flood control on the lower Ohio and Mississippi; the entire Tennessee River system can be 'turned off' until flood crests have passed, thus preventing millions of pounds of damage.

In order to prevent its reservoirs silting up, the TVA has had to tackle the problem of soil erosion. This has been accomplished through farm education schemes and by gaining the co-operation of the farmers in the head-water valleys. The steeper slopes have been terraced to check sheet erosion, while ploughing is done along the contours instead of across them, and crops with different harvest times are grown in alternating strips to avoid ex-

Figure 59   *The Tennessee Valley Authority area: industrial developments*

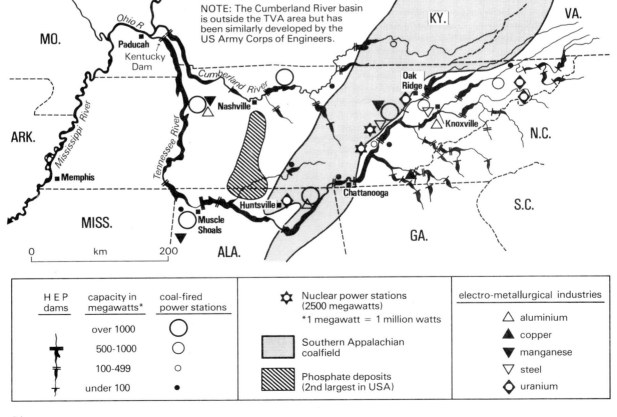

34 a and b *Hillside restored by TVA afforestation programme*

posing whole fields to torrential downpours. Farming has also been made more efficient by the provision of cheap electricity and fertilisers manufactured by TVA factories at Muscle Shoals.

Table 37   Monthly electricity bills: comparable industrial users

Location of factory	£
TVA area	2000
Chicago	3170
Boston	3890
New York	5670

The production of abundant cheap electricity has triggered off such an industrial boom in the region that the original HEP stations can no longer cope with the demand. To stave off a power shortage in 'Electricity Valley' the TVA has had to build a whole series of coal-burning plants which are now being supplemented by a new generation of nuclear power stations; the total capacity is expected to double within the next decade.

Among the region's electricity-hungry industries, of special note is the uranium enrichment and plutonium plant at Oak Ridge, where the first atomic bomb was built; and rocket research, development and testing at Huntsville, the northern point of NASA's 'Space Triangle'. Even more dramatic than the growth of industry has been the expansion of water-based recreational activities in a region where no natural lakes existed. With 16 000 km of shoreline, the 'Great Lakes of the South' now attract millions of visitors each year.

The TVA is widely regarded as a symbol of Southern progress and its work has received international acclaim. It has certainly brought higher living standards throughout the Tennessee Valley and shows what can be achieved by the combined efforts of federal and state governments and local communities. Strangely, however, this kind of action by the federal government is still regarded with political suspicion elsewhere in the USA, and the experiment has never been repeated.

Questions

Figure 59, the account and general

1. The TVA's authority covers an area four-fifths the size of England and spreads into seven states.
    a) Name the states.
    b) Why did the *federal* government have to tackle the job of developing the area?
2. *a)* How long is the Tennessee River's navigation channel?
    b) TVA river ports handle over 20 million tonnes of cargo each year. The principal commodities are: coal, grain, petroleum products, iron and steel, forest products and chemicals. Divide the list into (*i*) 'upstream' and (*ii*) 'downstream' commodities.
3. *a)* What is a 'multi-purpose dam'?
    b) Name the largest HEP station on the Tennessee River.

4. More than 75 per cent of TVA's electricity now comes from steam plants (coal-burning and nuclear) rather than dams.
    a) Why are the steam plants necessary?
    b) What are the locational advantages of the TVA area for (*i*) coal-burning plants and (*ii*) nuclear power stations?
5. *a)* What major type of industry has been attracted to the region? List the locational advantages.
    b) Account for the success of the TVA's fertiliser factories at Muscle Shoals.

Plates 34a and 34b and the account

6. Compare the two views. Explain why forests and pasture now take the place of cropland on such steep slopes.

Figure 60   *A 'staircase of lakes': profile of the Tennessee River*

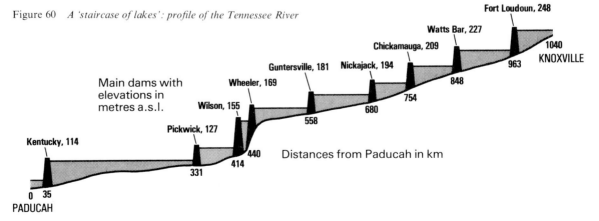

The South-Eastern States: industrial development and cities

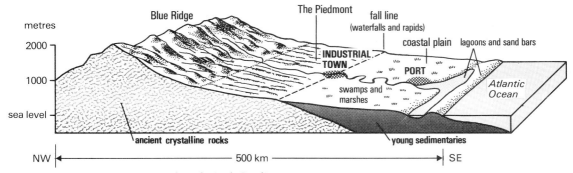

Figure 61 *Diagrammatic cross-section through North Carolina*

BIRMINGHAM (population 276 000, metropolitan area population 791 000). Birmingham is the centre of a relatively small but important iron and steel industry which began in the 1880s. Located on the southernmost extension of the Appalachian coalfield. 'The Pittsburgh of the South' benefits from proximity to good coking coal (lying in 1·5-metre thick seams near the surface). a lime-rich, self-fluxing iron ore, and supplies of extra limestone and dolomite for furnace linings. Despite low-production costs the industry was long disadvantaged by remoteness from the major iron and steel using centres. More recently, however, it has become crucial to the industrial development of the New South. It produces less than 10 per cent of the USA's steel total but specialises in pipes and tubes.

Figure 62 *Towns and industries of the Piedmont and Coastal Plain*

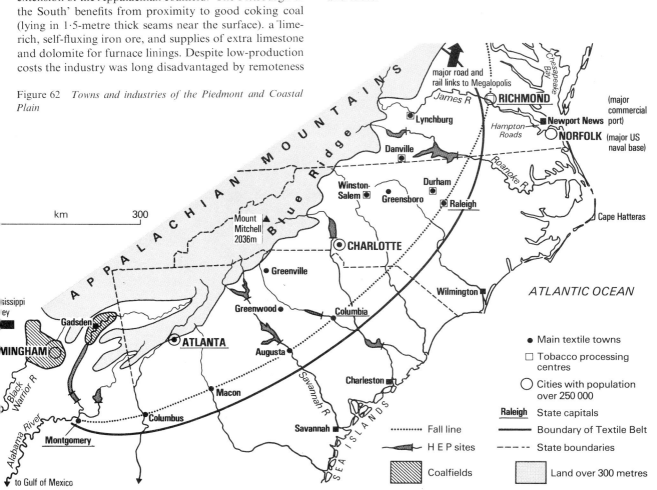

ATLANTA (436 000, metropolitan area population 1 790 000). Symbolic of the New South, Atlanta is the commercial, industrial and financial giant of the southeast and the regional capital. It was founded as a railway town in 1837, grew rapidly, and then was virtually destroyed during the Civil War. As the focus of road, rail and air networks it has become a major distributing and administrative centre with many warehouses and state and federal government offices. Its varied industries include motor vehicles, aircraft, rolling stock, textiles, chemicals and wood products. It is also the home of Coca Cola.

CHARLOTTE (281 000, metropolitan area population 593 000). This is the largest of the dozens of textile towns which are strung along the Piedmont zone between Lynchburg and Montgomery. The industry began in this area after the Civil War when New England mill owners were attracted by cheap labour, cheap power, soft water and local supplies of cotton. The decline of local cotton growing means that most of the raw material now has to be 'imported' from Texas and other western states. Even so, the industry has expanded to make the Piedmont the pre-eminent textile area in the United States. A few towns specialise in woollen goods, but recently many more have diversified into synthetic fibres, especially rayon derived from local timber.

Questions

Figure 61

1. *a*) Approximately how wide is (*i*) the Piedmont zone, and (*ii*) the Coastal Plain?
   b) (*i*) Account for the change in the nature of the river's course between the Blue Ridge and the sea (*ii*) Why did industrial towns grow up along the Fall Line?

Figure 62, an atlas and general

2. *a*) The textile belt lies in five states. Name (*i*) the states (from north to south), and (*ii*) their capital cities.
   b) Which of the capitals are Fall Line cities?

3. Chemical plants and paper mills have recently been established on the Piedmont. What modern locational advantages do these industries share with textiles?

4. Name (*i*) the canalised river system that links Birmingham to the sea, and (*ii*) Birmingham's seaport.

5. *a*) Why did Atlanta develop as the region's main route centre? (*hint:* Blue Ridge).
   b) What kind of services does Atlanta provide as regional capital?

The Gulf Coast and its industries

During the last few decades a zone within 80 km of the Gulf Coast has become one of the most heavily industrialised areas in the USA. Abundant deposits of salt, sulphur, oil and natural gas are among the most valuable in the world. Oil and gas are of special importance. Texas and Louisiana together account for approximately two-thirds of all US oil production and three-quarters of the natural gas. The first strike was made at Spindletop near Beaumont in 1901, after which many new oil and gas fields were discovered, some extending far out to sea.

WEALTH BENEATH THE WAVES

The first off-shore well was drilled in 1938, from a fixed platform in just a few metres of water. Since then the search for oil and gas has progressed farther and farther out on to the slope of the continental shelf, and floating rigs have become more common in recent years. In all there are now some 160 off-shore rigs in the Gulf of Mexico, about a third of the world total.

As British operations in the North Sea have shown, a modern self-contained drilling rig costs many millions of pounds. Apart from having all the necessary technical equipment and supporting services, a rig working in the Gulf of Mexico must also provide air-conditioned living quarters and recreational facilities for about 60 men, who usually spend alternate weeks at sea and ashore. The workers are evacuated by helicopter when hurricanes threaten, but the rig itself must be able to withstand the full fury of the storm. In particular the drilling platform must be kept stationary by raising it above the water, allowing the highest waves to pass underneath. Several techniques have been developed to achieve this objective. (See Figure 63.)

Apart from the cost of building and running the rigs, the oil and gas companies must pay a fee for exploration rights, an annual rental, and taxes amounting to one-sixth of all output. Small wonder that off-shore exploration and production is an extremely expensive business.

The very important question that had to be settled initially was: who should control the off-shore drilling and receive the revenues, the federal or the state government? Judgement was finally made in favour of the former, who decreed that most of the output should be piped to the Middle West and North East. However, there are many Texans and Louisianans who still feel that control of the oil and gas is rightfully theirs.

As with oil and gas, sulphur is now obtained from off-shore deposits. Most is extracted by the low-cost Frasch process, where superheated seawater is piped down to melt the sulphur, which is then pumped to the surface in liquid form. However, about a quarter of all sulphur output is a by-product of oil and gas wells. Its most important use is in the production of acids for fertilisers, insecticides and paints.

Questions

Figures 63, 64 and general

1. The limits of off-shore drilling have been extended thus:
   1955: 30 metres of water, 30 km from land;
   1977: 550 metres of water, 180 km from land (oil and gas at 7000 metres depth).
   a) Explain why different types of rigs have been developed.
   b) Why is it likely that the final limits of off-shore working may soon be reached?
2. What construction industry (named on Figure 64) benefited directly from the development of off-shore drilling? Explain your answer.

The account and general

3. *a*) Why have US oil companies played a major role in the search for, and production of North Sea oil?
   b) Compare the physical conditions of the North Sea and Gulf of Mexico. List (*i*) the similarities, and (*ii*) the differences likely to be experienced by the oilmen.
4. The question 'Whose oil'? has also arisen over North Sea production. Explain briefly the economic and political background to the dispute.

Figure 63   *Types of off-shore drilling rigs designed for work in the Gulf of Mexico*

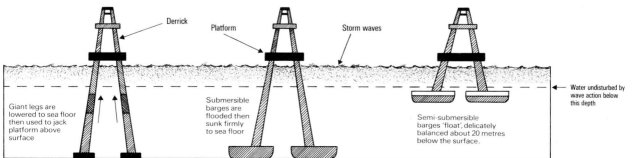

Modern industrial developments

Before the Second World War nearly all the region's output of oil and gas was sent by pipeline and tanker for refining and use in the north-east USA. This traffic is still important but the Gulf Coast is now the major centre of the nation's oil processing industry. Together with salt and sulphur, oil and natural gas provide the fuel and resource base for an extremely important petrochemical industry. Literally hundreds of different products are manufactured, including synthetic rubber, nylon and PVC. The waste product of one plant may be the essential requirement of another, and the whole region is criss-crossed by thousands of kilometres of pipelines through which materials are interchanged amongst factories.

Other industries with large energy requirements were established in the region by the government during the Second World War (e.g. iron and steel, and tin smelting). More have since been attracted to the area, principally by the availability of cheap fuel and sites with deep-water access. Indeed, both the Houston Ship Channel and the River Mississippi below Baton Rouge seem destined to be lined solid on both banks with oil refineries and chemical plants—interspersed with metals industries, power stations, and shipping and storage facilities. Such clusters of new industries have created great wealth throughout the Gulf Coast region.

Questions

Figure 64 and the account

1. 'Golden Crescent' and 'Spaghetti Bowl' are descriptions applied to the Gulf Coast industrial region. Explain why.
2. *a)* Name the three major concentrations of oil refineries.
   b) The region refines more oil than it produces. How is this achieved?

Plate 35 and general

3. *a)* List some of the site requirements of the oil refinery shown in the background. (hint: it has a river frontage)
   b) The presence of such an industry so close to Baton Rouge has both advantages and disadvantages for the city. What are they?

Figure 64 *The Gulf Coast oilfield and associated industries*

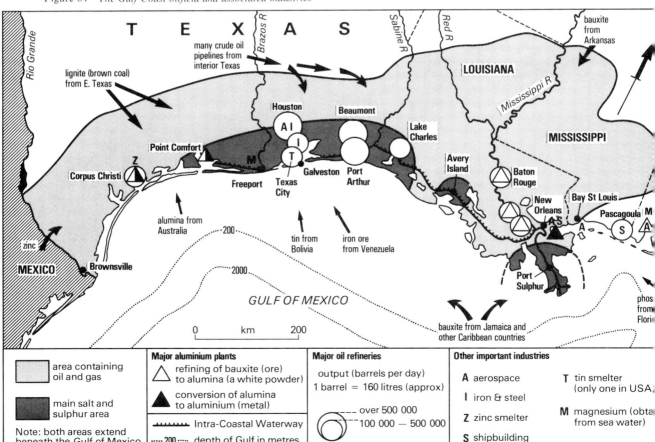

Figure 64

4. *a*) Name the commodity 'imported' by sea for use in the chemical industry.
   b) From where do the heavy metals industries of the following cities obtain supplies of ore: (*i*) Houston, (*ii*) Corpus Christi, (*iii*) Texas City?

Figure 64 and general

5. Aluminium production requires (*i*) huge quantities of cheap electricity, and (*ii*) a good location for receiving bulk shipments of raw materials.
   a) Account in detail for the fact that the Gulf Coast produces about 75 per cent of the USA's alumina and 25 per cent of its aluminium.
   b) Why does the Gulf Coast import bauxite from Jamaica but alumina from Australia? (*hint*: distance)

SPACE AGE INDUSTRIES

The latest arrival on the Gulf Coast is the aerospace industry. NASA's headquarters are in Houston, where at the Manned Spacecraft Centre capsules are developed and tested, and astronauts trained. At New Orleans (population 560 000) huge boosters for the largest rockets are manufactured, and at Bay St Louis (now converted to a space research centre) the boosters were static-tested before shipment to Cape Canaveral.

Despite the slow-down in manned-flight operations the American space exploration programme is continuing, so the region's research facilities and the manufacture of aerospace components remain important. Houston in par-ticular has also benefited from 'spin-off' industries such as electronic computers, data-processing machinery, printed circuitry and all types of electro-mechanical equipment. It is now the USA's fifth largest city and third largest port (population 1 357 000, metropolitan area 2 286 000).

Questions

1. What is meant by industrial 'spin-off'?
2. Houston is linked to the sea by the Houston Ship Channel (9 m deep and 90 km long). What other factors have contributed to its recent growth?

Plate 35 *Baton Rouge and neighbouring oil refinery*

The Mississippi : 'Old Man River'

The Mississippi River has one of the world's largest drainage basins, including all or parts of thirty-one American states and two Canadian provinces. Indeed, over 40 per cent of the continent's natural drainage funnels into the Mississippi, which annually carries to the sea over 500 million tonnes of material, mostly in the form of silt held in suspension. At the river's mouth the sediment is deposited faster than it can be moved by tides and currents. The result is a delta of marshes, lagoons and mud banks over which the Mississippi has repeatedly spilled sideways to form distributaries. The delta is constantly expanding seawards, modifying the Gulf coastline and locally depressing the earth's crust beneath the huge weight of deposits.

Below its confluence with the Ohio River, the Mississippi has created, over the course of many thousands of years, a valley varying in width from 50 to 200 km. Frequent flooding has deposited deep layers of fertile alluvial soil. However, the floods have sometimes been catastrophic. In 1927, for example, an area almost the size of Scotland was inundated, over 200 lives were lost and 637 000 people made homeless.

Following that disaster the federal government began a long-term project to provide effective flood control along the lower Mississippi. The main work has been the heightening and strengthening of the earthen embankments known as 'levees'. Many of these were constructed in the 1880s, but they were only 3 metres high and 16 metres wide at the base. Today, with the aid of modern earth-moving equipment, the ramparts are built 10 metres high and 96 metres wide. In all, there are now some 3500 km of levees along the Mississippi system, and they have successfully prevented major flooding on several occasions.

A secondary objective of the project was to improve the river's navigability. In the early nineteenth century the Mississippi became important as the principal means of transporting goods over long distances. However, its shallow, meandering and constantly shifting course always made navigation difficult, and its traffic declined rapidly with the advent of the railways. Since the federal project began, sixteen major 'cut-offs' have been excavated through meander necks, effectively straightening the river's course and reducing the distance travelled between Memphis and Baton Rouge by 270 km.

In addition, almost 1000 km of 'revetments' (overlapping concrete mattresses) have been laid across the soft river bed as far as the deep-water channel. Normally entire bends are revetted, stabilising the channel and thus protecting the vulnerable river banks from erosion. The main channel is dredged to a depth of at least 2·75 metres, creating over 3000 km of continuous navigable waterway for use by modern 'towboats' which push groups of barges transporting up to 50 000 tonnes at a time.

Figure 65   *The Mississippi Navigation System: ports and trade*

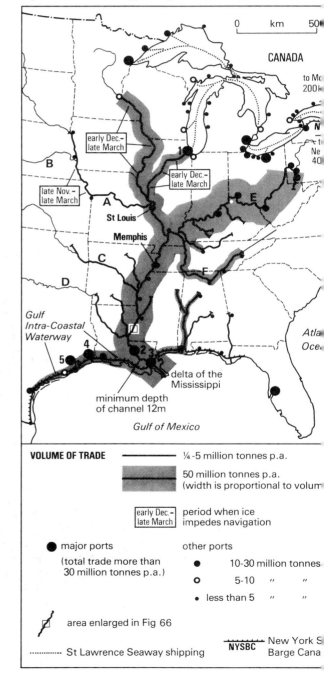

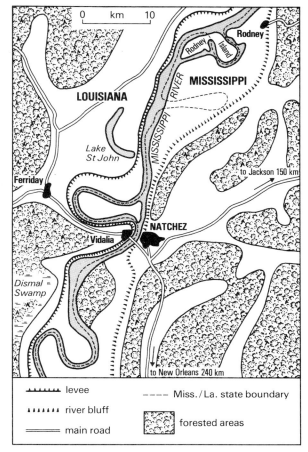

levee

river bluff

main road

---- Miss./La. state boundary

forested areas

Figure 66 *Riverside country in the Lower Mississippi Valley*

Without doubt, these improvements, coupled with regional economic expansion, have contributed greatly to the revival of water-borne commerce along the Mississippi and its tributaries. On the Ohio River alone annual cargo tonnage is now more than double that carried by the St Lawrence Seaway, while New Orleans, by total tonnage handled, is the USA's second largest port.

Questions

Figure 65 and an atlas

1. *a)* Name (*i*) the tributaries marked A–F, and (*ii*) the major ports numbered 1–5.
   b) Name the ports at the head of navigation on the Mississippi, Missouri, Ohio and Tennessee rivers.
2. *a)* What restricts the usefulness of the navigation system above St Louis?
   b) Why does the Ohio normally not suffer the same disadvantage? (*hint*: riverside concentrations of power stations, steelworks, etc.)

Figure 66

3. List the evidence which indicates that the river has changed its course several times in the past.

Figure 66 and the account

4. Why are *a)* Natchez, and *b)* Vidalia relatively safe from flooding?
5. Many cut-offs occur naturally.
   a) Describe where on the map a cut-off may next occur.
   b) With the aid of a labelled diagram explain how this may happen.

The account and general

6. How do improvements to the Mississippi River's navigability help to prevent flooding?

Figure 65 and general

7. Which section of the river is the most important commercially?
   a) What is the annual tonnage carried on this section?
   b) What major industry generates much of the traffic?

Figure 67 and general

8. Use the information on Figure 67 to construct a flow diagram illustrating the movements of cargoes handled by New Orleans. (*hint*: make the width of the 'arrows' proportional to the tonnages).
9. 'The Mississippi navigation system—economic artery of the eastern USA.' Using this title, write a detailed explanatory account of the waterway's regional importance.

Figure 67 *Trade of the port of New Orleans*

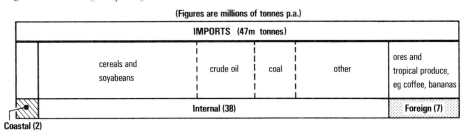

(Figures are millions of tonnes p.a.)

IMPORTS (47m tonnes)				
cereals and soyabeans	crude oil	coal	other	ores and tropical produce, eg coffee, bananas
Coastal (2)	Internal (38)			Foreign (7)

EXPORTS (65m tonnes)					
crude oil	other	crude oil	petroleum products	other	cereals and soyabeans	other—including manufactured goods
Coastal (16)		Internal (22)			Foreign (27)

Florida

A first look

Florida is widely acknowledged as the most dynamic state in the New South, and as such it deserves special attention. However, the question arises: is Florida truly 'Southern'? The state has been described as being 'in the South, but not of the South'. Geographically separated from its neighbours by swampland, the Florida peninsula also has a different historical and cultural background; it was hardly affected by the Civil War, and its black people are recent migrants rather than a legacy of slavery. Indeed, through its two most important single industries, Florida seems to

Figure 68 *Florida: selected natural and economic features*

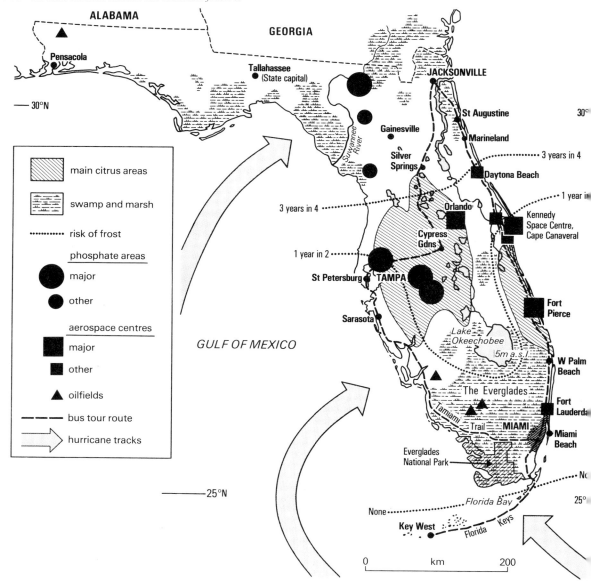

94

have stronger links with the more distant northern states, since these provide the major outlets for its agricultural products and most of the visitors for its tourist resorts.

Apart from its climate (see Chapter One), Florida has few natural resources of any consequence. Extensive pine forests, mainly in the north, cover nearly half the state's total area. Recent oil and natural gas discoveries may be important in the future but production is, as yet, very small. By contrast, rich phosphate deposits yield 75 per cent of the USA's total production and form the basis of an important fertiliser industry, with markets in Florida, in other states and overseas.

NASA's rocket assembly and launching facilities at Cape Canaveral, have generated important aerospace industries as well as phenomenal local population growth. In fact, Brevard County, where the Kennedy Space Centre is located, shot from 23 700 people in 1950 to a quarter of a million by the mid-1970s—a national record.

Much of Florida's recent economic expansion has been in the construction and service industries, which in turn are

Table 38   Florida and the South: population growth, 1950–1975

	Florida	The South	Florida as a percentage of
	(millions)		the South
1950:	2·77	33·79	8·2
1975:	8·25	47·19	17·5
Rate of increase			
1950–1975:	× 2·98	× 1·40	—

geared to the rapid rate of population growth in the state as a whole. Over 90 per cent of current increases are due to migration from other parts of the country, and this trend is expected to continue. As a result, the development of new residential areas has become a booming industry, especially in the south. Florida is particularly attractive to retired people, often wealthy, who bring with them savings and pensions earned elsewhere.

Questions

Figure 68 and an atlas

1. Elaborate on the statement that Florida is the 'nearest-to-tropical' part of the mainland USA.

Table 38

2. 'The most dynamic force in the New South'. How do the statistics support this description of Florida?

Plate 36

3. Describe the main features of the view. How are scenes like this linked with migration to Florida?

The account and general

4. *a*) Florida is the home of an above-average number of 'senior citizens'. Discuss the economic advantages and disadvantages for Florida.
b) Why do many senior citizens find the cost of living lower in Florida? (*hint:* climate).

An atlas

5. Long-range intercontinental ballistic missiles test-fired from Cape Canaveral fall into the South Atlantic Ocean near Ascension Island. Why is Cape Canaveral a good location for launching such missiles?

Plate 36   *Expensive new homes in Southern Florida*

Florida : sunshine playground

'Circular bus tours from Jacksonville or Miami visit Florida's most famous attractions in seven to twelve days. Going from Jacksonville to Silver Springs, you explore underwater gardens in a glass-bottomed boat and then drive south through orange groves. The water skiing show at Cypress Gardens is a thrilling spectacle, half ballet and half athletics. St Petersburg's Gulf Coast beach is highlighted by an elaborate outdoor aquarium with performing porpoises. The 25 km Sunshine Skyway crosses Tampa Bay to Sarasota, home of the Circus Museum.

The Tamiami Trail to Miami follows the edge of Everglades National Park, a swampy wilderness teeming with exotic birds. Brightly costumed Seminole Indians sell handicrafts by the roadside. Luxurious hotels at Miami Beach have nightclubs and private beaches, and the public beaches and golf courses are excellent. Boat tours pass private island estates, and 'party-boat' ocean fishing excursions are popular. Fishing is good everywhere in Florida. Hialeah Park, a race track, has tropical gardens with flamingos.

The island city of Key West is reached by the 160 km Overseas Highway, crossing long bridges between coral islets. Northbound for Jacksonville, you'll stop at the major resorts. Fort Lauderdale is a city of lagoons and canals. At Palm Beach, one of the magnificent vacation homes is now an art museum. Near Cocoa Beach, there is an outdoor exhibit of US Air Force space missiles, with Cape Canaveral in the distance. Automobile races are held on the smooth hard sand at Daytona Beach.

Underwater observation windows look into enormous aquariums of tropical fish at Marineland. Horse-drawn surreys show visitors St Augustine, oldest city in the USA, and its magnificent Spanish colonial fortress.'
(From *How To See The Southeast USA*, US Travel Service)

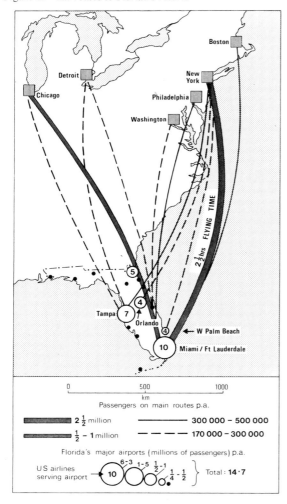

Figure 69   *Air routes to Florida's resorts*

Questions

The account and Figure 69

1. Approximately how far, in kilometres, is the coach tour (including the excursion to Key West)?
2. a) List (*i*) the natural attractions, and (*ii*) the other attractions mentioned in the tourist brochure.
   b) To what extent does each type of attraction depend on Florida's climate?

Plate 37 and general

3. The view shows a characteristic feature of Florida's Atlantic coastline—the off-shore bar or 'barrier beach', separated from the mainland by a narrow lagoon. Explain how the sand bar was formed.
4. Why are most of the major resorts located along this coast?

FLYING TO FLORIDA

Florida's main tourist season extends from October to June. The number of visitors has risen steadily from about five million in the early 1950s to twenty-five million in the 1970s, and the tourist industry has become the state's most important source of income.

New attractions are constantly being added to the old. In 1971, for example, Disney World was opened near Orlando. This huge entertainment park already attracts some nine million visitors each year—many arriving by air. Car ownership, the building of modern highways, higher personal incomes and more leisure time have all played their part in Florida's tourist boom. But there is little doubt that the major factor is the huge expansion of air travel during recent years. The popularity of Miami Beach and nearby resorts has made Miami International Airport one of the USA's busiest terminals. In fact jet aircraft now put Florida's resorts within half a day's travel of much of North America, and Europe too.

Questions

Figure 69 and the account

1. *a*) Where, in general terms, do the majority of Florida's tourists come from?
   b) What is the link between your answer to *a*) and Florida's specialisation in the winter tourist trade?
2. Orlando is planning to open a massive airport extension capable of handling 6 million passengers each year. Why is the extension necessary?
3. *a*) How has the development of air transport boosted Florida's tourist industry?
   b) What other social and economic factors have also played a part?

Plate 37   *Aerial view of Miami Beach*

Florida's citrus groves : a specialised form of agriculture

The importance of Florida's citrus groves may be gauged from two facts: the state produces one-third of the world's citrus crop; and the value of the Florida citrus harvest exceeds that of all other fruits grown in the USA.

The orange, first brought to Florida by the Spaniards in 1759, is today the most important single fruit in North America. The major producing region lies in Florida's central highlands, gently rolling hill country studded with hundreds of lakes and solution hollows but rarely exceeding 75 metres above sea level. Nevertheless frost is still a hazard, and in the 'big freeze' of 1976–77 over one-third of the crop was destroyed. Even in normal years local differences in the microclimate are so significant that a poorly sited grove can be wiped out overnight while nearby even the blossom on the trees remains unaffected. The most favoured location for a citrus grove is on the sloping southern or south-eastern side of a lake, but enclosed hollows are generally avoided. Soils are not a particularly important factor as modern fertiliser science ensures that practically any warm sandy soil can support a profitable grove.

Citrus cultivation involves much expensive machinery but the fruit itself must still be picked by hand, usually between November and April. This job is done mainly by thousands of migrant workers who, together with their families, move to Florida after harvesting other crops in states further north. Many landowners leave the day-to-day running of the groves, and the marketing of the produce, to specialised 'caretaking' companies.

Since the Second World War the longstanding contest with Californian growers for the great north-eastern market has swung in favour of Florida. Although fresh citrus fruit from California still sells better in the supermarkets than Florida's, producers in the latter state benefit from the fact that enjoying citrus in the convenient form of juice has become part of the American way of life. Thus the emphasis in Florida is now almost exclusively on processing citrus into canned juices and frozen concentrates. An added advantage is that the product can be sold all year round, avoiding glutting the market at harvest time and thus depressing prices.

Plate 38   *Irrigation in Florida citrus grove*

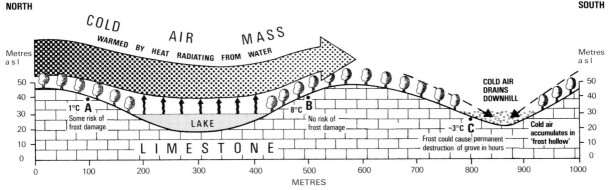

Figure 70 *Part of Florida's citrus region: diagrammatic cross-section showing winter conditions*

Questions

Figure 70 and the account

1. What is meant by 'microclimate'?
2. *a*) Account for the temperature differences at A, B and C.
   b) Why are such local differences important to citrus growers?

Plate 38 and the account

3. *a*) During what season of the year are irrigation systems most likely to be needed?
   b) Why is it worthwhile to install such systems?

The account

4. Why is the bulk of Florida's citrus crop sold in processed form?
5. What economic advantage do Florida's citrus producers have over their Californian competitors? (*hint:* location of main market)

General

6. Florida, with 2·5 million cattle, has become an important livestock producer. Suggest how the citrus processing plants have helped to boost the local cattle industry. (*hint:* 50 per cent of each fruit is waste—pulp, peel and pips)

The Everglades : swamp or farmland ?

Lake Okeechobee, having no natural outlet, simply overflowed along its southern rim, creating the swampy region known as the Everglades. Sawgrass, a tall, rough-bladed sedge, is the region's most characteristic vegetation. Beneath the sawgrass the water moves almost imperceptibly southward in a shallow 'river' about 100 km wide. Underlying the whole region is a saturated limestone bedrock on which the decaying sawgrass builds up a peaty soil. In many places limestone platforms protrude above the muddy water. On these islands, known locally as 'hammocks,' deeper soil has accumulated and swamp cypress, cabbage palm, mahogany, gumbo limbo and other trees grow close together.

Only on the hammocks, and where mangrove swamps flourish along the coast, do the Everglades ever resemble the tangled tropical growth of popular imagination. Most of it consists of open expanses of sawgrass with apparently limitless horizons. But the region contains a variety of unique plant and animal communities, including creatures such as alligators, crocodiles, manatees and aquatic birds rare or unseen elsewhere in the United States. In an attempt to protect at least part of this watery wilderness the Everglades National Park was established in 1947.

Outside the national park large areas have been reclaimed by digging more than 2000 kilometres of drainage canals and constructing a flood-protection dyke around the southern end of Lake Okeechobee. The drained peat soils are highly productive and the district has become an important farming area, favoured by the year-round growing season. Sugar cane is the most valuable crop but at least thirty varieties of winter vegetables are also grown.

Unfortunately, the peat soil dries out rapidly when exposed to the air and may be destroyed by fire or eroded by wind. Furthermore, the soil may shrink and subside at

99

Plate 39   *Everglades National Park*

rates of 2–3 cm a year. One official estimate is that by the year 2000 almost 90 per cent of the original soil will have been lost and much of the reclaimed farmland will have to be abandoned.

The natural ecosystems have suffered badly. In many places sea water has invaded the drainage canals, poisoning the soil, killing the plants and driving many animals out of their habitats. Elsewhere water levels have been lowered so much that the sawgrass is left high and dry, a flammable mass of dead vegetation.

Worse still, the diversion of the natural southward flow of water has created drought conditions in many parts of the Everglades National Park, with devastating effects on the water-dependent wildlife. It seems likely that the efforts to control floods and create new farmlands may eventually destroy this unique wilderness area.

Questions

Figure 68 and general

1. At what time of the year is Lake Okeechobee most likely to flood, and why?

Figure 68 and the account

2. *a*) Calculate the average gradient of the 'sawgrass river' between Lake Okeechobee and Florida Bay.
   b) How does your answer to *a*) explain the description of the river's flow?

Plate 39 and the account

3. Draw a labelled, explanatory sketch of the view shown. Indicate any relevant features mentioned in the account.

The account and general

4. *a*) What factors have made the Everglades an important farming region?
   b) What important agricultural region in Britain has soil problems similar to those of the Everglades?

5. Summarise the arguments for and against reclaiming the Everglades. Which side do you support, and why?

The Mountain West (USA)

A first look

The Rocky Mountains are a complex relief barrier made up of several dozen different ranges. To the west, the intermontane plateaus and basins, lying between 900 and 300 m above sea level are all characterised by aridity but otherwise their landscapes are extremely varied. Climate, and thus natural vegetation, also varies considerably in this immense region but everywhere, except on the higher mountain ranges, rainfall is less than 50 cm and amounts generally diminish southwards until in Arizona true desert is reached.

In this unpromising environment was originally the home of Indians—groups of nomadic hunters and small, highly organised farming communities. The first white settlers were the Spanish who established their colonial capital at Santa Fé as early as 1610 and, like the neighbouring Pueblo Indians, built *adobe* (mud-brick) houses and farmed by irrigation. The Spanish also introduced horses, sheep and cattle, the essential elements of western ranching.

In the nineteenth century a trickle of other white settlers passed through the Mountain West on their way to the Pacific coastlands, but no migrants made it their permanent home until the Mormons, seeking refuge from religious persecution, founded Salt Lake City in 1847. The Mormons created green oases of farmland by means of large-scale irrigation, and their influence took deep root in the Mountain West. But the isolation they sought was soon broken by the gold rush to California in 1849, the discovery of precious metals in the Rockies a few years later, and finally by the coming of the first transcontinental railway in 1869.

Questions

Figure 71 and the account

1. *a*) What is the maximum extent of the American Rockies
   (*i*) north-south, and (*ii*) east-west?
   b) Why is the description '*Mountain* West' not strictly applicable to the whole region?
   c) What is unusual about the drainage basins of the Great Salt Lake and the Humboldt River?

Table 39

2. Describe and account for *a*) the similarities and *b*) the differences between the climates of the three cities.

Figure 71 and an atlas

3. *a*) Identify the major cities marked by initial letters.
   b) Comment on the general location of the cities relative to the Rocky Mountains.
   c) Which city is likely to be the region's main service centre? Give reasons for your answer.

Plate 40   *The Great Basin, Nevada. In the Great Basin, movements in the earth's crust caused huge blocks to tilt and subside, creating a series of north-south mountain ranges separated by plateau ranges. This is known as 'basin and range' country.*

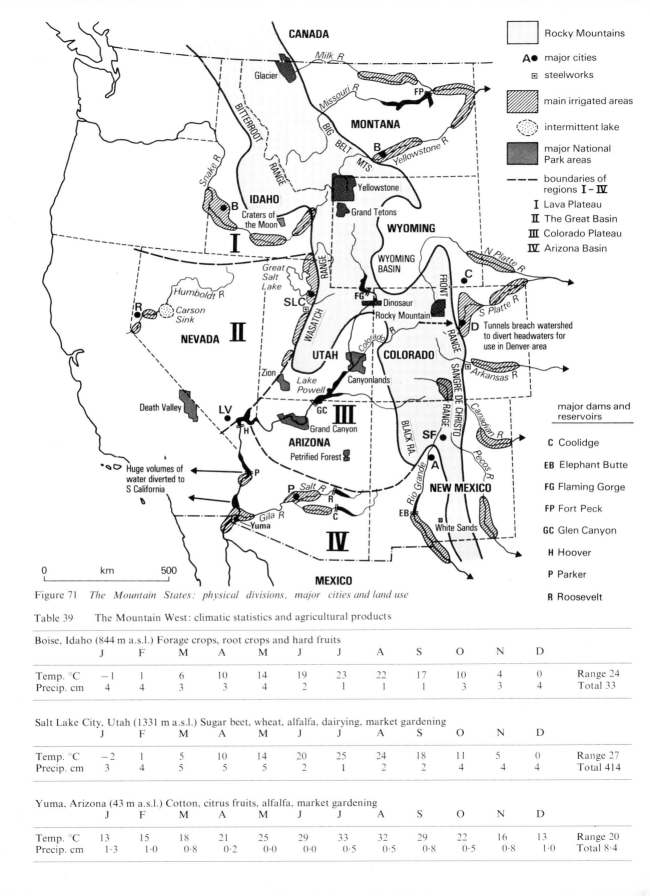

Figure 71   *The Mountain States: physical divisions, major cities and land use*

Table 39   The Mountain West: climatic statistics and agricultural products

Boise, Idaho (844 m a.s.l.) Forage crops, root crops and hard fruits

	J	F	M	A	M	J	J	A	S	O	N	D	
Temp. °C	−1	1	6	10	14	19	23	22	17	10	4	0	Range 24
Precip. cm	4	4	3	3	4	2	1	1	1	3	3	4	Total 33

Salt Lake City, Utah (1331 m a.s.l.) Sugar beet, wheat, alfalfa, dairying, market gardening

	J	F	M	A	M	J	J	A	S	O	N	D	
Temp. °C	−2	1	5	10	14	20	25	24	18	11	5	0	Range 27
Precip. cm	3	4	5	5	5	2	1	2	2	4	4	4	Total 414

Yuma, Arizona (43 m a.s.l.) Cotton, citrus fruits, alfalfa, market gardening

	J	F	M	A	M	J	J	A	S	O	N	D	
Temp. °C	13	15	18	21	25	29	33	32	29	22	16	13	Range 20
Precip. cm	1·3	1·0	0·8	0·2	0·0	0·0	0·5	0·5	0·8	0·5	0·8	1·0	Total 8·4

Modern developments

Throughout the region ranching is still the main form of land use. Cattle predominate but some ranches, especially in Montana and Wyoming, carry large flocks of sheep. Only in Idaho and Montana is lumbering an important industry. Elsewhere the extensive, but often thin, forest cover is more valuable as summer grazing and as a means of checking soil erosion and conserving water.

In the twentieth century the construction of huge multi-purpose dams by the federal government has transformed agriculture in many parts of the region. But such schemes are not without their problems. In particular, the extension of irrigated cropland has severely reduced the amount of water available so that even the region's largest river, the Colorado, can no longer meet all the demands placed upon it and often reaches the sea as a mere trickle.

The exploitation of the region's vast mineral wealth is likely to remain very important for many years to come. During the Second World War, steelworks were built at Provo in Utah and Pueblo, Colorado, both using local coal supplies. Steel production has since formed the basis for a wide range of manufacturing industries including electronics, missiles and other 'defence' products. With the expansion of employment opportunities, the region's cities

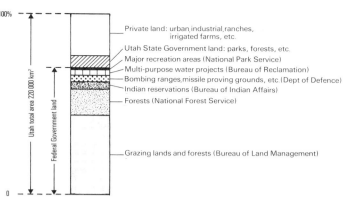

Figure 72   *Land use and ownership: a typical Mountain State (Utah)*

have grown rapidly in recent decades, throwing an additional strain on the scarcest of all local resources—water.

Even so, most of the Mountain West remains very sparsely populated, so much so that in July 1945 the New Mexico desert was used to test the first atomic bomb. The region also contains some of the most spectacular scenery in North America and large tracts have been set aside as national parks and recreation areas. With a greatly improved highways network the Mountain States are 'invaded' by millions of Americans each summer and tourism has become a major industry.

Plate 41   *Lake Powell, Utah*

Questions

Plate 40 and the account

1. Explain *a*) why 40 hectares or more may be required to feed one animal, and *b*) why transhumance (usually by truck or train nowadays) is often necessary.

The account and Figure 71

2. *a*) Why does the Colorado River fail to reach the sea? Give a detailed answer.
   b) There are inter-state (and international) disputes over entitlements to Colorado water. Why?

Plate 41

3. *a*) Describe and account for the main landforms. (*hint:* 'plateau', 'canyon', 'mesa' and 'butte' are key words.)
   b) How can you tell that the photograph was taken in summer?

Table 40   The Mountain West: approximate areas and population 1970

State	Area (km²)	Population (1976)	Population per km²
Arizona	294 000	2 270 000	7·7
Colorado	270 000	2 583 000	9·6
Idaho	216 000	831 000	3·8
Montana	381 000	753 000	1·9
Nevada	286 000	610 000	2·1
New Mexico	315 000	1 168 000	3·7
Utah	220 000	1 228 000	5·6
Wyoming	253 000	390 000	1·5
Mountain West Total	2 235 000	8 282 000	4·4
Great Britain (for comparison)	230 000	54 405 000 (1975)	236·5

c) Why has Lake Powell become a major recreational facility? (*hint:* the photograph was taken 225 km upstream from Glen Canyon Dam.)

Figure 71 and Table 39

4. *a*) Account for the different crops raised on irrigated land in the Boise, Salt Lake City and Phoenix/Yuma areas.
   b) What evidence is there that irrigation and ranching are closely linked?

Figure 71 and general

5. *a*) How do the names of the national parks reflect the variety of scenery in the Mountain West?
   b) What other tourist attractions does the region have?

Table 40

6. *a*) What is remarkable about (*i*) the size of individual states, and (*ii*) the total population of the Mountain West, compared with Britain?
   b) Elaborate on the statement that the Mountain West remains very sparsely populated.

Figure 72 and general

7. *a*) The proportion of land in the Mountain West still owned by the federal government ranges from 30 per cent in Montana to 87 per cent in Nevada. Why are the figures much higher than in most other regions of the USA?
   b) (*i*) What percentage of Utah is owned by the federal government? (*ii*) Which two government bodies control over half the state's area?

Figures 71, 72 and general

8. Under the headings Great Basin, Colorado Plateau, Rocky Mountains and Wasatch Piedmont (immediately west of the Wasatch Range) list the major types of land use shown in Figure 72. Explain each list. (*hint:* some types of land use appear in more than one physical region)

THE BINGHAM CANYON COPPER MINE

In the nineteenth century mining in the Rocky Mountains was usually for gold and silver. Many fortunes were made from these small-scale enterprises, but the most accessible lodes were soon exhausted and the settlements which had mushroomed in the mining districts were quickly abandoned. Today, such 'ghost towns' are visited only by tourists.

As the old mines declined so new ones, often large-scale and highly mechanised, opened up to exploit the deposits of lead, zinc, copper and other metals. Typical of this later type of development is the Bingham Canyon copper mine in Utah, which began operations in 1904. Since then mining activities have transformed what was once a large mountain into a huge pit reputed to be the world's largest man-made excavation.

The mine's present appearance results from two important factors: the ore averages less than 1 per cent of copper, and 2·5 tonnes of waste material must be removed before one tonne of ore can be mined. For decades long trains of slow-moving railway wagons circled for kilometres around the terraces carrying tonne after tonne of waste material to dumping areas outside. Now the trains

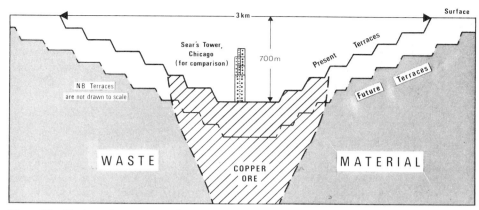

Figure 73   *Bingham Canyon Mine: diagrammatic cross-section*

Plate 42   *Bingham Canyon Mine*

have been replaced by giant diesel trucks capable of carrying as much as 110 tonnes of material up steeper gradients without resorting to 'switch-backing'.

However, the company continues to use trains for hauling ore from the mine to its processing plants near the Great Salt Lake, 25 km to the north. There the ore is crushed, concentrated, smelted and refined to produce about 200 000 tonnes of copper every year—nearly one-fifth of the USA's total. In addition, small quantities of other metals are recovered during the refining processes.

Questions

Plate 42 the account and general

1. Why are large-scale operations necessary at Bingham Canyon mine?
2. *a*) What do the by-products of the refining processes indicate about the nature of the ore body at Bingham Canyon?
   b) Why is molybdenum, one of the mine's valuable by-products, used in the steel industry?

3. Why is the copper processed near the mine rather than in the major market areas in the eastern USA?

Figure 73

4. *a*) Why is it necessary to remove so much waste material to extract the ore?
   b) Why will the proportion of waste material to ore increase in future years?

Figure 74 *Minerals of the Mountain West*

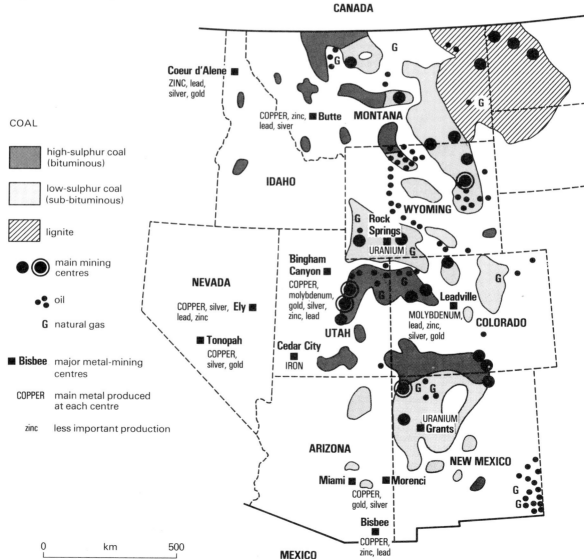

COAL: THE WEST'S NEW MINERAL WEALTH

In 1970 the federal government passed an anti-pollution law forbidding the burning of fuels with a high sulphur content in the most populous parts of the country. As the new law affected most of the coal of the eastern states the mining companies began a search for 'clean' coal, which turned attention on the immense reserves lying between Arizona and Montana.

Previously, few companies had exploited these deposits, mainly because the coal was too far from the biggest markets. Yet after 1970 much of the coal in the Mountain West became more attractive simply because it has a low (less than 1 per cent) sulphur content. Many of the deposits lie in extensive 30-metre thick seams just beneath the surface; all a company has to do is remove the overburden of soil and rocks and extract the coal by means of large excavators. Mining costs per tonne are so low that even after transport to the East the coal can compete in price with that of Appalachia.

As a result, the coal industry has drawn up ambitious plans for developing the Western deposits. Besides scores of new mines, many plants for converting local high-sulphur coal into natural gas will be established in the region, together with dozens of new coal-burning power stations, some of which already send electricity to cities as distant as Los Angeles and El Paso. To transport the huge quantities of low-sulphur coal the railway companies are buying thousands of new wagons and locomotives to form unit trains. In addition, the mining companies plan to build long-distance pipelines to carry slurry (coal mixed with water) from mines to users. The new developments are eventually expected to attract over 500 000 people into the sparsely populated region.

By 1976 over 110 million tonnes of coal a year were being produced in the Mountain West—more than a sixth of the national output. However, a major environmental problem must be solved before the region's full potential can be realised. By spending up to £10 000 per hectare mining companies can restore opencast land in the East to its former appearance. However, successful revegetation of coal lands in the West is likely to be much more difficult because of the low rainfall. The federal government has recently framed a law which, in effect, states that if land cannot be restored it must not be mined. Since much of the potential coal supply lies under federal land, some mining operations have been seriously delayed.

Questions

Figure 74

1. *a)* Which state contains the most extensive deposits of low-sulphur coal?
   b) What is lignite?
   c) What other mineral fuels are found in the Mountain West?

The account and general

2. *a)* Give two reasons why coal became more attractive in the 1970s. (*hint:* oil prices)
   b) List the factors (*i*) which make the coal easy to exploit, and (*ii*) which have delayed production.

Plate 43 and the account

3. Draw a simple 'field-sketch' of the mining scene. Label the sketch to indicate some of the features of coal-mining in the Mountain West.

The account and Plate 43

4. *a)* Why will reclamation of opencast land be especially difficult in the Mountain West?
   b) What effect will reclamation have on the price of coal?
   c) Do you think a reclamation law is necessary? Give your reasons.

Plate 43   *Open-cast mining*

The American Indian, past and present

When Columbus discovered North America the native Indians numbered perhaps a million. Divided into over 300 tribal groups and scattered thinly across the continent they lived in harmony with the natural environment by hunting, fishing and farming. After the coming of the white man the Indian story was one of war, loss of land and diminishing numbers. Pushed back by the advance of white settlement the Indians were eventually forced on to reservations occupying remote, poor-quality land for which the newcomers had no other use. Today, although free to move anywhere they choose, two-thirds of the USA's 800 000 American Indians still live on reservations, most of which are located west of the Mississippi. Thus the present distribution of the Indian population is very different from the original pattern.

Most reservations are still held in trust for the Indians by the federal government and the tribal lands are controlled by the Bureau of Indian Affairs in Washington, DC. This control means that although Indians are full citizens of the United States they do not possess all the freedoms enjoyed by other Americans. Many Indians resent being treated like irresponsible children and a civil rights campaign began in the 1960s. Perhaps still the poorest and least privileged of minority groups, the Indians have made significant progress in recent years. With much public sympathy, and financial backing from the government, many tribes are beginning to share more fully in modern American life.

NAVAHO POWER

The Navaho Reservation in the 'Four-Corners' area was allotted to the tribe in 1868, after the Indians had been heavily defeated by the US army. Although scenically spectacular, most of the reservation is semi-arid and suitable only for grazing limited flocks of sheep, the mainstay of the traditional economy. Today the reservation is the largest in the USA and the 150 000 Navahos are the largest tribe. In 1972 the Bureau of Indian Affairs granted the Navahos limited self-government, and the reservation became virtually a separate nation-state subject to neither state laws nor taxes. From their capital at Window Rock the Navaho Tribal Council began the task of transforming the reservation's rural economy to an industrial one.

The tribe has gone into business on a large scale, operating an industrial estate, roads, sawmills, banks, motels, restaurants, craft centres and supermarkets. The Tribal Council has also gained control of 130 trading posts on the reservation, requesting the 'Anglo' owners to sell out to Indians. In the reservation's Utah section, scenic Monument Valley, the setting of many screen 'Westerns', has been opened as a tribal park, organised along the lines of the national parks run by federal government. Most important of all, vast tracts of land are being leased to companies prospecting for oil, gas, coal and uranium. By 1985 Navaho revenues from such leases are expected to total £25 million a year and mineral exploitation should provide thousands of jobs for the Navahos, helping to reduce the usual 30 per cent unemployment rate.

Plate 44 *Navahos selling jewellery at the roadside*

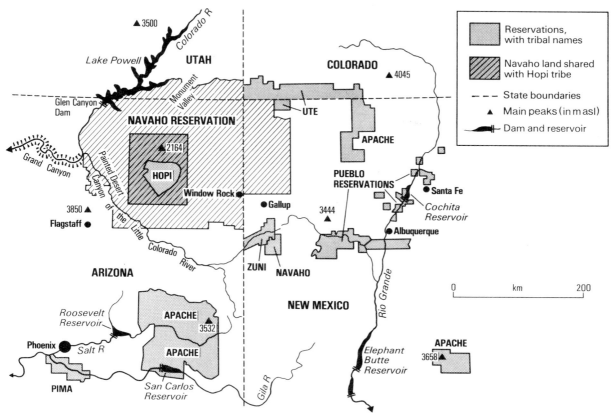

Figure 75 *Indian reservations in the Four Corners area*

Other aspects of tribal life are also changing. The traditional Navaho house was built of logs, adobe and rocks —whatever came to hand. Such a house, called a *hogan*, was practical and comfortable, warm in winter and cool in summer. A family group would cluster its hogans at a given location but these settlements were never large enough to be termed villages. Now the new wealth is helping to build modern standardised homes and the Navahos are becoming increasingly urbanised as new towns spring up on reservation land.

As the Navahos move into the modern world, traditional crafts, such as making jewellery and weaving beautiful rugs and blankets, are slowly losing ground. Similarly the younger Navahos have little regard for the tribe's ancient rituals and ceremonials; as the Navaho medicine men and religious elders die few are trained to take their place and more traditional customs pass into oblivion. Despite these losses the new prosperity and political power have brought a fresh sense of pride in being Indian. As the Navahos' leader says: 'The white people in the south-west are going to have to get rid of their negative attitude and learn to accept us'.

Questions

Figure 75

1. *a)* Why is the Four Corners area so called? (*hint:* state boundaries)
   b) Calculate the approximate area of the main Navaho Reservation.
   c) (*i*) Name the other Indian tribes living on neighbouring reservations. (*ii*) Which of the tribes have the best land for cultivation? Explain your answer.

Plate 44 and the account

2. *a)* Describe the physical environment of the Navaho Reservation.
   b) Explain (*i*) how the physical environment hampered the Navahos' traditional economic pursuits, and (*ii*) how the new economy is less restricted by the physical environment.
3. List the ways in which the Navahos profit from the tourist trade.

The account

4. *a)* What have the Navahos (*i*) gained, and (*ii*) lost as a result of the recent changes? List all the relevant points.
   b) Do you think the changes are for the better? Justify your answer.

Yellowstone : the world's first national park

Figure 76   *Yellowstone National Park*

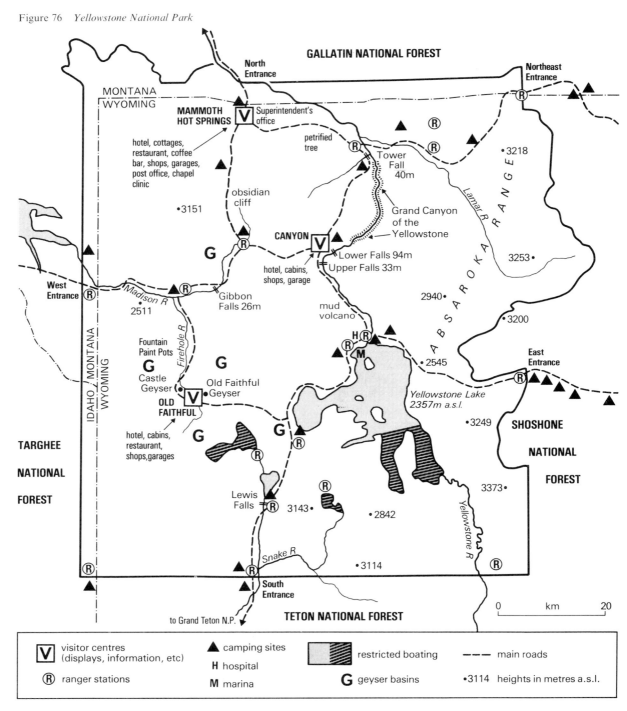

Plate 45   *Castle Geyser erupting*

Yellowstone gained this distinction in 1872 when a group of scientists persuaded the federal government to preserve this part of the great western wilderness in its unspoiled natural condition. Accordingly, the park was created for the benefit and enjoyment of the general public, a most unusual idea for those times.

Almost half the size of Wales, Yellowstone National Park is the largest in the United States. Within the park the government has banned all settlement and every kind of economic activity as well as major roads, railways, airports, and even power and telephone lines. However, because the park is for people, some developments related to the tourist industry have been allowed.

The centre of the park is a broad volcanic plateau with an average elevation of about 2700 metres. Around its margins are mountain ranges rising above the general level of the tableland. Extensive forests of lodgepole pine and meadows of alpine flowers provide the natural environment for elk, bison, moose, bear and many other species of animals and birds offering a display of wildlife unsurpassed in the United States. All these creatures are protected by law, and hunting is forbidden.

Yellowstone also contains over 10 000 thermal features, of which the most spectacular are the many geysers. Each eruption of Old Faithful, the most famous geyser, projects 40 000 litres of water and steam 50 metres into the air approximately every hour. Hot springs, mud volcanoes, heated rivers and brilliantly coloured pools of boiling water are other features of great interest. Many of the thermal areas are covered by a thin crust of minerals deposited by water brought to the surface by geysers and springs. Where a geyser has erupted for many years a cone of fragile 'sinter' may be built up.

How geysers work

Geysers require a combination of three factors—water, heat and rocks strong enough to withstand the pressures generated during an eruption. After steam has formed (see Figure 77), it pushes some of the water up out of the geyser vent in a small preliminary eruption. This overflow immediately reduces the pressure on the superheated water lower down in the geyser tube. The boiling point is rapidly lowered and the water flashes into a vast volume of steam which surges upwards with irresistible force, hurling the overlying water into the air in a spectacular eruption.

Figure 77   *First stage of a geyser eruption*

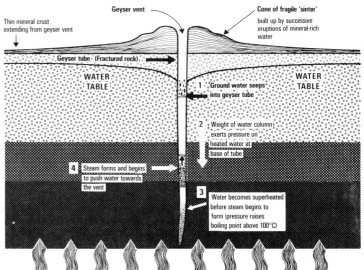

PEOPLE IN THE PARK

Yellowstone is run by the National Park Service whose rangers have the difficult job of preserving the park's natural character and at the same time ensuring that the public can enjoy the scenic wonders in safety. During the summer months an average of 60 000 visitors enter the park each day. A staff of 700 are employed to provide the many services required. Most visitors arrive by car and Yellowstone has more than 800 km of public roads giving access to most of the major features. Relatively few people stray far from the air-conditioned comfort of their vehicles, but for the more adventurous over 1600 km of trails lead to remote areas of the park.

In the more frequented areas the impact of people on the wilderness has become very marked; for example, 90 tonnes of rubbish have to be disposed of every day. Motorists are responsible for importing a variety of other 'urban' problems into Yellowstone. Although the park roads are intended for leisurely driving, hundreds of car accidents occur each year. Traffic jams have also become frequent—especially when bears are sighted by the roadside.

People have lured many animals away from their natural habitat by carelessly leaving food lying around in camping areas, or even more foolishly, offering biscuits, sweets and popcorn to bears waiting along the road. Despite their tame appearance the bears are wild animals, and each year dozens of people are injured in such encounters. Troublesome bears have to be trapped and removed to remote areas of the park; in extreme cases they must be destroyed. The sight of bears roaming freely in Yellowstone may become rare if some visitors continue to behave irresponsibly. The thermal features can also be hazardous, especially if visitors ignore warning notices and the leaflets handed out by park rangers. The thin crusts of sinter often conceal pools of boiling water which have claimed the lives of several people unwise enough to stray from the boardwalks and signposted trails.

For the vast majority of visitors, however, Yellowstone is a very enjoyable experience, well worth the small entrance fee. The idea of making an area of outstanding beauty or interest into a National Park has spread rapidly. Nowadays the National Park Service administers some 12 million hectares of land in the United States, and there are over 1200 national parks elsewhere in the world.

Questions

Figure 76 and an atlas

1. *a)* Calculate the approximate area of Yellowstone National Park.
   b) In which state is most of the park located?
   c) How far is Yellowstone from major centres of American population, such as (*i*) Los Angeles, (*ii*) Chicago, (*iii*) New York?

Figure 76 and the account

2. *a)* Make a list of the various services provided for visitors.
   b) Do you agree that such services should be allowed in Yellowstone? Justify your answer.

Figure 77 and the account

3. Use Figure 77 as the basis for two similar diagrams illustrating the intermediate and final stages of a geyser eruption. Label the diagrams to explain what happens during each stage of the eruption.

Plate 45 and Figure 76

4. *a)* Describe the general scene.
   b) (*i*) What is the name of the river in the foreground?
   (*ii*) Why is the name appropriate?
   c) How does the thermal feature in the foreground differ from Castle Geyser?
   d) Why have some of the trees died before reaching maturity?

The account and general

5. Write the warning notes for a leaflet that the National Park Service might issue to visitors, advising them of the potential dangers of Yellowstone and how they should be avoided.

6. *a)* List the ways in which Yellowstone differs from national parks in Britain.
   b) Account for as many of the differences as possible.

California

Early growth and recent trends

When Mexico ceded California to the United States in 1848, the territory contained little more than 2000 American settlers. Attracted by the best farmland west of the Mississippi River, these hardy pioneers had survived the hazardous overland trek which began at towns such as Independence and Kansas City, and which usually took several months to complete.

In January 1848 gold was discovered at Sutters Mill on the American River, a tributary of the Sacramento. This single event transformed California from a remote backwater into the world's El Dorado almost overnight. Within a year thousands of 'forty-niners' were pouring along the California Trail or arriving in San Francisco by sea. The effects were dramatic. The massive influx of people triggered rapid economic development and in 1850 California became the thirty-first state of the Union, quickly earning its nickname, 'The Golden State'.

The trend started by the Gold Rush has seldom slackened. The population has approximately doubled every 20 years since 1860, with migration as the biggest contributing factor. Indeed, between 1950 and 1970 migration added, on average, more than 1 000 people each *day*. In 1970 the Census confirmed that, with a population of approximately 20 million, California had become the largest state in the Union.

However, California's rapid population increase and widespread affluence have created many social and environmental problems. These, coupled with a recent downswing in the state's economic fortunes, have severely reduced California's general attractiveness. Consequently, annual migration rates in the 1970s have been very much lower than in previous years. Moreover, a recent opinion poll shows that a third of the State's permanent residents would leave if given the chance. It remains to be seen if such trends will become permanent or if they are merely a temporary weakening of California's proven magnetism.

Figure 78   *California: main physical features*

Plate 46   *Spanish mission, San Diego, California*

Questions

Atlas

1. Between 1542 and 1821 California was ruled by Spain. How does Spanish influence show up on a modern map of the state?

Plate 46

2. *a*) Why does the church have white-washed walls with few windows?
   b) Why did the Spanish build such mission stations in California?

Atlas and general

3. *a*) Suggest the easiest route for the overland trail to California.
   b) Describe the major geographical obstacles and hazards encountered by settlers using the trail.
4. *a*) Approximately how long (in kilometres) was the California Trail?

b) Suggest one important reason why the journey normally took several months.

5. *a*) Name two sea routes from New York to San Francisco that were used as alternatives to the overland trail. (*hint:* one route involved some overland travel)
   b) In each case list the geographical difficulties that had to be overcome.

The account and general

6. *a*) What is meant by 'El Dorado'?
   b) Why were the 'forty-niners' so called?

The account

7. *a*) What may California's population total be in 1990 if the trends of the past continue?
   b) Is this total likely to be reached, and why? (*hint:* in 1976 the state's estimated population was 21 520 000)

Figure 79 *California: annual rainfall and climatic regions*

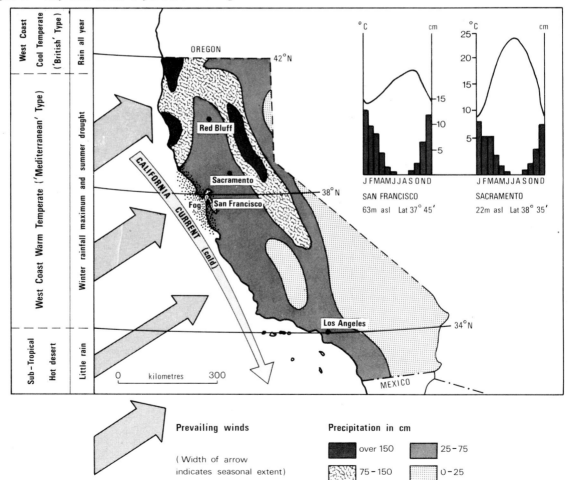

Questions

Figures 78 and 79

1. *a*) Account for the west-east variations in rainfall distribution across California at the latitude of (*i*) Red Bluff, and (*ii*) Los Angeles.
   b) Give reasons for the variations.
2. *a*) Name one major relief region, most of which lies in a 'rain shadow' area.
   b) By means of a labelled cross-section, show how the rain shadow is caused.

Figure 79

3. *a*) Between what latitudes, approximately, does the 'Mediterranean' climate region extend?
   b) What common rainfall feature indicates that both Sacramento and San Francisco have a Mediterranean-type climate?

4. *a*) Approximately how far apart are San Francisco and Sacramento?
   b) Which city has the smaller annual temperature, range, and why?
   c) What special feature is responsible for San Francisco's relatively low summer temperature?

Plate 47, Figure 79 and general

5. San Francisco's summer fogs are caused by on-shore breezes in the afternoons.
   a) Why do such breezes occur?
   b) Explain in more detail how the fogs are caused.

Figures 78 and 79

6. Name the major relief regions having the following types of natural vegetation:
   (*i*) giant redwoods and other coniferous trees;
   (*ii*) cacti.

Plate 47   *San Francisco fog*

Agriculture

CENTRAL VALLEY IRRIGATION SCHEMES

Since the 1940s large areas of the Central Valley have been transformed from almost completely unproductive semi-desert into one of the most efficient and prosperous farming regions in the world. The key is irrigation.

The basic problem is that the north has two-thirds of the Central Valley's water but only one-third of the irrigable land; by contrast, the south has two-thirds of the irrigable land but only one-third of the water. To overcome this problem the federal government has constructed an elaborate system of dams and canals to transfer surplus water from the Sacramento River and boost the inadequate flow of the San Joaquin River. The scheme has been so successful that water from the upper course of the San Joaquin can now be diverted to the southern end of the Central Valley where it irrigates a previously barren area.

There are now some two million hectares of irrigated land in the Central Valley—over 60 per cent of the total farmland. Even so, great quantities of potentially valuable floodwater flow unused to the sea each year. To harness some of this water, further dams and canals are being constructed. The most important of the new developments are the Oroville Dam (250 metres—the highest in the USA) and the California Aqueduct, key features of the State Water Project, a separate scheme designed primarily to transfer water to southern California for domestic and industrial purposes. However, the aqueduct also delivers, en route, additional irrigation water to the San Joaquin valley. The completion of the full State Water Project in 1990, will add considerably to the Central Valley's total area of irrigated land.

Although extremely successful, these schemes will not solve all the problems of farming in California's dry areas. In the first place, the costs of building and maintaining such large-scale dams and canals are enormous. Farmers who use water provided by the projects have to pay heavy charges, and this makes their crops expensive to produce. Secondly, the dams regulate the flow of water, but they also trap great quantities of silt which the rivers would normally carry downstream. The silting up of reservoirs can reduce their useful life to as little as fifty years, since there is as yet no cheap method of removing the silt.

Thirdly, in the driest areas, evaporation of irrigation water draws underlying salts into the top-soil. Crop growth is thus prevented unless the salts are flushed out by extra flows of water. Finally, large tracts of the Central Valley are unsuited to irrigation and will almost certainly remain unproductive in the future.

Plate 48   *The Delta-Mendota Canal*

Questions

Figure 80, the account and general

1. Which part of the Central Valley benefits most from the Central Valley Project? Explain your answer.
2. *a)* Why does the Sacramento River carry more water than the San Joaquin River?
   b) (*i*) In what region do the two main rivers and most of their tributaries rise?
   (*ii*) Why do the rivers carry plenty of water during the early part of the dry season?
3. The main purpose of the Central Valley Project is to provide irrigation water but there are several additional benefits. List as many as you can.

Plate 48 and Figure 80

4. *a)* In what general direction was the photograph taken?
   b) In which part of the San Joaquin valley is the area located—northern or southern? How can you tell?
5. *a)* Name the other artificial watercourse shown in the top left of the photograph.
   b) Suggest why both channels follow a zig-zag course.
6. *a)* Describe the main features of the farming landscape.
   b) Why is the San Joaquin valley so well suited to irrigation agriculture?

PATTERNS OF FARMING

The expansion of commercial fruit and vegetable growing in California undoubtedly owes much to the development of irrigation. However, the coming of the railways and the invention of refrigeration and canning were also very important, since the main markets for this produce are in the eastern states. Lowland California now contains some of the world's most intensively farmed areas, ranging across several degrees of latitude. This allows over 200 kinds of crops to be grown—including nearly half the USA's fruit and vegetables. Californian farmers employ the most modern machinery and scientific techniques. Productivity continues to increase and California easily leads all other states by value of farm products (£3 700 million in 1974).

Citrus fruits are perhaps California's best known agricultural product. The orange growers, many of whom belong to co-operatives such as 'Sunkist', use giant electric propellers to ward off the threat of frost at blossom time. Large-scale 'smudging'—heating the air by burning oil in pots—is still practised, although the thick black smoke of former years is nowadays prevented by special re-circulating devices. Other citrus fruits are even more sensitive to frost, and production is confined to the warmest areas and to 'thermal belts' above valley floors.

Grapes are the state's second-ranking crop by value. Vineyards cover valley floors and hill slopes throughout the 'Mediterranean' part of the state. About 90 per cent of all American wine is produced in California. Raisin grapes are dried outdoors in the sun, and about 20 per cent of raisin production is exported. Britain is an important overseas customer for raisins.

Cotton, however, is the most valuable of California's crops. The cotton is of high quality and benefits from the long growing season, the dry picking season and the conveniently flat land, which allows the use of machinery for most operations. The crop is less subject to disease, and yields are much higher per hectare than in the Cotton Belt of the Deep South. About a quarter of total US production is now obtained from California.

Figure 80   *Central Valley irrigation schemes*

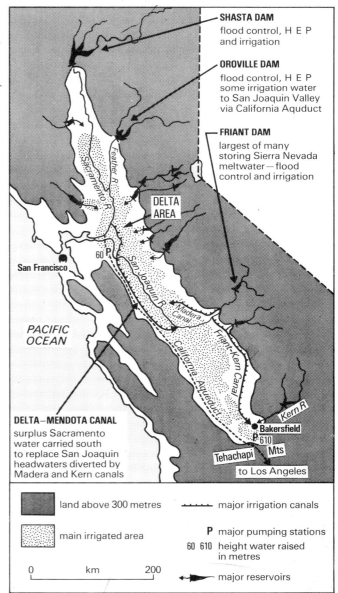

SHASTA DAM
flood control, H E P and irrigation

OROVILLE DAM
flood control, H E P some irrigation water to San Joaquin Valley via California Aquduct

FRIANT DAM
largest of many storing Sierra Nevada meltwater—flood control and irrigation

DELTA AREA

San Francisco

PACIFIC OCEAN

DELTA–MENDOTA CANAL
surplus Sacramento water carried south to replace San Joaquin headwaters diverted by Madera and Kern canals

Bakersfield
Tehachapi Mts
to Los Angeles

land above 300 metres
main irrigated area

major irrigation canals
P major pumping stations
60 610 height water raised in metres
major reservoirs

0   km   200

Plate 49 *Citrus growing in the San Bernadino Valley*

California is also important for its livestock, although nearly all the five million beef and dairy cattle are reared in feedlots occupying relatively small areas of land. Alfalfa, grown on irrigated land and transported to the cattle, is now the most important fodder crop. As one field of irrigated alfalfa may produce six or more 'harvests' each year the number of cattle that can be kept may exceed that of a whole ranch in other parts of the state. Poultry farming is also highly specialised. Intensive 'factory farming' methods have increased productivity and made poultry and eggs the least expensive of foods derived from animals.

Questions

Figures 81 and 78

1. *a*) Name the three main irrigated areas outside the Central Valley.
   b) For each area name the source of water used for irrigation.
   c) How long is (*i*) the Los Angeles Aqueduct, and (*ii*) the All-American Canal?
2. *a*) What is the general relationship between the irrigated areas and crop production?
   b) (*i*) Name three farm products produced on non-irrigated land. (*ii*) For each, name the area of production.

Table 41 and the account

3. Under the headings 'Temperate' and 'Sub-Tropical' list all the crops included in the table.
4. What makes normally low-value crops, such as lettuce and celery, so profitable to Californian farmers? (*hints:* market and season)

Plate 50 and general

5. *a*) Name the mountain range in the background.

b) The valley is a flat-bottomed alluvial trough. Explain (*i*) the exact meaning of this description, and (*ii*) the advantages to farms in the valley.

Table 41 California's share of total US production of certain fruit and vegetables

More than 90 per cent	45–90 per cent
lemons	broccoli
figs	lettuces
almonds	peaches
artichokes	melons
dates	cauliflowers
olives	tomatoes
prunes	pears
walnuts	asparagus
grapes	celery
plums	strawberries

(*US Abstract of Statistics, 1977*)

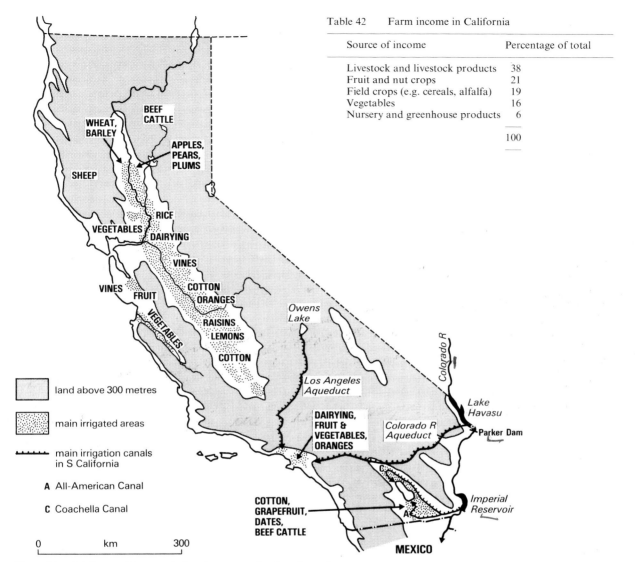

Table 42   Farm income in California

Source of income	Percentage of total
Livestock and livestock products	38
Fruit and nut crops	21
Field crops (e.g. cereals, alfalfa)	19
Vegetables	16
Nursery and greenhouse products	6
	100

Figure 81   *California: Main agricultural areas and selected products*

Figure 81, the account and general

6. *a)* Name (*i*) two citrus fruits other than oranges, and (*ii*) the areas specialising in their production.
   b) Explain why these fruits are grown in the areas named.

The account and general

7. With the aid of a diagram explain how orange growers combat the threat of frost with *a)* electric propellors and *b)* smudge pots.

Table 42

8. Draw bar graphs or a divided circle (pie graph) to illustrate the statistics.

9. *a)* What is the most important source of income for California's farmers?
   b) How does the combined value of fruit, nuts and vegetables compare with your answer to *a)*?

119

Plate 50   *Irrigated farmland, Salinas Valley: the 'salad bowl of America'*

AGRIBUSINESS AND ITS PROBLEMS

TECHNOLOGY AND THE TOMATO

Recent changes in demand have made the humble tomato the most valuable of all California's fruit and vegetable crops. As such it was quickly subjected to intensive 'agricultural engineering'.

'The engineers designed a machine that picked tomatoes by lifting up the vine and shaking it. That was efficient, but not efficient enough; because the fruit ripened on different days, the machines had to go through the fields three or four times to harvest all the tomatoes. The solution was to put all the tomatoes on the same time-table. A mowing machine trims the tops off all the young plants, causing them to multiply their branches, and later on to bear fruit which ripens simultaneously.

This solved the picking problem; but it created a packing problem. Tomatoes were traditionally packed in a field box, which held 56 pounds (25 kg). The new machines picked the tomatoes faster than they could be packed in the old boxes. So the engineers invented a 'bulk bin',

Plate 51   *'Ethion Stops Mites': a roadside billboard showing the variety of fruit grown in California*

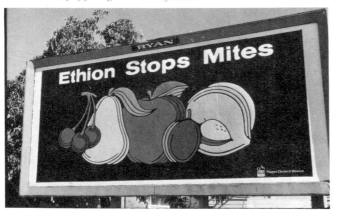

which was much larger. But then the tomatoes raining down into the big bin tended to get squashed, so, as an engineer explained 'We had to design a tomato to fit the bin: a tomato with a rougher skin; easier to handle, and—to save space—not so round: in fact, a tough oblong tomato! Even so that isn't the final solution of the problem, the stalk end of each tomato, when packed in a bin, may pierce the skin of its neighbour, so that now an attempt is being made to develop a tomato which leaves its stalk on the plant.' (From: *In the Future Now* by Michael Davie, Hamish Hamilton, 1972)

The machine almost halved the costs of harvesting tomatoes and the engineers went on to achieve similar success with melons, strawberries, sweet potatoes, and numerous other crops which demanded 'stoop labour' previously provided by the *braceros*, migrant workers from Mexico.

As Californian agriculture becomes more technical so it requires amounts of capital investment which are beyond the resources of the small farmer. As a result, farms of less than 40 hectares are steadily disappearing. Despite government aid the number of small Californian farms was halved between 1950 and 1970. These bankrupt holdings were quickly added to other farms, so that their average size has increased steadily to about 220 hectares. Ownership has often passed to large companies with sufficient financial backing to afford the modern practices which have turned traditional farming into something better described as 'agribusiness'. Such companies now dominate Californian agriculture: 7 per cent of the farms occupy 80 per cent of the arable land, while 2 per cent of the farms employ 60 per cent of the workers. As farms increase in size ('spreads' of around 1000 hectares are commonly regarded as the most efficient nowadays) so too does the average size of fields—in order to make the best use of the machinery. And as mechanisation increases, the number of employees diminishes.

Where livestock is concerned, widespread factory farming means that many animals spend the whole of their lives in extremely unnatural conditions. Some people regard these practices as inhumane, believing that the end product —cheaper food—cannot justify the methods used to obtain it. Also, the large-scale use of fertilisers and in-secticides for improving crop yields is now known to pose a considerable biological threat to the balance of nature. Nowhere is this threat greater than in California, where the application of chemicals to farmland is intensive.

A final fear is that, in the long run, the choice of fruit and vegetables grown by Californian 'agribusiness' will be decided not by what people want to eat, but by what the machines can best handle. Even if the crops can be mechanised they will be cultivated either for freezing or for canning. Eventually, fresh fruit and vegetables may become a luxury that, even in California, only the very rich can afford.

Questions

The account

1. Describe briefly what the Californian agricultural engineers might define as 'the ideal tomato'.
2. Who benefited, and who suffered as a result of the success of the new harvesting machine?
3. Explain what is meant by the term 'agribusiness'.
4. Draw bar graphs to illustrate how large company farms dominate Californian agriculture.
5. Argue the case for and against the factory-farming of livestock.
6. Summarise the problems caused by the search for increased agricultural efficiency in California.

Plate 51 and Figure 81

7. *a)* Who might buy the product being advertised?
   b) Name the fruits depicted on the advertisement.
   c) In what part of the Central Valley was the photograph taken?

Plate 51 and the account

8. Argue the case for and against the use of pesticides such as the one advertised.

The industrial explosion

Lacking coal and with only small deposits of iron ore, California for long remained primarily an agricultural region. Its early industries were based on processing the products of its farms, forests and fisheries. These activities are still important, but manufacturing industries now produce the majority of goods and employ many more people. In recent decades the rapid development of electronic and other ultra-modern industries has made California the most prosperous of the 50 states. Indeed, judged as a separate country, California would be ranked ahead of Britain among the world's leading economic powers.

Table 43   Production of goods in California, by value

	Percentage share
Manufactured products	81
Agricultural products	14
Fish and mineral products	5
	100

THE DEFENCE AND AEROSPACE INDUSTRIES

The spectacular rise of California's industries dates from the Second World War, when the state became the main base for American military operations against the Japanese. In 1942 a strategically located steel works was built at Fontana, east of Los Angeles. By using coal from Utah (1300 km away), some iron ore from Eagle Mountain (180 km away) and much local scrap the problems of supplying raw materials were overcome. The Fontana works provided steel for the expansion of a whole range of 'war industries' centred mainly in southern California.

In addition to the state's strategic location, California's climate was an important factor in the development of the aircraft industry. Outdoor storage and assembly work were possible for most of the year, thus saving on the costs of factory buildings, heating and lighting. In addition the Mojave Desert offered ideal conditions for test flying at all seasons.

After 1945 the aircraft industry continued to enjoy such advantages and expanded rapidly. The growth of civil aviation provided huge new markets for passenger aircraft while American involvement in Korea and Vietnam gave further boosts to the production of military aircraft. With rapid expansion into the field of rockets and satellites for both defence and space exploration, the manufacture of aerospace equipment has become California's most important industry, accounting for well over one-third of the value of the state's industrial products.

The major aerospace companies depend on a large number of specialist engineering firms for the supply of a wide variety of electronic gadgetry and other sophisticated components. The industry is also closely related to a great deal of scientific and technical research employing thousands of highly-qualified and skilled personnel. However, practically the only customer for aerospace products is the United States Government and, with such heavy dependence on defence contracts, any easing of international tension or major changes in government policies could directly affect California's overall prosperity.

In an attempt to reduce the industry's dependence on defence contracts, the direction of research nowadays is towards miniaturised computers for business firms, laser techniques for industrial purposes, and advanced navigation and signalling equipment for passenger aircraft and surface transport (e.g. BART). The marine sciences which are now developing at Long Beach, San Diego and Monterey, are of special interest. Recent discovery of manganese nodules and other mineral deposits on the sea bed means that the exploration and exploitation of the 'inner space' of the Pacific Ocean may become as important to California as any of its present industries.

Table 44   Jobs in California's manufacturing industries

Electrical equipment and supplies	235 400
Transportation equipment (especially aircraft)	222 800
Food and allied products	169 600
Machinery, except electrical	141 400
Fabricated metal products	113 000
Printing and publishing	91 300
Clothing and other textile products	72 700
Ordnance and accessories	66 900
Primary metal industries	59 200
Chemicals and allied products	55 100
Stone, clay and glass products	51 100
Lumber and wood products	48 000
Rubber and plastic products	42 800
Paper and allied products	36 800
Furniture and fixtures	36 300
Instruments and related products	35 700
Miscellaneous manufacturing industries	33 800
Petroleum refining and related industries	29 100
Textile mills products	10 500
Leather and leather products	6 500
Total:	1 558 000

ENERGY SUPPLIES

Figure 82   *California's sources of energy*

HEP from Pacific NW
from Alberta
oil from Alaska
HEP
HEP
HEP
HEP
HEP
HEP
Sacramento
Rio Vista field
GAS
Richmond (R)
HEP
Stockton
HEP
• Fresno
GAS
SAN JOAQUIN BASIN
(R) Bakersfield
from New Mexico
Hoover Dam (HEP)
from New Mexico (coal source)
Colorado R.
LOS ANGELES BASIN
San Pedro (R) Long Beach
from Texas and New Mexico
oil from Venezuela, Indonesia, Middle East

oilfields
(R) major refineries
◀— oil pipelines
(GAS) natural gas fields
⇐ natural gas pipelines
HEP main hydro-electric power areas
◀—× electricity imports
■ nuclear power stations in operation by 1990

0   km   300

Questions

Table 43

1. Comment on the relative importance of manufacturing industry and other economic activities in California.

Table 44 and the account

2. *a*) What are the primary metal industries?
   b) Why are such industries relatively unimportant in California?

3. *a*) List those industries which are wholly or partly associated with defence and aerospace.
   b) How many people are employed in this group of industries?
   c) Express your answer to *b*) as a percentage of the total.

The account

4. Describe (*i*) why, and (*ii*) how the aerospace industry is reducing its dependence on government contracts.

Questions

Figure 82

1. Oil is California's major energy resource. Name:
   a) the two largest oilfields;
   b) the location of the major oil refineries.

Figure 82 and Table 44

2. Oil and gas provide the raw materials for the petro-chemical industry.
   a) Suggest two likely centres of this industry in California.
   b) How many people are employed in industries associated with petro-chemicals?

Figure 82 and general

3. Draw up two columns headed 'HEP Stations' and 'Nuclear Power Stations'. Under each heading list the following:
   a) the region of California in which most of the stations are located;
   b) the reasons why the stations are located in the region named (*hint:* water).

Figure 82

4. Elaborate on the statement that 'Imports of energy are now essential to California'.

The tourist industry

California attracts some 16 million visitors each year; obviously tourism has become an important industry. San Francisco, perhaps the most beautiful of American cities, is a major attraction with its coastal setting, hilly streets, Victorian cable cars and Chinatown—a colourful world of temples, tearooms, restaurants and exotic shops. In the Los Angeles area the famous 'movie' industry was located in Hollywood at the beginning of this century when most films were shot outdoors, because bright sunlight was essential. Today, tours are arranged to film studios and to Beverly Hills where many famous stars have their homes. At Anaheim, Disneyland, an offshoot of the film industry, is a popular entertainment centre with over five million visitors every year. The old British liner, *Queen Mary*, now permanently moored at Long Beach, is also proving a profitable attraction. Containing hotels, restaurants and museums, the great ship is the town's principal asset in its bid to become a major tourist resort.

But California's 'great outdoors' is its most important tourist asset. With deserts, forests, mountains and beautiful beaches California is the most physically diverse state

Plate 52   *Cable car, Chinatown, San Francisco*

Plate 53 *Camouflaged oil rigs, Long Beach, California*

in the Union. The climate encourages practically every known outdoor sporting and leisure pursuit—a morning's skiing on fresh snow can be followed by ocean surfing in the afternoon. An excellent system of camp sites, picnic and motoring facilities gives easy access to recreational areas, especially the huge parks and forests run by the state and federal governments. In all, about one-third of California's total area provides land for recreation.

YOSEMITE NATIONAL PARK: COPING WITH CONGESTION

'In recent years Yosemite gained a reputation as over-crowded and as fast developing such urban problems as traffic congestion, smog and crime.

Three years ago, the National Park Service placed portions of the park off limits to automobiles and established a free shuttle bus system.

As a result, motor vehicle traffic has been reduced substantially, and there is a much less urban aura to the park. And this year, Yosemite, applying a technique introduced last summer in several other parks, has reduced congestion on trails in the back country as well.

Park rangers divided remote areas of the park into 48 sections and placed a limit on the number of people permitted into each area daily.

The back-packers must sign in advance for admittance to these areas, a system that according to park officials spreads hikers throughout the park more evenly.

A telephone-computer reservation system for campground sites introduced here and in 20 other national parks now allows campers to know in advance whether they will have a place.'
(*New York Times*, 5 August 1974)

As California's own population increases, and as more out-of-state visitors arrive, further over-use of tourist facilities seems inevitable, so that in more and more areas the number of visitors will have to be limited.

124

Questions

The account, Figure 78 and general

1. Imagine that you are a travel agent's employee, and you are required to promote 'California for the tourist'. Make a list of the places you would advertise with a short description of each.

The account

2. *a*) Why was the film industry originally established in California?
   b) What locational advantages does California offer to the modern industry? (*hint:* physical diversity)

Plate 53 and the account

3. *a*) Why have the drilling platforms been camouflaged?
   b) How have the various features of the platform been disguised?
   c) What features of the oil-drilling operations will be sensed by people in Long Beach despite the landscaping and soundproofing?

Plate 54

4. *a*) Describe (*i*) the summit surface of Half Dome, and (*ii*) the valley side.
   b) What type of erosion created the view shown?
5. *a*) Describe the vegetation on the valley floor.
   b) Why will the forest probably never be exploited commercially?

Newspaper extract

6. *a*) What measures have been taken to reduce over-crowding in Yosemite National Park?
   b) Describe (*i*) how the measures operate for different kinds of recreation, and (*ii*) the benefits gained by visitors.

Plate 54   *Yosemite National Park*

Los Angeles

Los Angeles is essentially a city of the twentieth century. Its only initial advantages were a sunny climate and an oilfield, but it grew rapidly as the centre of developments such as petroleum refining, film making, the processing and distribution of fruit and vegetables, and later, the defence and aerospace industries. As a result of such growth, Los Angeles has become California's major industrial area, the economic capital of the Pacific and South-West regions, and the United States' second largest population cluster (10 350 000 in 1975).

Situated in a very dry region, Los Angeles has a huge thirst. The problem of water supply has been 'solved' twice this century by building aqueducts from the Owens River (1913) and from the Colorado River (1941). However, the large increases in both population and industry since the Second World War have created a further water shortage. The ambitious State Water Project (see Figure 80) is the latest attempt to remedy the situation. Deliveries of water to Los Angeles began in 1975 and the full flow should be available by 1982. But even this expensive scheme will eventually prove inadequate and there are plans to channel supplies from water-abundant areas as far away as western Canada. Probably the best scheme for the future is the distilling of sea water. Experimental plants are already in operation but the process is, as yet, very expensive.

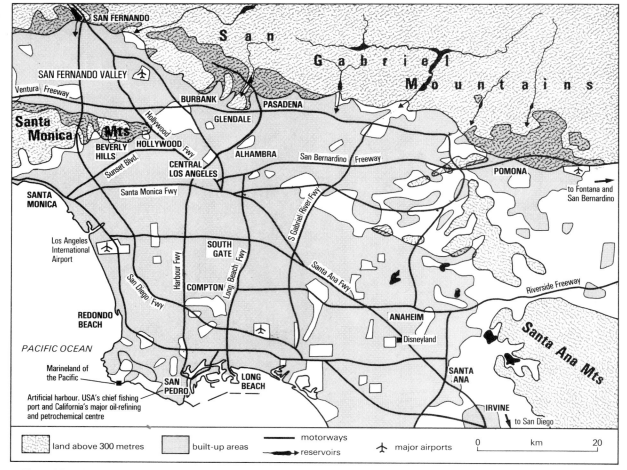

Figure 83   *The Los Angeles Region: 'suburbs in search of a city'*

Questions

Figure 83 and the account

1. *a*) Using transparent graph paper, or a grid drawn on tracing paper, calculate the size of the built-up area of Greater Los Angeles.
   b) What physical features have limited the urban sprawl?

2. How has Los Angeles (*i*) tried to solve the problem of thirst; and (*ii*) remedied the lack of a harbour?

A CITY ON WHEELS

In Los Angeles life is based on the use of cars more than anywhere else in the world. The city grew up in the automobile age and never really had any adequate public transport. In the production of cars Los Angeles is second only to Detroit. Most of the components are made outside California and shipped to factories where the cars are assembled. This system is economic mainly because of the huge demand for cars in California. There are now 90 cars for every 100 people of driving age and

an elaborate system of limited access freeways (motorways) has been laid out in the form of a giant grid. Over 800 km of freeways already exist and another 1000 km will be completed in the 1980s. But every kilometre of new freeway generates more traffic and rarely eases congestion. Even though about 80 per cent of central Los Angeles is devoted to the needs of the automobile, the city is notorious for its traffic jams and parking problems. By 1985 Los Angeles may contain 12 million people and 9

Plate 56 *Rush hour traffic, Los Angeles*

million cars—generating future problems which can hardly be imagined. However, few people appear to object to the dominance of the automobile, merely accepting it as the normal, almost essential means of getting about. There is little enthusiasm for improving the almost non-existent public transport system.

Each day the cars of Los Angeles emit thousands of tonnes of carbon monoxide and other pollutants into the atmosphere, despite laws obliging manufacturers to fit anti-pollution devices to the engines of all new cars. Even on clear days when poisonous gases can disperse into the atmosphere the dangers are obvious enough, but on 340 days of the year a temperature inversion exists over Los Angeles, and on 150 days it is low enough to trap the pollution, which accumulates as 'smog', a brownish-yellow haze, painful to eyes and nose and harmful to general health.

SUBURBS IN SEARCH OF A CITY

Cars and the freeways have transformed Los Angeles into the world's most extensive urban area. Indeed, Los Angeles is more accurately described as a multi-centred metropolis than a city in the traditional sense. Held together only by the freeway network, the Los Angeles area clearly shows how a gigantic formless sprawl can develop if widespread use of the private car goes unchallenged.

Recent attempts to revitalise the city centre as a cultural, commercial and residential area have failed to stem the flow of people to the suburbs, which in many ways have become more important than the city itself.

Suburban living often means commuting to the city over long distances, but in many cases jobs are available locally since industries have also been abandoning the inner city for more favourable locations in the suburbs. Shops, too, have followed the trend to suburban sites where many hypermarkets (very large supermarkets selling extensive ranges of goods) have sprung up in recent years. However a new law 'freezing' California's agricultural land is designed to halt the unfettered growth of suburbs.

At Irvine, suburban development has reached its ultimate form—a completely planned satellite city for 430 000

Plate 57   *New housing development at Irvine*

inhabitants. Jobs are provided on a huge industrial estate served by freeways, a railway and an airport. Community facilities include a recreation and sports complex, and an enormous one-stop shopping precinct. Irvine is the latest example of a suburban centre which is within the orbit of Los Angeles but almost completely independent of it.

Questions

Plate 55 and general

1. How can the Central Business District (CBD) be identified?
   a) Why is the Los Angeles CBD much smaller than is usual in a city of this size?
   b) Describe the general height of buildings outside the CBD area.
   c) Indicate how the area is dominated by cars.

The account and general

2. Make a list of the problems caused by the widespread use of the car in the Los Angeles area.

3. Explain a) how the car has transformed Los Angeles into the world's most extensive urban area; and b) why the car is important to the majority of suburban residents.

Plate 56

4. a) How does the pattern of Los Angeles' rush hour traffic differ from that of other cities? (*hint:* direction)
   b) Account for the difference.

5. a) Look at the fifty vehicles nearest the camera and moving towards Exit 24. How many of the vehicles are (*i*) private cars, (*ii*) buses, (*iii*) vans and trucks?
   b) Use the results of your vehicle count to construct a bar graph showing the composition of the Los Angeles rush hour traffic. (*hint:* convert results into percentages by multiplying by two)

Plate 57

6. a) Comment on (*i*) the design of the individual houses, and (*ii*) the layout of the estate.
   b) For people of what income group is the development intended? How can you tell?

Plate 57 and the account

7. Why is California's State Government attempting to limit the spread of suburban housing like that in the photograph?

129

San Francisco

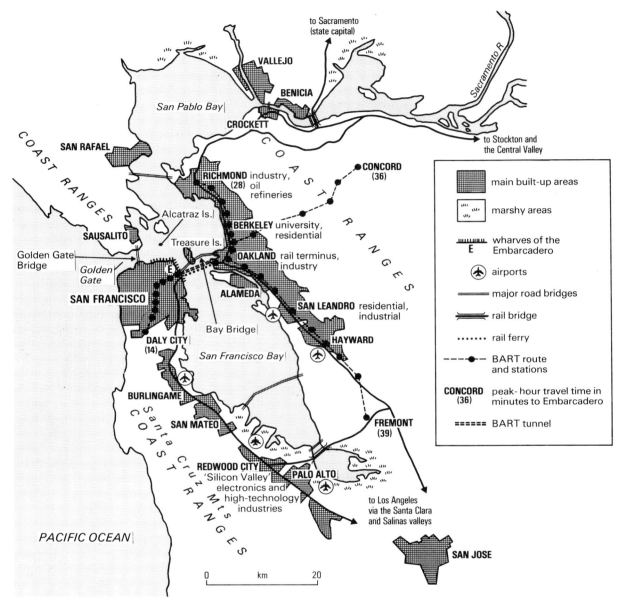

Figure 84   *The San Francisco area*

Questions

Figure 84 and an atlas

1. Describe the physical setting of San Francisco.
2. Name the two natural features which have enabled San Francisco to become the largest port on the Pacific coast of North America.

3. *a)* Name San Francisco's main hinterland in California.
   b) Suggest the kind of products that form the bulk of San Francisco's exports.

4. Why was the opening of trade through the Panama Canal in 1914 important to San Francisco?

Plate 58 and Figure 84

5. *a*) In what direction was the photograph taken?
   b) What details on the photograph indicate that San Francisco is a great port?

c) Why has the city not developed on the land to the north of the Golden Gate?

Figure 84

6. Why has much of the industrial and residential development taken place in the bay-shore suburbs?

BART—A NEW TRAIN SERVICE

San Francisco is still the Bay Area's main cultural, commercial and business centre and generates heavy commuter car traffic from the suburbs. Traffic problems are heightened by the limited number of access points to the city. As traffic volumes increased, freeways began to appear as they had in Los Angeles. San Franciscans, however, were concerned that the new highways, and the inevitable torrent of cars, would do irreparable damage to the special character of their city. So they voted in favour of building BART—the Bay Area Rapid Transit System.

Fully operational since September 1974, BART is the world's most advanced passenger train service and the first completely new rapid transit system in the United States for over 60 years. It was designed by Californian aerospace companies, and has been acclaimed as a '21st century concept', the product of ultra-modern electronic technology. Its electrically powered computer-controlled trains run at speeds of up to 130 kph with only 90 seconds between trains at peak periods. Every function, from the opening and closing of doors to speed and

Plate 58   *Aerial view of San Francisco*

Plate 59 *BART train, San Francisco*

distance control, is completely automatic, though a driver in each train can take over in an emergency. The interiors of the light-weight aluminium coaches are air-conditioned, close-carpeted and colour co-ordinated, with a guaranteed seat for every passenger—more like a jet airliner than a commuter railway. Stations are particu-larly bright and pleasant, while fares are lower than for bus trips of equivalent distance.

The whole idea is to attract passengers and so reduce, if not eliminate, the jams, noise and air pollution caused by commuters' cars. The saving in journey time can be as much as 80 per cent on the key section of the route which runs under the Bay. This makes Oakland to San Francisco a nine-minute journey compared with the 30 to 45 minutes needed to get through the nerve-jangling tangle of rush-hour traffic on the Bay Bridge. Eventually BART could be carrying 200 000 passengers a day, about 10 per cent of the present commuter traffic.

Unfortunately, BART has experienced a number of technical problems which have plagued its initial operations. These unforeseen difficulties have made the trains much less reliable than originally hoped. Indeed, it has been estimated that for every passenger carried the BART system loses about £3. Clearly, this threatens the project's long-term prospects of success, and it remains to be seen whether BART's trains can live up to original expectations.

Questions

The account and Figure 84

1. *a*) Why are San Francisco's car commuter problems increased by the city's location?
   b) Name the two main access points by road to San Francisco.
   c) How does BART cross the bay?

The account and general

2. *a*) What special technical feature makes BART different from most other rail systems?
   b) Why is it no surprise that such an ultra-modern transport system should be developed in California?
3. Calculate the present total number of commuters in the San Francisco area. (The total is expected to double by 1990!)

4. *a*) List the advantages which BART was intended to offer commuters, compared with using their cars.
   b) What, in practice, has made the project less advantageous than originally expected?

Figure 84

5. Calculate (*i*) peak-hour travel time from the most distant BART station to downtown San Francisco (Embarcadero); (*ii*) the approximate distance, in kilometres, along the same route; (*iii*) the average speed of the BART train covering the route.

California and the earthquake threat

Modern research indicates that the outer layers of the earth's crust are made up of large 'plates' which fit closely together although they are moved around by gigantic forces. The places where earthquakes often occur are along plate boundaries. In California the notorious San Andreas Fault is the boundary where two huge plates, the American and the Pacific, slide past each other, with tendencies here and there to pull apart or press together. If the sliding took place evenly the northward movement of the Pacific plate would average 5 cm each year, but the fault tends to stick and then to slip, suddenly releasing the accumulated strain and sending shock waves through the surrounding land.

Both of California's major cities are at risk but the biggest threat is to San Francisco, which was destroyed by movement of the San Andreas Fault in 1906. Now, another major earthquake seems imminent. The catastrophe may aready have happened before you read these words, or

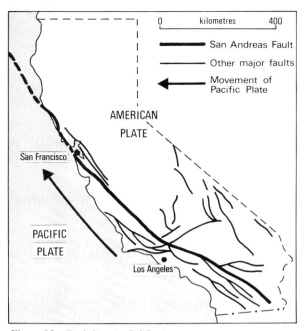

Figure 85 *Fault lines in California*

Plate 60 *The San Andreas fault in Southern California: view looking north*

it may be delayed another half-century. The longer the delay the worse the earthquake will be because strain is steadily building up in the rocks year by year. In the San Francisco area the rocks have locked in an ominous way and could have to make a 'jump' of up to 4 metres. If these enormous forces are suddenly unleashed, the destruction of San Francisco seems certain. Pessimists predict a death toll of 50 000 in San Francisco next time, and damage costing £50 000 million.

American scientists believe that San Francisco can be saved. They have discovered that movement along fault lines can be encouraged by 'fluid-injection'—pumping water into the rocks to act as a kind of lubricant. Equally important, they can 'apply the brakes' by pumping water out of the rocks. Using these principles, seismologists have devised a scheme to cause a long series of minor earthquakes whose violence would be kept within

tight limits. After practical experiments in an earthquake zone remote from centres of population the plan, if successful, will then be applied to the San Andreas Fault. These may seem desperate measures, but the alternative is the almost inevitable large-scale destruction of California's cities.

(Based on *The Restless Earth* by Nigel Calder, B.B.C. Publications, 1972)

Questions

The account

1. Explain in your own words:
   a) why, without human intervention, the destruction of San Francisco seems inevitable;
   b) why the timing of the disaster cannot be accurately predicted;
   c) how scientists are attempting to prevent the disaster.

Figure 85

2. *a*) Name the plate on which is located (*i*) San Francisco, and (*ii*) Los Angeles.

   b) Assuming smooth, continuous movement along the San Andreas Fault: (*i*) how far north will the Pacific Plate move during the lifetime of an average Californian (70 years)? (*ii*) how long will it take for Los Angeles to arrive on the same latitude as San Francisco?

Plate 60

3. *a*) Identify the plates to the left and right of the fault.
   b) What evidence is there on the photograph that movement has taken place along the fault?

The Pacific North-West (USA)

Introduction

Compared with California, the two north-western states have been 'late developers' in the economic life of the USA. In 1843 settlers began arriving along the Oregon Trail but the region had no gold rush to stimulate early development. Instead, timber supplies and salmon fishing became the economic mainstays, although the latter is now of comparatively minor importance. In recent years other resources have been developed, especially the water supplies and power potential of the Columbia River. As a result, the region now has a range of manufacturing industries of which the Boeing aircraft works at Everett is the most important. Even so, the present-day population remains relatively small and nearly half the people live in the three metropolitan areas of Seattle, Tacoma and Portland.

Seattle is the 'mainland' USA's major trading and communications link with Alaska. Developments in the 49th State, have always directly benefited the port, which now has much to gain as the terminus for some of the tankers carrying Alaskan oil from Valdez. But the problem of piping the refined oil over great distances to the major American markets will remain. Indeed, the cost of transporting its products to the main centres of population in the eastern states has always been the Pacific North-West's biggest economic handicap.

Table 45   Three Pacific states: a comparison of size and population

State	Area (km²)	Population (1976)
Washington	176 540	3 612 000
Oregon	251 072	2 329 000
California	410 837	21 520 000

(*US Abstract of Statistics, 1977*)

Plate 61   *Seattle, Washington*

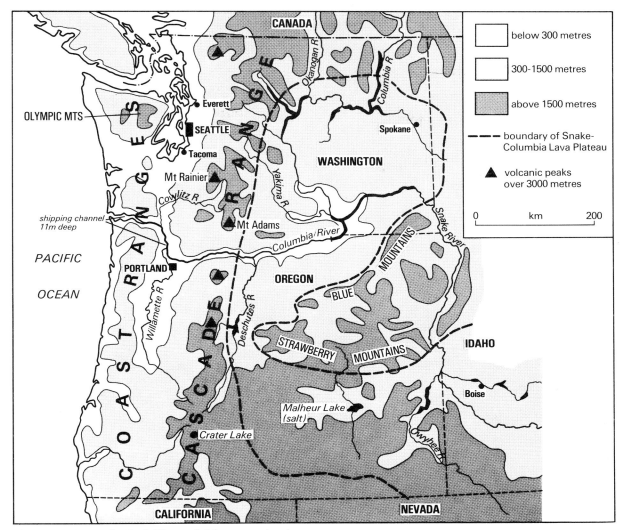

Figure 86　*The Pacific North West: relief features and major towns*

Questions

Figure 86

1. Compare the positions of Seattle and Portland. Explain why *a*) Seattle is the largest port, and *b*) Portland is the regional capital of the Pacific North West (*hint:* communications).

Plate 61 and Figure 86

2. *a*) Identify the mountains in the background.
   b) Comment on the general layout of Seattle. How typical is it of US cities?

The account and general

3. *a*) Name one major US area with large centres of population which is *not* remote from the Pacific North-West.

b) Which of the Pacific North-West's resources will this heavily populated region be most interested in?

Table 45

4. Express the information in 'blocks', using squared graph paper.
   (*i*) Round off the figures as necessary.
   (*ii*) Make one square of the graph paper represent x km^2.
   (*iii*) Use one dot to symbolise y people.
   (*iv*) Space the dots in the appropriate blocks as evenly as possible.

Figure 86 and an atlas

5. What countries in Europe occupy a position equivalent to the Pacific North-West region?

135

A volcanic landscape

Physically, the Pacific North-West forms the link between California to the south and British Columbia to the north. The valleys and mountains in the western half of the region are simply northward extensions of the major relief features of California. However, the Snake–Columbia lava plateau is a distinctive area which has no counterpart further south.

The lava plateau is one of the world's largest-scale examples of volcanic activity. At various times during the last 20 million years tension in the earth's crust opened up fissures through which molten rock welled out. One outpouring followed another, smothering the original surface under vast sheets of basalt hundreds of metres thick. Later, rivers flowing across the plateau excavated gorges deep enough in places to expose the ancient surface beneath the basalt layers. Elsewhere, the Blue Mountains and other peaks project like 'islands' through the basalt.

Other volcanic landforms of more recent origin occur in the Cascades. Successive outpourings of lava and explosive eruptions of ash, cinder and pumice built up 'composite cones' of classic volcanic shape. Several of these majestic peaks reach over 3000 metres in height and one of them, Mt Baker, erupted as recently as 1870. In the southern Cascades alone there are at least 120 other volcanoes, extinct or dormant. This is a volcanic landscape that has only recently spent its energies—and is likely to be heard from again.

CRATER LAKE

One of the region's most interesting volcanic features is Crater Lake, 9·6 km wide, the deepest (590 m) and perhaps the loveliest of all American lakes. It crowns a volcano once considerably higher than it is today. Within the last 7000 years a tremendous explosion ripped off the top of the mountain, and great quantities of lava spewed out over the surrounding countryside. The cavity which resulted could no longer support the weight of the cone, which collapsed into the void. After the destruction of 'Mount Mazama', additional activity within the caldera produced Wizard Island. This cinder cone rises from the floor of the cavity to a height of 233 m above the surface of the lake, which is itself 1885 m above sea level.

Plate 62   *Lava Plateau and the Columbia River*

Plate 63   *Crater Lake and Wizard Island*

Questions

Atlas

1. *a*) Name the regions of California of which the following are the northward extensions: (*i*) the Cascade Mountains, (*ii*) the lowland of the Willamette and Cowlitz valleys.
b) In what form do the Coast Ranges continue into British Columbia?

The account and Plate 62

2. Compare the Pacific North-West's two types of volcanic landforms, using the following headings:
   a) location, *b*) age, *c*) mode of formation, *d*) geological composition, *e*) scale, *f*) present general appearance, *g*) likelihood of future volcanic activity.

The account and general

3. *a*) Explain how Crater Lake itself was formed.
b) The depth of the lake is almost constant. Why?

The account and Plate 63

4. *a*) Calculate the *total* height of the Wizard Island cinder cone, i.e. from base to summit.
b) Estimate the height of the caldera rim above the lake surface.

General

5. With the aid of a simple sketch, explain how it is possible to show that the height of the former Mount Mazama was approximately 3700 m. (*hint:* slopes)

Climatic considerations

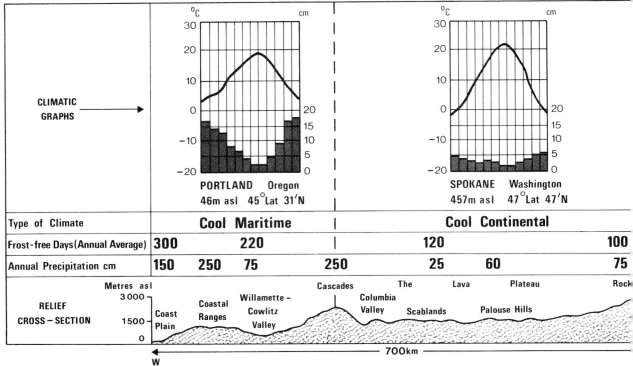

Figure 87 *Contrasts between the coastal and interior areas*

Questions

Figure 87

1. Study the climatic graphs of Portland and Spokane.
   a) Describe the differences.
   b) Account for your observations.
2. a) Using the figures provided, draw a rainfall graph to show west-east variations.
   b) Compare the rainfall graph with the relief cross-section. What general relationship do you notice?

3. a) (i) Explain why the interior is so much drier than the areas nearer the coast. (ii) Why is the precipitation lowest in the Scablands?
   b) Explain why the growing season decreases eastwards.

Forestry

Coniferous softwood forests occupy over half the total area of the Pacific North-West. The region now contains the bulk of the USA's remaining commercial timber reserves and accounts for over one-third of the nation's total lumber production. The importance of timber to the Pacific North-West can be gauged from two other facts: this industry is the region's major employer, and its products are worth more than twice those of agriculture.

Due to the heavy rainfall and mild temperatures the tree-line lies at 1500 m on the Coast Ranges and even higher on the Cascades (see Figure 88). It is here that most of the large-scale felling is now concentrated, but such mountainous terrain creates problems of access to the timber. Often it is difficult and expensive to cut and remove selected trees, so an area of perhaps as much as 15 hectares is felled completely. This practice is called 'clear-cutting'. After an area has been cleared, strict laws require programmes of replanting, not only to replace the forest resources but to keep soil erosion to a minimum. Natural regeneration of the clear-cut areas would take longer and lead to trees of uneven age and a mixture of varieties in one area.

The rugged terrain has led to the development of a range of special machines for cutting the trees and transporting them to sawmills and other processing plants. Recently even helium-filled balloons have been used to lift batches of five or six large felled trees—each weighing over a tonne—and then deliver them to road-side depots. This method saves the time and cost of building access roads through the forest. Elsewhere, slides are constructed down which the logs are rolled, either to rivers or to points where heavy tractors or multi-wheeled trucks can

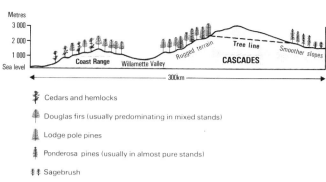

Cedars and hemlocks

Douglas firs (usually predominating in mixed stands)

Lodge pole pines

Ponderosa pines (usually in almost pure stands)

Sagebrush

Figure 88   *Section through the forests of Western Oregon*

retrieve them. Most logs are carried to the mills by road but the broad rivers and sheltered inlets still provide a cheap means of transport. Large log rafts are a common sight on Puget Sound and on the Columbia River throughout the year. The various dams across the river may appear to present a problem but this is overcome by a tug and raft travelling through the navigation locks together.

The rivers are also essential to the region's pulp and paper mills. Great quantities of water are used for the various mill processes and then returned to the rivers in a very polluted state. Although such pollution can be prevented the extra expense would make the industry uncompetitive compared with other centres nearer the main markets.

Much research is carried on into the more efficient use of wood products. For example, instead of being burned, the sawdust and trimmings from sawmills are now turned into the familiar chipboard and blockboard. More recently, methods have been devised to convert mill waste into alcohol, protein-rich foodstuffs, and even a tobacco substitute.

Plate 64   *Part of Seattle harbour*

Questions

Table 46 and Figure 88

1. *a*) (*i*) Name the region's two most commercially important species of trees. (*ii*) What proportion of the total do these two species together represent?
   b) Name one species of trees included in 'Others'.

Table 46   Timber cut in the Pacific North-West

Species	Percentage of total
Douglas fir	59
Ponderosa pine	13
Hemlock	9
Cedar	7
Other	12
Total	100

Figure 88

2. *a*) Account for the fact that the tree line is lower on the eastern slopes of the Cascades than on the western slopes.
   b) Why is the tree line much higher in Oregon than in Britain?
3. Give two reasons why the felling and transport of Ponderosa pine is generally less difficult than that of Douglas fir.

The account and general

4. Describe, in your own words, the problems of the timber industry in the Pacific North-West. How, and to what extent, have they been solved?

Plate 64

5. *a*) Describe the three different cargo-handling methods used in the dock area shown.
   b) What kinds of cargo are likely to be associated with each handling method?

Farming

The marked climatic contrasts of the Pacific North-West directly affect farming within the region. In particular there are sharp differences between the well-watered western lowlands and the drier interior plateau areas.

In the nineteenth century most of the early settlers were attracted to the alluvial soils of the Willamette-Cowlitz-Puget Sound lowlands where dairying and mixed farming were developed, mainly to support the local population. This is still the most important farming area and, although summer irrigation has recently increased the range of products, the major national markets are so distant that most of the output is still sold locally. Only apples (for which Washington is the leading state), cherries, raspberries and similar specialist crops, often in canned or processed form, are sent to other states—although Japan has emerged as an increasingly important customer in recent years.

After 1900 the lava plateau was opened up for the commercial production of winter wheat and other cereals. The volcanic rocks have often weathered into fertile soil, rather like the loess deposits which cover some parts of the plateau. However, this advantage is offset by the plateau's low rainfall, particularly in the Scablands. Dry farming techniques are used to conserve moisture in the soil, but the yields from each hectare are relatively low. To compensate for this, the farms are large, mostly between 800 and 1200 hectares.

Questions

Figures 86 and 89

1. Name the type of livestock, and the livestock products produced in: *a*) the Willamette Valley; and *b*) the interior plateau.

The account

2. *a*) List the advantages of the lava plateau for cereal production.
   b) Explain, in your own words, why the area's farms are so large.

The Columbia Basin Project

Paradoxically, the interior has a surplus of water—the problem is that it flows deep in the flat-floored valleys of the Columbia River and its major tributaries. Providing irrigation water for farmland in the valleys is a relatively easy matter, but the problem of raising water from the Columbia River on to the Scablands was solved only when the federal government built the Grand Coulee Dam, the key feature of the multi-purpose Columbia Basin Project. Work on the dam began in 1933 and took eight years to complete. Today it is still the largest concrete dam in the western hemisphere.

The engineering problems were formidable. Basically, some of the HEP generated at the dam is used to raise water over 80 metres from Lake Roosevelt into Banks Lake, which occupies part of the Grand Coulee Valley. From Banks Lake the water is pumped southwards in canals and tunnels to irrigable areas where it has brought new life to over 400 000 hectares of previously semi-arid farmland.

The first water began flowing in 1948. Since then about 10 000 small farms have been located on the newly irrigated areas. The size of farm is limited by law because the government planned the project as a family-type development, with each farm just large enough to support 'an average-sized family at a suitable level of living.'

Irrigation has enabled a wide range of crops to be grown despite the altitude of the farmland and the shortness of the growing season. Some of the crops are used as fodder for livestock, an increasingly important aspect of the new farming.

Table 47   Crops grown on Project land

	Percentage of total area
Hay and forage crops (mainly alfalfa)	30
Pasture	10
Field crops (especially potatoes and sugar beet)	28
Fruit and vegetables (especially apples, peas and beans)	20
Cereals (mainly wheat)	12
Total	100

Plate 65   *The Grand Coulee Dam*

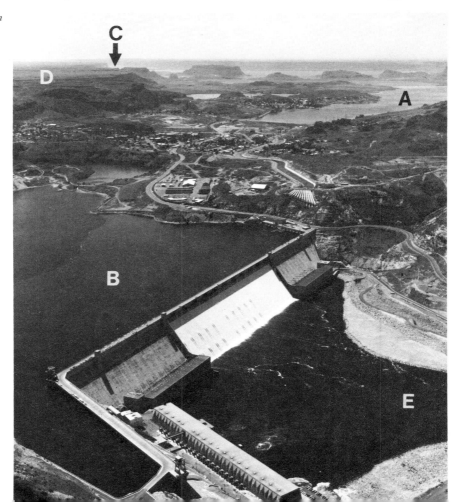

The project has also stimulated much-needed industrial growth in the area. Many food-packing and processing plants have been established to handle the new products, while improved road and rail links connect the area with Pacific ports and elsewhere. In addition, the Columbia River is navigable by barges as far as Pasco.

Compared with adjacent non-irrigated areas the project is undoubtedly a success; hectare for hectare its farms now have incomes and yields twenty times higher than land to the east. However, although sales of HEP from the Grand Coulee Dam are expected eventually to return a profit, the farms themselves will probably never repay the enormous total cost of providing the irrigation water— perhaps as much as £500 million. (By comparison, the development of Concorde, the Anglo-French supersonic airliner, cost over £1000 million.)

Questions

Plate 65, Figure 89 and the account

1. *a*) Name the features indicated by the letters A–E or the photograph: lakes A and B, valley C, plateau D, river E.
   b) Through what links is water transferred from Lake Roosevelt to Banks Lake?
   c) A third power-house was completed in 1976. What structural changes to the dam's original design did this addition necessitate?

The account

2. *a*) What agricultural improvements resulted from the building of Grand Coulee Dam?
   b) How did the completion of this dam, and others in the region, cause the loss of farmland? (*hint:* Figure 89)
3. *a*) Calculate the average size of farm on the project land.
   b) Why were the project's farms deliberately limited in size?

Table 47 and the account

4. *a*) What proportion of the total project area is devoted to producing food for livestock?
   b) Give two factors which limit the range of crops that can be grown, even on the irrigated land.

The account

5. *a*) Who *really* paid for the Columbia Basin Project?
   b) Do you agree with the view that the spending of so much money can hardly be justified when the number of people who benefit directly is so small? Justify your answer.

The Columbia River and hydro-electricity

The Columbia, by volume of water, is the fifth largest river in North America. Precipitation in much of its catchment area is continuous throughout the year and run-off, at least in the south of the basin, is not seriously affected by winter freezing. Consequently, the river is the most important in the continent for the production of HEP—both actually and potentially. Many dams have already been built across the American section of the Columbia and others are under construction. International co-operation is important since 40 per cent of the water originates in Canada. Recently-built dams on the Canadian section of the river provide better flood control and a more even flow of water south of the border. As a result of these developments, the Pacific North-West is the only area west of the Mississippi that has sufficient HEP to satisfy demand for years to come.

One important use of the plentiful and relatively cheap HEP is the smelting of alumina to produce aluminium. Most of the alumina is transported by rail from Gulf Coast plants which use bauxite from Arkansas; the remainder comes from Tacoma, which processes bauxite imported from the Caribbean area. Once at the smelters the alumina is subjected to electrolytic processes requiring huge quantities of electricity. More than a quarter of all US aluminium is now produced in the Pacific North-West.

Hydro-electricity is widely used in other industries including the smelting of copper (from Idaho and South America) and lead (from Idaho) at Tacoma; shipbuilding and railway rolling stock at Seattle (steel mainly from scrap); and aircraft manufacturing at Everett.

Despite the many benefits, the damming of rivers like the Columbia is a cause for concern. Apart from the danger of new industries polluting the river, the upper reaches are salmon breeding grounds and catches on the rivers have fallen to only 15 per cent of original levels. Approximately £100 million has been spent in an effort to maintain the salmon runs on the Columbia River by building special 'fish ladders' around the newer dams and by providing hatcheries and research stations.

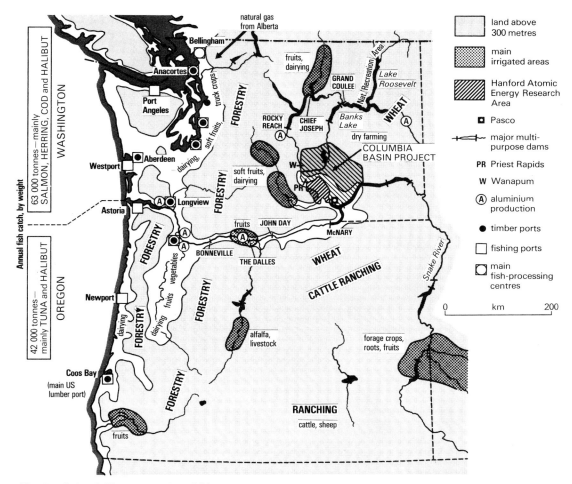

Figure 89   *Pacific North West: economic activities*

Questions

The account and general

1. Explain in detail why the Columbia is North America's most important river for HEP production.

Figure 89 and Table 48

2. Draw a large-scale sketch map to show the American section of the Columbia River. On it mark the locations of the dams listed in Table 49 and at each location show the present and ultimate outputs by means of either concentric proportional circles or by bar graphs. (*hints:* (*i*) round off all the statistics, (*ii*) choose an appropriate scale)

Figure 89 and the account

3. *a)* Account for the location of aluminium smelters in the Pacific North-West.
   b) Name one industry in the region that is a major user of aluminium.

Figure 89

4. Name two other sources of energy (apart from HEP) used in the region.

General

5. Summarise *a)* the advantages, and *b)* the disadvantages resulting from the multi-purpose dams built across the Columbia River.

Table 48   Major HEP plants on the Columbia River

| Name | Date of completion | Output in megawatts* | |
		Present	Ultimate
Grand Coulee	1941	2025	9771
John Day	1968	2160	2700
Chief Joseph	1956	1024	2073
The Dalles	1957	1119	1813
McNary	1953	986	1406
Wanapum	1963	831	1330
Priest Rapids	1959	789	1262
Rocky Reach	1961	712	1215

*1 megawatt = 1 million watts.

143

The Boeing Aircraft Works

The Boeing company occupies a large site at Everett, 50 km north of Seattle. The availability of timber was an important location factor during the early days of flight, when planes were made mostly of wood. However, as in California, it was the Second World War which speeded the industry's growth. With government aid, varied testing grounds and security from enemy attack the company was soon producing large numbers of B17 bombers—the famous 'Flying Fortresses'.

After 1945 production diversified and expanded and now includes hydrofoils, electronic devices and 'Cruise' missiles. Even more important are commercial jet aircraft such as the huge 747, the 'jumbo jet' which can carry 380 passengers. With this aircraft, and others in its production range, the company has succeeded in capturing a large share of international markets. In recent years Boeing has built half the world total of new passenger jets. Not surprisingly, 'transportation equipment' ranks first in Washington State for both employment and value of products, while the Boeing company is the Pacific North-West's largest single employer.

Questions

The account and general

1. List the factors which have contributed to the growth of the Boeing aircraft industry *a*) before 1945, and *b*) since 1945. (*hint:* recent economic developments in the region.)

Plate 66

2. *a*) Which of Boeing's passenger aircraft is shown? (*hint:* it is the largest made by the company)
b) Comment fully on the scale of operations inside the factory.

General

3. Why is the Pacific North-West's remoteness from major markets of little disadvantage to the Boeing company?

Plate 66 *Inside the Boeing Aircraft Company, Seattle*

The Arctic Fringe

Physical and climatic features

Table 49   Northern Baffin Island: climatic information

	J	F	M	A	M	J	J	A	S	O	N	D	
Temp. °C	−31	−31	−27	−19	−7	2	6	5	−1	−11	−21	−26	Range 37
Precip. cm	1·0	0·8	1·0	0·8	1·0	1·3	1·8	3·1	2·3	1·8	1·0	0·8	Total 16·7
	F	F	F				NS	NS			F		

▲ Average date of the break-up of pack ice   ▲ Newly formed pack ice covers coastal waters completely

F: Frostbite conditions are expected—the severe chilling of the body by wind at low temperatures.

NS: The only two months when snow does not normally fall

The vast Arctic fringe extends from the Atlantic to the Pacific coast and from the southern part of Hudson Bay to within some 6° latitude of the North Pole. It forms one of the world's most inhospitable regions with severe climatic conditions to be endured or avoided. The information in Table 49 indicates typical features of the true Arctic zone.

The high pressure system of cold air over the Arctic region repels other influences for most of the year and total precipitation is generally low. Sometimes, however, the high pressure gives way to inrushes of air from the Pacific and on such occasions the Northlands experience some of the worst blizzards on earth. The highest snowfall totals occur in the Alaskan mountains to the west of the region. Elsewhere, the dry powdery snow is blown around for much of the time giving extremely poor visibility, for which the term 'white-out' has been coined.

Another measure of cold is the permanently frozen ground, or 'permafrost' which underlies the whole of the true Arctic. Past and present climates have frozen all moisture in the ground to depths of 200 metres and more in the northern islands. The top 20 to 25 cm of the ground thaws out annually in the brief summer, but refreezes again a few weeks later.

Unfortunately, modern construction work has often resulted in the thawing out of the deeper layers of permafrost, completely saturating the area with oozing mud and destroying the natural habitat of many plants and animals.

In addition to these adverse climatic conditions the

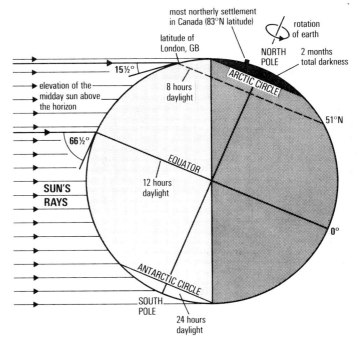

Figure 90   *Daylight hours on 21 December*

Northlands also experience extremes of summer daylight and winter darkness. In the earth's orbit around the sun, the Northern Hemisphere is tilted away from the source of both heat and light between September and

145

Figure 91 *Daylight on 21 June, Arctic Circle:*
view looking north

March, giving the winter half of the year. On 21 December, the winter solstice, the Arctic Circle has 24 hours of darkness, while the North Pole endures a three-month period without daylight (Figure 90). In the summer season the North Polar Region is tilted towards the sun and the 'top of the world' enjoys 24 hours daylight. But the sun does not rise far above the horizon and temperatures remain low. Consequently, frozen areas of land and water are slow to thaw (Figure 91).

Questions

Table 50 and general

1. *a*) Construct a single line graph to show the temperature statistics of northern Baffin Island.
   b) On your graph draw horizontal lines to illustrate the following features: (*i*) freezing point; (*ii*) a line to separate off the months without normal snowfall.
   c) Why do the months of pack ice and those with average temperatures below 0°C not coincide? (*hint:* land/water differences)

The account and general

2. *a*) Why is the snow dry and powdery, unlike that experienced in Britain?
   b) Suggest why the term 'white-out' was coined.
   c) (*i*) What 'past climate' was mainly responsible for the vast depth of permafrost? (*ii*) Do you think the permafrost is likely to thaw permanently given present temperatures? Give your reasons.

Figure 90 and the account

3. *a*) (*i*) By how many degrees is the earth's axis tilted?
   (*ii*) Give the latitude of the Arctic Circle.
   (*iii*) What is the relationship between (*i*) and (*ii*)?

   b) (*i*) If the axis of the earth's rotation were vertical at all times, what would the length of daylight be along the latitude of London (51°N), and along the Arctic Circle.
   (*ii*) What conclusions can you draw from the answers to (*i*)? (*hint:* seasons)

4. *a*) On 21 December, how many hours are there between sunrise and sunset at (*i*) the Equator, (*ii*) the Arctic Circle, (*iii*) London?
   b) Confirm by reference to a diary or almanac that the British amount is approximately correct.

5. Explain why on 21 December the sun's rays:
   a) are warmer at the Equator than at 51°N;
   b) give no warmth to the Arctic regions.

Figures 90, 91 and the account

6. Imagine that the earth in orbit has moved to the other side of the sun six months later, giving conditions of the opposite season. Draw a diagram, including all details from Figure 90, to show the daylight hours on 21 June. (Omit the angle of the midday sun.)

Alaska : the American northland

A FIRST LOOK

Bought from Russia in 1867 for about £2 million, Alaska was administered as an American territory until 1959 when it became the 49th State of the Union. In size, Alaska dwarfs all other states in the Union: its remote and separate position in the north-west of the continent tends to conceal the fact that Alaska is equal in area to one-fifth of the entire area of the continental United States.

In the 1890s the lure of gold attracted people of many nationalities to the Klondike, but few remained when the major veins and gold-bearing river gravels were exhausted. Alaska had few enduring attractions to outsiders until the

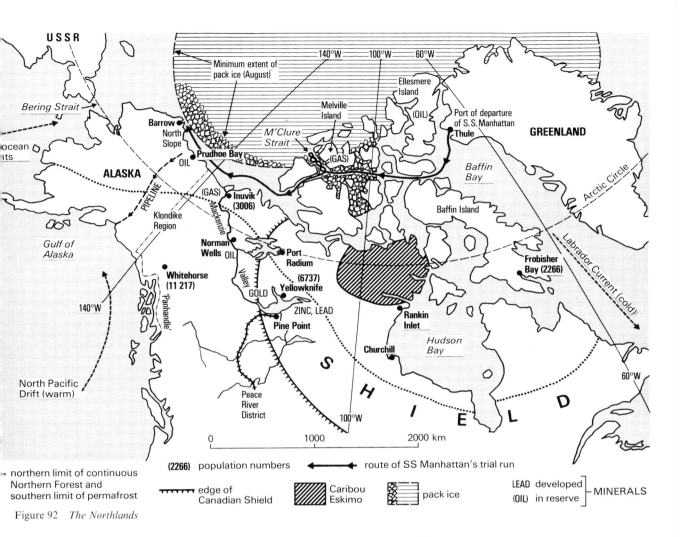

Figure 92 *The Northlands*

Map labels:
USSR
Bering Strait
ocean rts
Minimum extent of pack ice (August)
140°W 100°W 60°W
Barrow
North Slope
OIL
Prudhoe Bay
ALASKA
M'Clure Strait
Melville Island
(OIL)
Ellesmere Island
Port of departure of S.S. Manhattan
Thule
GREENLAND
(GAS)
Baffin Bay
PIPELINE
(GAS)
Inuvik (3006)
Mackenzie
Klondike Region
Baffin Island
Arctic Circle
Gulf of Alaska
Norman Wells OIL
Valley
Port Radium
(6737)
Yellowknife
GOLD
Frobisher Bay (2266)
Labrador Current (cold)
140°W
'Panhandle'
ZINC, LEAD
Pine Point
Rankin Inlet
North Pacific Drift (warm)
S H I E L D
Whitehorse (11 217)
Churchill
Hudson Bay
60°W
Peace River District
100°W
0   1000   2000 km

(2266) population numbers   ←——→ route of SS Manhattan's trial run

• northern limit of continuous Northern Forest and southern limit of permafrost
edge of Canadian Shield
Caribou Eskimo
pack ice
LEAD developed
(OIL) in reserve } MINERALS

middle of the twentieth century, although by 1930 the white population had slowly increased in size until it equalled the numbers of the native Indian and Eskimo groups. With the arrival of military and defence personnel during the Second World War and, more recently, of the many thousands linked with the exploration and development of oil, the Alaskan population has almost tripled. Now native groups comprise only about 15 per cent of the 382 000 total population.

Physically Alaska is made up of two mountain areas, extensions of the Pacific Coast Ranges and the northern-most Rockies. Between the two mountain ranges are plateau-like areas which become lower towards the Bering Sea, especially in the Yukon Valley. Climatically a distinctly warmer area, the Pacific-facing slopes and valleys contrast with the inhospitable central and northern parts of the state (see Table 50).

Table 50   Alaska: selected climatic statistics

		Juneau (Pacific coast)	Fairbanks (Yukon valley)
Average temp. °C	Jan.	−2	−11
	July	14	15
Precip. cm	Jan.	29·0	2·0
	July	8·9	3·9
	Annual total	231	30

THE DEVELOPMENT OF ALASKA

The 'better' southern district of Alaska was quite late in attracting settlement. Its main resources of fish and timber were not sought out until those of the Pacific North West were becoming depleted. Alaska held little attraction for

147

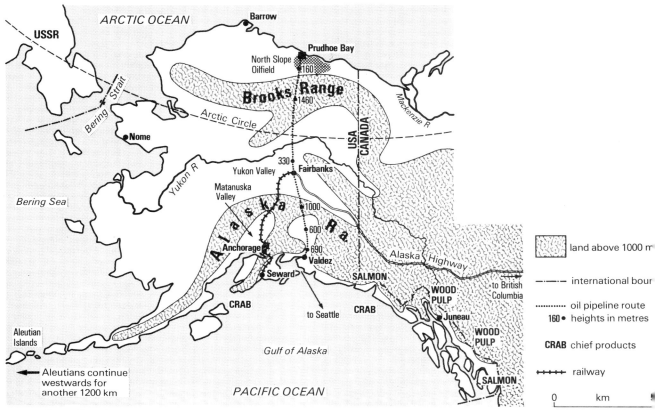

Figure 93 *Alaska*

those who did clear the ground and farm it; attempts at commercial agriculture usually ended in failure. However, developments in fishing and lumbering were growing and by the middle of the twentieth century, Alaska was a world leader in the canning of salmon. Present catches are worth some £50 million annually. But overfishing of salmon stocks led to a search for alternative catches and sales of king crabs are now very important. These crabs weigh up to 11 kg and can measure 2 metres from claw to claw. Before the oil boom began almost half the state's income came from fish, £20 million per year from the sale of king crabs.

Since the 1950s the forestry developments have been transformed from small, localised saw-mills to major operations exporting lumber. Also, three large pulp and paper mills have been established in the 'Panhandle' area, where all the timber, mainly hemlock and spruce, is near to the coast. The 1970 value of forest products was £50 million, and one of the important buyers is now Japan.

Since 1941 this corner of the continent has had an important strategic value. After Japanese troops had landed on the outermost Aleutian Islands in the Second World War (see Figure 93) an invasion of the mainland of North America seemed possible. To counter this threat the United States Army hurriedly built the Alaska Highway

across Canada. This new road was used to carry heavy weapons to protect Alaska and also to take supplies to the Russian ally across the Bering Straits. Strategic needs still require almost 70 000 military personnel and civilian staff to be based in Alaska—although nowadays the USSR is the potential enemy.

In the 1960s great quantities of oil and gas were discovered beneath the Alaskan North Slope, overlooking Prudhoe Bay, and economic considerations became important again. However, the location of the mineral fuel in the extreme north posed a problem in the transport of the product to market. For the first time it was necessary to examine a route from Alaska other than the Pacific coastal link to the port of Seattle or the landward route across Canada, the Alaska Highway.

Table 51   Alaska and Norway: population comparison

	Approximate latitudinal extent (°N)	Area (km²)	Population
Alaska	58–72	1 518 120	382 000
Norway	58–72	323 886	4 017 000

(*Statesman's Year Book, 1977*)

Questions

Figure 93

1. Construct a cross-section from south to north along the Alaska pipeline, naming the major relief features on the route.

Table 50, Figure 93 and general

2. Examine the two climatic regions of Alaska shown in Table 50. Under the headings of temperature and precipitation: (*i*) note any important differences; and (*ii*) account for these differences.

The account and general

3. Account for the erratic nature of Alaska's development during the twentieth century.

Table 51

4. *a*) Compare and contrast the information about Alaska and Norway.
   b) What does the information suggest about the potential size of Alaska's future population? Will it ever be numbered in millions? (*hint:* climatic considerations)

A TEST RUN THROUGH THE NORTH WEST PASSAGE

'On 2 September 1969 the *SS Manhattan*, a specially strengthened ice-breaker of oil tanker size (150 000 tonnes), turned her huge armoured bow section into the broken pack-ice near Baffin Island. All off-watch hands looked out as the *Manhattan* cut into the first ice floe, in seas where so many ships had gone down in the past. But the steel prow cracked off a chunk of ice 2500 square metres in size and sailed on without a quiver.

As the blocks ahead grew larger the ship developed more speed. Gigantic floes cracked and heaved as the *SS Manhattan* moved on. Then the ship bore down on a massive sheet of ice over one kilometre across and almost 20 metres thick. Crew members gripped the deck rail hard and awaited the shock. The armoured bow struck and a plume of salt spray shot higher than the ship and huge chunks of ice flew in arcs on each side of the vessel. There was a deafening explosion as the great floe shattered; blocks the size of bungalows turned over and scraped along the ship with agonizing shrieks.'
(From *National Geographic Magazine*, March 1970)

Plate 67   SS Manhattan *in the North-west passage*

It was to test the capability of modern technology that this unusual trial run took place through the pack ice of the North West Passage. The description shows the successful start of the *Manhattan's* voyage, in passing through the broken edge of the pack ice (Figure 92). The main pack ice further north represents many centuries of freezing and is up to 10 metres thick and unbroken to the horizon, even in summer. Since it was a trial voyage, the easier route was left behind and M'Clure Strait was entered for the real test of strength. After gaining only 150 metres per hour even the powerful *Manhattan* became locked in thick ice. The basic problem lay in the design of the engines, which developed the full 32 000 kw going forward, but lacked the ability to do so in reverse. Thus the ship could not pull away from the pack ice into the newly forming ice at the stern. Other icebreakers assisted in freeing the *Manhattan* and Prudhoe Bay was reached by returning to the more open route nearer the mainland. The return from Alaska to the home port of New York took just over a month and a token barrel of Alaskan oil was delivered.

THE EXTRACTION AND TRANSPORTATION OF ALASKAN OIL

Soon after the voyage of the *SS Manhattan* the Alaskan government made the decision to ignore the North West Passage and proceed with the laying of a pipeline across the state to the Gulf of Alaska. Little was done for a number of years while the Washington government considered the objections of conservationists, who argued for the tundra regions to be left alone. In 1974, however, the 'go-ahead' was given, and since then Alaska's most valuable resource has been exploited with all possible speed. In mid-1977 the pipeline began carrying its first oil to Valdez for onward shipment to the 'Lower 48 States', mainly via California, to supply much-needed energy to the United States.

THE CONSERVATIONISTS' CASE AGAINST DEVELOPMENT

Despite many forms of extractive economy, such as hunting, fishing and mining, most of Alaska is still a frontier land or 'wilderness'. It owes this to its remoteness and its great size.

The tundra areas consist of a delicately balanced set of ecological conditions on the surface of the permanently frozen ground. The grasses, mosses and animals, such as caribou, are well adapted to their environment (see Plate 68). Many cases are on record of great damage to the natural ecological balance caused by digging through the permafrost to make roads and foundations. The Alaska Highway, built thirty years ago, still has problems of waterlogging and unstable foundations. It is often forgotten that workcamps, airstrips and supply roads must first be built before the pipes can be brought into position —not an easy task when the pipe sections are over one metre in diameter. Even surveying parties did much accidental damage by diverting caribou off their migration tracks, and by blocking salmon streams when excavating gravel for foundations.

The 1300 km long oil pipeline itself is a potential danger to the environment. For example, the oil will have to be heated to make it flow, and any heat which escapes will thaw the supporting permafrost. The pipe, left unsupported over a considerable length, may fracture, causing a disastrous seepage of oil. In the tundra, such damage to the fragile environment would be impossible to make good. Most alarming of all, the pipeline will be crossing an area well known for its destructive earthquake. In 1964, Anchorage, the largest city of the whole Northland, was severely damaged by violent tremors.

Why create all these problems, and damage one of the world's last wilderness areas when it will supply oil to the USA for only an estimated 20 years?

Plate 68　*Caribou herd on the Alaskan North Slope*

THE ECONOMISTS' CASE FOR DEVELOPMENT

The United States consumes 30 per cent of the world's energy, which includes 5000 litres of oil per year for each American. Despite the huge output from the continental United States, in 1976 over 40 per cent of the oil consumed had to be imported, mainly from the Middle East, Canada and Venezuela. For political reasons, future supplies from the Persian Gulf could be uncertain, and oil bought from the OPEC producers will be at a high price.

The Alaskan oilfield is the biggest that the United States possesses. It is believed to equal in size the largest fields of the Persian Gulf. After many years of exploitation, most other oilfields within the USA are running out, so the Alaskan oil is vital to the nation's requirements.

Because the Prudhoe Bay field is located within the tundra zone, oil companies have employed many scientists from the start of operations to ensure that the environment is little affected. Further south the pipeline route has been carefully sited, taking account of the effects on existing forests and animal populations (see Plate 69). The pipe is buried for over half of its 1280 km length. Although the oil has to be heated to keep it flowing, in the most critical sections the pipeline is insulated by jackets filled with brine to prevent heat loss which could damage the permafrost.

Any scheme for shipping out oil through the North West Passage would need about 40 tankers of 200 000 tonnes, all strengthened to work in the pack ice, like the *SS Manhattan*. Even if such a fleet could be provided, the coastal environment would still be at risk from oil spillage. Also it is very doubtful whether the Canadian

Plate 69 *The Alaska pipeline under construction near Valdez*

government would allow US tankers to pass through their territorial waters on commercial routes.

To move the oil by pipeline is the only solution. Its construction has provided much-needed employment in Alaska and offers the state good chances of long-term industrial growth based on revenues from the oil developments.

Questions

Plate 67

1. *a*) (*i*) Suggest what advantage was gained by slightly raising the armoured bow of the *Manhattan* above the water level. (*ii*) Why were helicopters particularly useful as an aid to navigation?
b) What particular hazard would there be if a fully laden oil tanker was in the position shown in the photograph?

The account

2. In your own words explain,
a) the reason for the *Manhattan's* journey, and
b) what the actual journey showed.

Figure 92 and general

3. *a*) Down which coast will the pack ice extend farthest in the winter season? Give a reason for your answer.
b) What does your answer to *a*) indicate about the length of the navigation season in northern waters?
c) Confirm your answer to *b*) by quantifying your statement, using the Baffin Island climatic statistics (Table 49).

Plate 68 and the account

4. *a*) (*i*) What evidence is there that this is the tundra area? (*ii*) List any activities shown which will probably upset the tundra environment. In each case justify your answer.
b) Why do the caribou spend winter in the forested zone to the south?

Plate 69 and the account

5. *a*) Compare this land surface with the tundra section of the pipeline.
b) How easy is the construction of the pipeline, from the evidence shown?

The account

6. *a*) Debate the two sides of the pipeline argument in class.
b) Explain your own attitude in written form, justifying your point of view.

The Canadian northland

THE DEVELOPMENT OF THE CANADIAN NORTH

The Northland of Canada covers almost one half of the country's total area but the population density of one person per 50 square kilometres is extremely low. As in Alaska the exploration and development of Arctic Canada have brought very rapid changes to native communities, and the future of Eskimo and Indian groups is very much an issue yet to be settled.

In common with many other Canadian regions it was the fur trade which attracted white settlement to all the inhabited districts of the Northland. From the late seventeenth century the Hudson's Bay Company had been trading in the area, and early this century they established many trading posts, particularly in the eastern Arctic where 20 posts existed by the 1920s. From this date southern Canadians also began to set up churches, schools and police posts in a dispersed pattern across the Northland. The new communities were European in nature, Eskimos were not encouraged to settle around them, and life in the Arctic continued much as before, with only the trading of white fox pelts added to the traditionally self-sufficient way of life.

When surveillance of the Arctic Ocean from radar bases and military stations brought hundreds of newcomers to the Northlands, there was a rapid development of air transport to support the new bases. A vast quantity of government money was poured into the Arctic Zone to set up the 'DEW-line' (Distant Early Warning) facilities. Eskimos had many opportunities to earn a wage in construction work and in the late 1950s, over 1000 moved home to be near the new developments.

It is with the extraction of minerals that the economic future of the region probably rests. The annual value of metals from the Canadian Shield section of the Northland is already one hundred times that of furs. Western sections of the Shield have produced gold since 1935, for example at Yellowknife (Figure 92). From the remoter region of Great Bear Lake copper and silver are extracted at Port Radium. At Rankin Inlet on Hudson Bay an attempt was made to cut the costs of mining operations by training Eskimo workers, instead of bringing miners hundreds of kilometres from the south. Unfortunately the nickel ran out more quickly than expected and the economically successful operation ceased. At the time the mine closed almost 80 per cent of the workforce were Eskimos, employed in all aspects of the work except the drawing-office.

On the edge of the Northland the largest lead and zinc deposit in Canada has been opened up at Pine Point, Great Slave Lake. This development produces two-thirds of the total value of all the minerals of the Northland, but a new 700 km railway line had to be built to make the project possible.

The last two decades have witnessed the use of newer forms of transport—helicopters in the Arctic Islands and hovercraft in the Mackenzie Delta. Much of the activity is supported by the funds of oil and gas companies who are exploring a vast area very rapidly. Over 5000 permits have been issued for the investigation of the Arctic Islands alone. Expectations are that the value of gas extracted from the northern coastal areas will soon exceed that of metals.

Plate 70   *DEW-line radar station*

Questions

Figure 92, Plate 70 and the account

1. *a)* Why was the DEW-line constructed along the northern rim of Canada?

   b) Measure the approximate distance from Ellesmere Island through the northernmost Canadian Islands to Prudhoe Bay.

   c) List two difficulties of constructing radar bases along this 'edge of the continent'.

2. In 1974 a very curious event took place under the pack ice at the North Pole, when Canadians placed a flag of tough material to mark their sector of the Arctic Ocean. Why is the Canadian government interested in this sector of pack ice, icean water and sea bed? (*hint:* economic and strategic factors)

3. *a)* List the past and present metal-producing localities and the minerals produced in the Shield area.

   b) In general, why are the costs of Northern mining so high?

3. Write a short account of modern transport developments in the Northlands of Canada and Alaska.

THE ESKIMO

For thousands of years the Eskimos or *Inuit* (The People) have survived the harshness of the Arctic by using each animal resource to the utmost. Seals provided meat, skins and oil and were the chief target of the hunt. Polar bears and whales were sometimes fearlessly tackled by the inhabitants of larger villages, giving a plentiful meat supply if the hunters were successful. The Eskimo people lived in scattered settlements wherever food was likely to be found. Most of the Arctic Coast was occupied, though one large group lived inland where they hunted caribou.

The old way of life depended on the ability of the group to move around to obtain food: dog teams and sledges were used on the pack ice and snowy ground, kayaks or larger whaling boats in the water. In winter, igloos were built for overnight camps, but tents of animals' skins usually served in the summer months. The environment was usually little disturbed, and alterations in the food chain were small.

The Eskimo was sometimes in difficulty when the food chain was disturbed. For example in the 1950s the number of caribou dropped rapidly to 250 000—only a quarter of the population of the previous decade. The Canadian government had to assist starving Eskimo groups where caribou failed to appear. The animals have now multiplied to 500 000, largely because licences have been issued to restrict white people from shooting them, and also because the caribou migration routes are left undisturbed.

Other problems were met by those Eskimo hunters who depended on the Hudson's Bay Company as buyers of their furs. The price of white fox pelts dropped catastrophically in the 1950s, when fashions in garments changed. However, seal fur came into vogue in the 1960s and Eskimos were again able to use their hunting skills with high powered rifles and motorised sledges (snowmobiles) to obtain a good income. The sale of seal skins then declined following publicity campaigns against the wearing of animal products.

The really important changes in the Arctic came with the acquisition of large amounts of money and the development of new facilities and communities. The wages which attracted Eskimos did not last, however. Once the military bases had been completed or the oil company moved on, there was little work an Eskimo could find. If a family had sold its team of dogs and its hunting equipment it was impossible to return to the old ways of trapping. Even those with snowmobiles did not find it very profitable to return to seal hunting. In 1975 the maintenance and running of such equipment cost £1000, but seal pelts sold for an average price of only £10.

The Canadian government has helped the Eskimos in many ways. At first they gave unemployment money to needy families, but this practice was soon replaced by the state development of Eskimo-run co-operatives to exploit

Figure 94   Arctic food chains

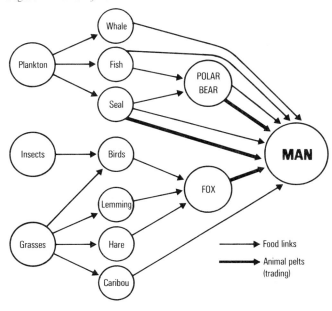

153

resources such as caribou, seals and fish. Village artists have also been encouraged to develop handicrafts, such as carving, printing and needlework, for sale in the south. Over 40 such co-operatives now exist in the Canadian Arctic.

In many districts new settlements have been created by the Canadian government to accommodate the expanded population. Inuvik, which partly replaced an older town, is a community of 3000 people in the Mackenzie Delta area (see Plate 71). Its facilities are generally better than the recent re-settlement schemes for island groups further away to the north-east. Even the remotest villages of Baffin Island have completely urbanised Eskimos requiring homes.

Older Eskimos have found it difficult to adjust to life in towns like Inuvik, and many would prefer to return to their traditional way of life. However, the younger generation sometimes act and think very differently. Many teenagers prefer to ride motor bikes and tune their transistor radios to Eskimo disc-jockeys. The traditional skills of igloo building, fishing and hunting are not being learnt and the general life-style is an urban one. Does the land really belong to The People any more?

Questions

Figure 94 and the account

1. *a)* Why was the 'food chain' scarcely affected by traditional Eskimo hunting?
   b) What probable drastic alteration was made in the grass-caribou-human chain during the 1950s (*hint:* 'outsiders')?
   c) (*i*) In the peak period of seal hunting explain what changes probably occurred in the food chain.
   (*ii*) What could have been the consequences if seal fur prices had remained high for many decades?

The account

2. *a)* Write a short account of commercial trapping and hunting in the Arctic since 1930.
   b) What future is there for trapping in the Canadian Northlands?

Plate 71

3. *a)* Town services for water, electricity and steam central heating are carried along the surface in boxed 'utilidors'. (*i*) Describe the 'utilidors'? (*ii*) Why are the services provided in this way?
   b) What evidence is there from the photograph to suggest that Inuvik is a planned town? Base your answer on (*i*) the houses, (*ii*) other buildings.

The account

4. *a)* Explain why Eskimo co-operatives were founded in the Arctic.
   b) Is it likely that the success of co-operatives will continue for many years? Give reasons for your answer.
5. Comment on the new settlements in the Canadian Northland with regard to:
   a) the reasons for the settlements;
   b) their success.

Plate 71   *Inuvik : a summer view of a planned community on the margin of the true Arctic*

The Northern Forest Belt

Introduction

South of the Northlands the summer becomes sufficiently long for trees to grow, forming a vast coniferous forest belt. The original inhabitants of the area were small groups of Indians who lived in balance with the natural environment by fishing, hunting and gathering the forest resources. The first Europeans to arrive were interested mainly in fur trading. By coincidence, much of the forest grows on the mineral-rich Canadian Shield and since the early part of the nineteenth century, timber and minerals have been increasingly exploited. Today there is deep concern about the use of the Northern Forest Belt and action is being taken to ensure that its resources are replenished for the future.

Figure 95   *The Northern Forest Belt*

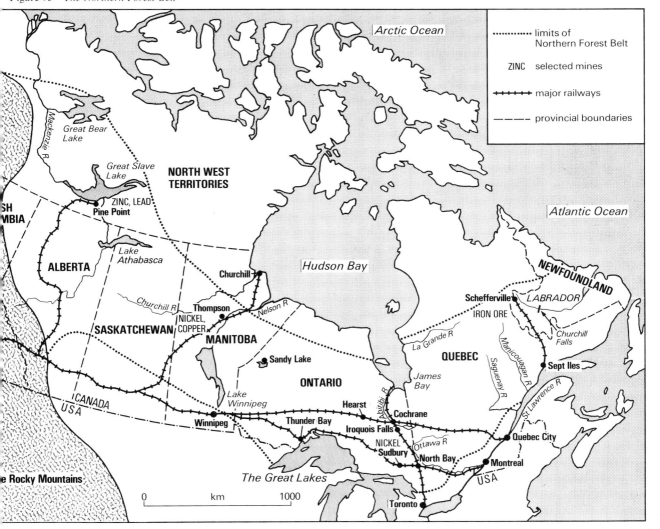

Plate 72   *Transporter crossing a muskeg (swamp)*

Questions

Plate 72 and Figure 96

1. Describe the natural features shown in the photograph.

Figure 95 and an atlas

2. In the Northern Forest Belt:
   a) Which river system forms the most extensive lowland area?
   b) Comment on the extent of other freshwater areas.

General

3. Why was the Northern Forest Belt a rather neglected area until well into the nineteenth century?

Figure 96   *Section through part of the Northern Forest Belt*

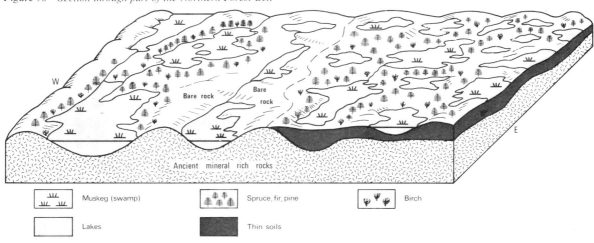

The Indians of the Northern Forest

For over 300 years the Hudson's Bay Company has obtained animal pelts from Indian groups, chiefly the beaver from the vast forest zone. The beaver's habit of controlling water levels by building dams resulted in immediate discovery of the animal with its subsequent decimation by trappers. However, in remoter areas the traditional way of life has continued up to the present time, as both the table and the following extract indicate.

Table 52	Production of furs from the Northern Forest (Annual value)
Beaver	£2 930 000
Muskrat	£1 400 000
Wild Mink	£ 350 000
Marten	£ 272 000
Red Fox	£ 268 000

(For comparison, the only animal reared successfully in captivity, the mink, raised £9 800 000.)

THE SANDY LAKE INDIANS OF NORTH-WEST ONTARIO

'Patched tents and tarpaulin shelters were springing up beside the cabins as more and more families arrived for Treaty Day pay-out. Grey-white huskies were chained back in the bush behind the cabins and everywhere there seemed to be the smell of beaver smoking. Most cabins had two or three of the scraped pelts stretched on willow frames up on the roof. The meat was draped on a tripod arrangement of poles over the fire. One bent old crone . . . was smoking sturgeon, and the roe hung in pink clusters, a small fortune in the caviar world, and commonplace here.'
(From *Without Reserve*, by Sheila Burnford, Hodder & Stoughton, 1969)

Plate 73   *Indian trappers of the Northern Forest*

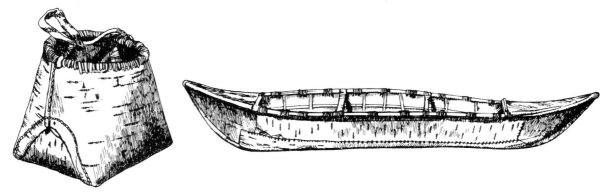

Figure 97   *Birch bark canoe and cooking vessel*

In neighbouring Quebec, the traditional way of life was threatened by the James Bay Project, a scheme to produce HEP from the rivers flowing into James Bay. After a long legal tussle with the Quebec government, hunting, fishing and trapping rights were safeguarded. In addition £75 million, plus royalties on the HEP are to be paid to the native groups in the area, comprising 6000 Cree Indians and 4000 Eskimos.

Despite this success the everyday situation for Indians is not encouraging. There are few jobs near the Reserves and the average Indian income is only one-third that of other Canadians. Consequently, many Indians have decided to leave the tribal lands to live and work in ordinary communities, where they believe that better opportunities are available.

Table 53   Residence of Indians in Canada

Location	Total number	30–34 age group
1. On the Reserves	176 457	8857
2. On Crown Lands*	25 442	1345
3. In ordinary Canadian communities	74 534	5382

*Certain Indian rights still apply.

Questions

Plate 73 and the account

1. *a)* Give two reasons why the beaver develops a thick pelt.
   b) What advantages do snowshoes have compared with ordinary footwear, e.g. fur boots?

Table 52 and general

2. *a)* State briefly how the figures for beaver production compare with (*i*) other wild forest animals and, (*ii*) ranch-raised mink.
   b) What advantages and disadvantages occur from breeding fur-bearing animals in captivity?

The account and general

3. *a)* (*i*) Name two non-coniferous trees that grow in the Northern Forest. (*ii*) What use do the Indians make of them?

   b) (*i*) What special advantages has the canoe in the Shield area of Canada? (*ii*) Give two hazards of canoe travel in the region.

The account

4. The Treaty Day pay-out amounts to a few pounds for each Indian. Suggest what the tribes gave up in return for this annual fee. With whom was the Treaty made?

The account and Table 53

5. *a)* What factors encourage Indians to leave their reserves?
   b) Why does the 30 to 34 age group have the greatest proportion of people living in ordinary Canadian communities.
   c) List the kinds of difficulties that may face Indians living and working in ordinary communities.

Forestry and forest products

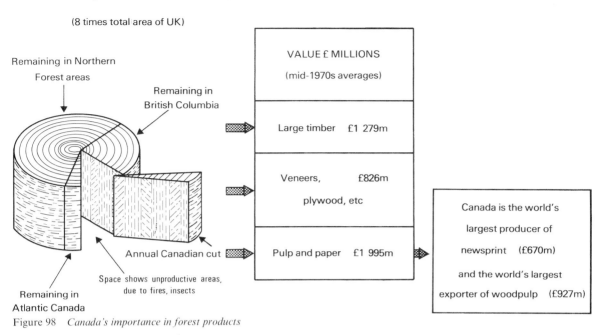

(8 times total area of UK)

Remaining in Northern Forest areas

Remaining in British Columbia

Annual Canadian cut

Space shows unproductive areas, due to fires, insects

Remaining in Atlantic Canada

VALUE £ MILLIONS
(mid-1970s averages)

Large timber   £1 279m

Veneers,   £826m
plywood, etc

Pulp and paper   £1 995m

Canada is the world's largest producer of newsprint   (£670m) and the world's largest exporter of woodpulp   (£927m)

Figure 98   *Canada's importance in forest products*

Figure 99   *How newsprint is made*

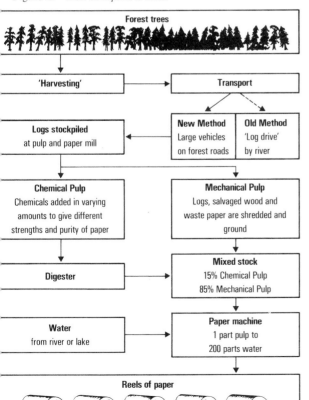

Forest trees

'Harvesting' → Transport

Transport → New Method: Large vehicles on forest roads / Old Method: 'Log drive' by river

Logs stockpiled at pulp and paper mill

Chemical Pulp: Chemicals added in varying amounts to give different strengths and purity of paper

Mechanical Pulp: Logs, salvaged wood and waste paper are shredded and ground

Digester

Mixed stock: 15% Chemical Pulp, 85% Mechanical Pulp

Water from river or lake

Paper machine: 1 part pulp to 200 parts water

Reels of paper

The search for timber suitable for ships' masts brought the nineteenth-century lumbermen into the southern part of the Northern Forest by way of the Ottawa Valley. By the latter part of the last century trees were being cut for American railways, for town construction and for the rapidly developing pulp and paper industry. The government of Ontario became so alarmed at the rate of extraction in the early years of this century that it put aside many areas as Crown Forests, in which there were restrictions on the scale of forestry operations.

As smaller kinds of trees gradually become usable in the pulp and paper industry, so the industry has spread northwards throughout the huge forest area. However, the slow rate of tree growth is a disadvantage—one hundred years of growth of fifteen trees (spruce or pine) provide only one tonne of newsprint. Consequently trees have to be replaced; in the northern forest several million are planted every year, usually two-year-old seedlings.

Table 54   The expansion of Canada's pulp and paper industry

	1900	1940	1970
Pulp and paper mills	53	103	139
Number of workers	6000	34 000	80 000

159

Most of Canada's pulp and paper mills are located in the Northern Forest Belt. Recently processing has been under strict control. In 1975 the world's first pollution-free pulp and paper mill was opened at Thunder Bay, Ontario.

Recent changes in forestry operations have affected both lumberjacks and methods of transport. Modern machines now work in the forest and load directly on to road transport, making work outside possible for all but the worst winter period. There is, therefore, a regular supply of wood to the pulp and paper mills throughout the year.

Questions

Figure 98

1. Use the diagram to compile notes on the importance of forestry products to Canada.

Figure 99 and the account

2. *a*) List some items of different strengths and purity which are made at paper mills.
   b) (*i*) What is re-cycled paper? Where could it fit into the diagram? (*ii*) What is the link between re-cycled paper and the planting of two-year old seedlings?

Figure 100

3. *a*) (*i*) What is the purpose of the branch lines that appear to end 'nowhere'? (*ii*) Why is the area on the map well placed to serve likely markets?
   b) Use the key on the map to indicate the sequence in which the clearance of trees occurred, during the opening up of northern Ontario: (*i*) first clearance; (*ii*) next clearance; (*iii*) recent clearance.
   c) Comment on the value of the 'mature forest' areas for future logging. (*hint:* Figure 96)

Figure 100, Plate 74 and Figure 99

4. *a*) Suggest two possible industrial advantages of the site at Smooth Rock Falls.
   b) What aspect of the production may cause pollution problems?

Plate 75. Table 54 and the account

5. *a*) List three specific operations that the 'harvester' does.
   b) How have the new kinds of machines affected the number of workers in the forest?
   c) Comment on changes in the number of workers per mill in this century.
   d) In what way do the answers to *b*) and *c*) support or contradict each other?

The account and general

6. Discuss the ways in which the forestry industry of the Northern Forest has changed from the nineteenth century to the present time.

Plate 74   *Traditional method of moving logs*

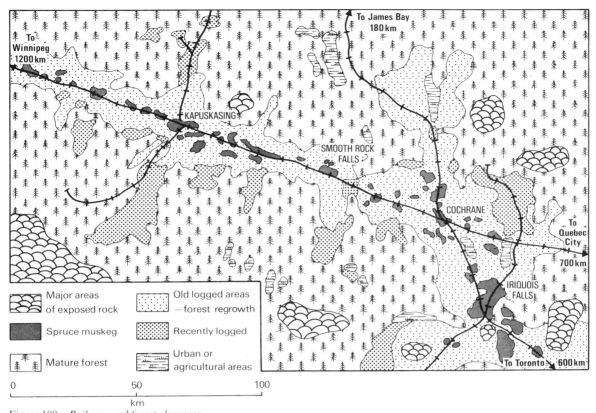

Figure 100 *Railways and forest clearance*

Major areas of exposed rock

Spruce muskeg

Mature forest

Old logged areas — forest regrowth

Recently logged

Urban or agricultural areas

0   50   100

km

To Winnipeg 1200 km

To James Bay 180 km

KAPUSKASING

SMOOTH ROCK FALLS

COCHRANE

To Quebec City 700 km

IRIQUOIS FALLS

To Toronto 600 km

Plate 75 *A modern forestry harvester at work*

Mineral developments in the Northern Forest

Table 55   Canadian Production of Major Metals in 1976 (£million)

Copper	British Columbia	206	Nickel	Ontario	497
	Ontario	195		Manitoba	119
	Quebec	91			
			Zinc	Ontario	133
Iron	Newfoundland	322		New Brunswick	71
	Quebec	162		North West	
	Ontario	132		Territories	60
				Quebec	51
				British Columbia	47

(The total value for all types of metallic minerals was £2600 million, exceeded by the combined value of gas and oil at £3300 million.)

In the twentieth century the demand for industrial metals has stimulated the extraction of minerals from remoter Canadian areas, particularly the Canadian Shield. Copper, nickel and iron have been the most important items, but even localities well endowed in mineral deposits have been worked out. At worst the mining community becomes a 'ghost town' and forests gradually conceal the buildings and mining scars.

The search for workable deposits goes on with great speed and efficiency, and over 200 mines are now operating in the Forest Belt. Exports to the USA, Western Europe and Japan are increasing in quantity and value all the time and are a most important source of Canadian income. A fifth of the value of all Canadian exports consists of mineral products, earning £3900 million per year.

Plate 76   *Residential district, Thompson, Manitoba*

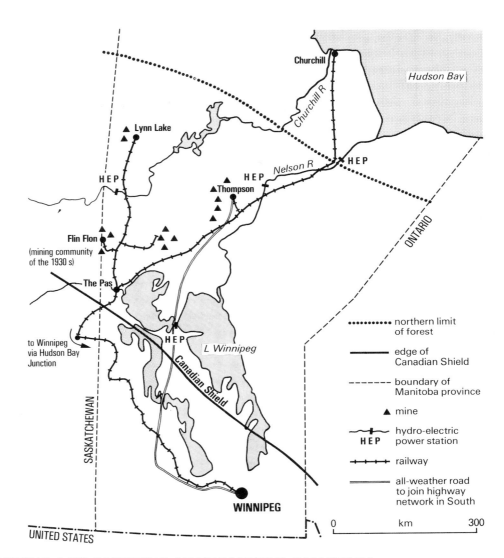

Figure 101
Northern Manitoba

MINING AND SMELTING AT THOMPSON, MANITOBA

Thompson is an example of a modern community in a relatively remote area. Unlike most earlier mining settlements this is a planned lay-out including homes, shopping areas and industrial estates as well as the mining and smelting works.

The material dug from the ground is put through a concentrator, where the crushed rock is separated into nickel, copper, zinc and waste. Thompson also has a smelting plant where metals are further purified. Apart from mining and metal-working other kinds of work are available, such as government clerical work and light engineering.

The town is now well established, with a population of over 20 000. However, the location of Thompson does not encourage people to settle permanently. A survey of the workforce taken a few years ago showed that approximately a quarter of the people were born outside Canada.

In order of numbers the countries of origin were: West Germany, Great Britain, Yugoslavia, and other countries of southern Europe. Excluding those from Great Britain, the numbers of foreign-born inhabitants are far above the expected level for a town of Thompson's size.

In order to find sufficient workers within Canada, the mining company assists families with removal expenses and the worker receives sound training for the new job. Despite all the help that is given a very rapid turn-over of workers occurs, as many as one-third of the workforce leaving in a year. An important development was the construction of an 'all-weather' road to link the town with the existing highway systems that lead to Winnipeg (see Figure 101). The feeling of isolation was reduced when it became possible to drive to the big city, rather than wait for infrequent trains.

163

Questions

The account and general

1. *a*) Why is the town of Thompson in a better economic position than towns which have only a mine?
   b) Why are many foreign-born people prepared to work at Thompson, whereas many Canadians would not wish to do so?

Plate 76, Figure 101 and general

2. *a*) (*i*) What building material predominates at Thompson, and (*ii*) why hasn't the material come from the local area? (*hint:* position near northern limit of forest)
   b) (*i*) Find evidence on the photograph for one service provided to this street, and (*ii*) from Figure 101 indicate the source of this service.

Figure 101, Plate 76 and the account

3. List the advantages and disadvantages of living in a settlement like Thompson, as far as a teenager is concerned.

Figure 101 and the account

4. Successful smelting requires the following conditions:
   a) a large labour force;
   b) adequate capital to finance the operation;
   c) good transport links with (*i*) the mineral supply and (*ii*) the market (customers);
   d) huge quantities of electricity.
   Which of these conditions apply at Thompson?

The Sudbury Basin : a northern farming area

Mixed farming is carried out in scattered areas in the Forest Belt to supply the local markets in mining, lumbering and recreational communities. However, the climatic conditions make successful farming very uncertain. For example, in an exceptional year the first frost occurred as early as 3 September, ruining most of the crops. The best conditions for agriculture are found in those districts with better soils, which are not typical of the true Canadian Shield. One such area is in the Sudbury Basin near the southern margin of the Forest Belt. Sands were deposited around the margins of an Ice Age lake, while finer sediments collected on the lake floor. Today the soil of the area is a silty loam, very free from stones.

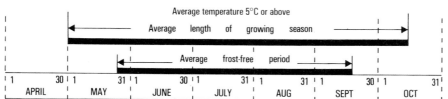

Figure 102   *Temperatures in the Sudbury Basin*

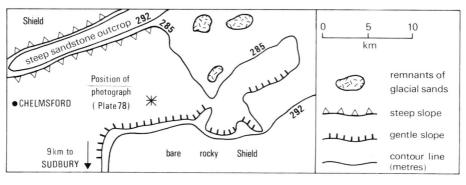

Figure 103   *A productive valley in the Sudbury Basin*

Plate 77 *Potato growing in the Sudbury Basin*

Questions

Plate 77 and the account

1. *a)* Why is the soil particularly suitable for root crops?
   b) (*i*) Suggest two ways in which the view indicates an *old lake floor.* (*ii*) What problem for the farmer may result from this situation? (*hint:* snowmelt)

Figure 103 and the account

2. *a)* Explain why the Shield does not appear in the centre of the map.
   b) By what processes have the glacial sands been reduced in size since the Ice Age?

Figure 102 and the account

3. *a)* (*i*) At what approximate date will the first frost normally occur? (*ii*) How long is the average frost-free season in days?
   b) (*i*) How long is the growing season in days? (*ii*) Will any frosts occur in the growing season? Explain your answer.

Figure 104a *Variation in the flow of the Saguenay River*

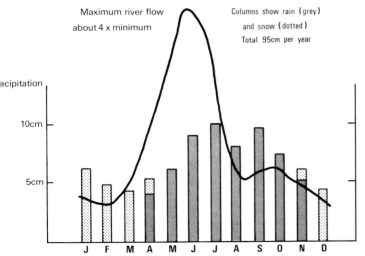

Maximum river flow about 4 x minimum

Columns show rain (grey) and snow (dotted)
Total 95cm per year

Figure 104b *Power production (megawatts) in Quebec and Newfoundland*

St Lawrence	(Montreal area)	1500
Ottowa		1000
Saguenay		750
Manicougan		3500
Churchill	(Labrador)	5000
La Grande	(not yet complete)	10 000

Plate 78 *HEP plant in Saguenay Valley*

Questions

Figure 104a

1. *a*) (*i*) State the difference between the highest and lowest monthly totals for precipitation, and (*ii*) comment on the distribution of precipitation through the year.
   b) What is the probable cause of (*i*) the minimum flow of rivers in the late winter, and, (*ii*) the maximum flow in the late spring?
   c) Why does the graph of river flow come to a peak very quickly?

Plate 78 and Figure 96

2. Describe how the landscape shown in Plate 78 differs from most of the forested Canadian Shield. Account for the differences noted.

Figures 105 and 104b

3. Construct a diagram to show the power transmission lines. At the appropriate river locations draw squares in proportion to the power produced. (La Grande would be the largest square.)

Figure 105 *Selected HEP developments*

British Columbia

A first look

British Columbia became part of Canada over one hundred years ago, and was linked with the rest of the country by the Canadian Pacific Railway in 1885. However, its sense of isolation lasted well into the twentieth century, until the advent of long-distance aircraft, better Canadian highways and improved trans-Pacific trading links. Physically, the province is similar to the American states of Washington and Oregon to the south. High mountain ranges and plateaus are common, but British Columbia has few areas of low ground. The province receives large amounts of rain and snowfall, particularly on the coastal mountains and islands. Only the deep, sheltered valleys of the interior lack water.

The resources of the extensive forests provide the main

Plate 79 *The Columbia River flowing through the Rocky Mountain Trench*

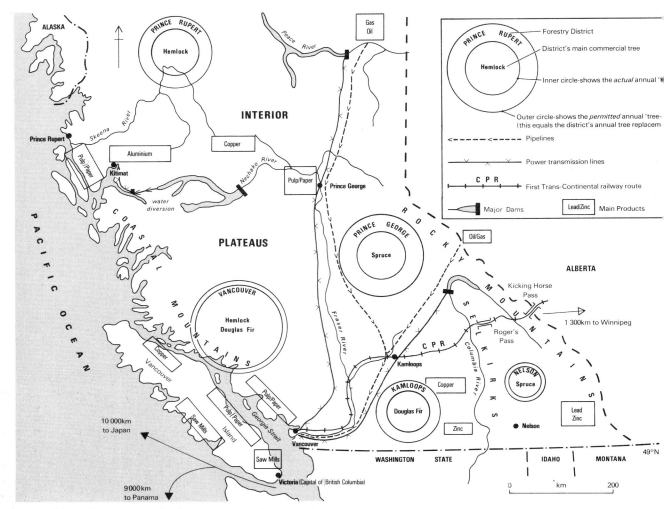

Figure 106 *British Columbia: routeways and major products*

income of British Columbia, since the combination of heavy rainfall and lack of suitable lowland areas makes farming difficult. The plentiful rainfall has been stored in many dams which provide hydro-electric power, irrigation water and flood control, partly under an agreement with the USA. Locally, new developments have in some instances reduced the catches of the magnificent Pacific salmon. Mineral resources are of considerable value to British Columbia; copper, lead and zinc occur in a continuation of the mineral zone of the American Mountain West. In addition, coal, oil and gas are being rapidly de-veloped in the Peace River District, which is an extension of the sedimentary rocks of the Prairies.

The population of British Columbia increased quite rapidly from 1950 onwards and the main settled area, around Vancouver, is now overcrowded. Of the two-and-a-half million people in the province about one million live in the Greater Vancouver area. The lower Fraser Valley is the only easy route to the Pacific and has attracted many industries. There are tremendous contrasts between this region and the 'empty' interior of British Columbia.

Questions

Plate 79

1. *a*) Explain in detail how the area shown presents ob-stacles to land transport crossing from east to west.
   b) (*i*) In what ways is the word 'Trench' a suitable description of the valley of the upper Columbia River?

   (*ii*) Comment on the nature of the channel of the river.
   c) State briefly what impression people have made on this landscape.

The account and an atlas

2. What is meant by saying that British Columbia suffers from a 'sense of isolation'?
3. *a*) Measure the approximate length of the Columbia River. How much of its course is (*i*) in Canada, and (*ii*) in the USA?
   b) Comment on the unusual course of the Columbia River.

Figure 106 and an atlas

4. *a*) (*i*) How far from the Pacific Ocean is the source of the Peace River?
   (*ii*) Where is the river's mouth located?
   b) In what way is this river course unusual?
5. What artificial diversion of a river does the map show? Attempt an explanation of the purpose of the diversion.

Questions

Plate 80, the account and general

1. *a*) Are the weather conditions shown typical of the British Columbia coast? Explain your answer.
   b) What kind of surface do these planes require for take-off?
   c) List some of the area's physical conditions which cause hazards to aircraft.

Figure 106 and general

2. In the Pacific Coast area:
   a) for what kinds of activities will aircraft with floats be especially suitable; and
   b) why might a sense of isolation still exist?

Plate 80   *Aircraft on Vancouver Island*

The Canadian Pacific Railway

When British Columbia joined Canada rather than the USA it was conditional upon the building of a railway to link it with Ontario and Quebec. The enormity of the task was revealed by the London *Times* which said that Canada could no more build the railway than tunnel the Atlantic. Although the Canadians were only attempting what had already been done by American transcontinental railways, the proposed line was about 4700 kilometres long and it had to be built in a virtually unpopulated area—only 70 000 people lived in the vast western half of Canada.

The railway route crossed three kinds of region. First came a long, difficult construction task across the Canadian Shield north of the Great Lakes. Next, the level surfaces of the Prairies region allowed rapid progress and gave the Canadian Pacific Railway Company a share of excellent lands which could be used to attract settlers. Finally, in British Columbia itself there were over 800 kilometres of wild mountains and plateaus, much of which was unexplored. To enter the province the crest of the Rockies had to be crossed at Kicking Horse Pass, followed by a rapid descent to the Rocky Mountain Trench beyond. When the track was first built the gradient was as steep as 4·5 per cent (1 in 22) in places, and there were severe curves to aggravate the problem.

After the Rocky Mountain Trench a climb over the Selkirk Range brought the problem of severe winter conditions. At the summit of the Roger's Pass the snow depth was about 15 metres and avalanches were frequent. Newly laid track, materials and men were constantly being lost. In the end the railway company built a series of snowsheds, totalling 10 kilometres in length, and employed 150 men with snowploughs and mechanical blowers to keep the lines clear.

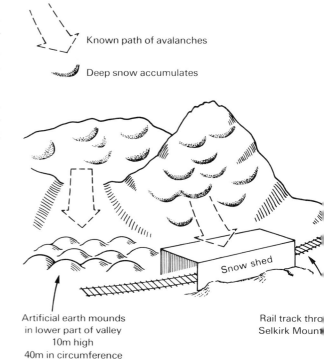

Known path of avalanches

Deep snow accumulates

Snow shed

Artificial earth mounds in lower part of valley
10m high
40m in circumference

Rail track throw Selkirk Moun

Figure 108 *Defences against avalanches*

The lower ground in the plateau areas of British Columbia offered difficulties of a different kind, those of squeezing the track through the wild, narrow river valleys. The engineers frequently resorted to tunnelling or widening the gorges by blasting, especially along the middle Fraser Valley.

Figure 107 *Gradients on the CPR in British Columbia*

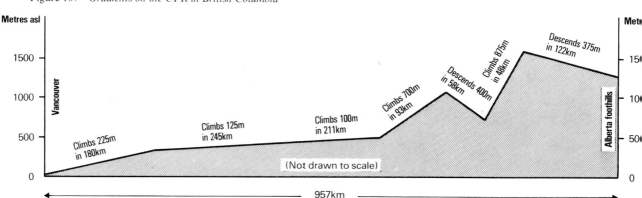

Metres asl

1500

1000

500

0

Vancouver

Climbs 225m in 180km

Climbs 125m in 245km

Climbs 100m in 211km

(Not drawn to scale)

Climbs 700m in 93km

Descends 400m in 58km

Climbs 875m in 48km

Descends 375m in 122km

Alberta foothills

Metr

150

100

50

0

957km

The completion of the remote sections of track in British Columbia became a financial struggle that almost brought the CPR to bankruptcy. Little income came from the virtually uninhabited interior of the province and construction costs were vast. At the Kicking Horse Pass the engineering and construction work to build an easier gradient of 2·2 per cent (1 in 45) had to wait until years later when more money was available. Ingenious spiral tunnels were then cut through the rock extending the line but reducing the gradient. Remarkably, in 1885, after four years of construction, the Canadian Pacific Railway reached Vancouver—well ahead of schedule.

The railway company still finds it difficult to make a profit. The daily Super Continental passenger train of the Canadian National Railway Company loses £7 per kilometre on its slightly different route from Montreal to Vancouver (4660 km).

Questions

The account and general

1. *a*) Name the regions of Canada along the route of the CPR from the St Lawrence Valley to the Pacific Coast.
   b) What knowledge of Canada's geography was *The Times* reporter using as the basis for such scathing comment?
2. Publicity was important, but the CPR would not allow scenic photographs with snow to appear. Why did considerable care have to be taken about the kind of publicity that reached Britain and Europe?

Figure 107 and the account

3. *a*) Use the vertical and horizontal scales shown on the graph to construct an accurate profile of railway gradients in the manner illustrated.
   b) On your profile name: The Rocky Mountain Trench; British Columbia Plateau; Selkirk Mountains; Canadian Rockies; Roger's Pass; Kicking Horse Pass.

Figure 108 and general

4. *a*) (*i*) Explain what the snow sheds are intended to do.
      (*ii*) What is the purpose of the mounds?
   b) How are the trains equipped to deal with snow on the track?

The account and general

5. Why was the construction of the CPR across British Columbia particularly slow and expensive?

The account

6. *a*) Calculate the total loss made by the Canadian National Railway on every journey of the *Super Continental* from Montreal to Vancouver.
   b) The Canadian government keeps the *Super Continental* running by subsidising it. Why?

Resources in demand

THE PACIFIC SALMON

The five varieties of salmon of the Pacific Coast provide attractive, nutritious food which retains its flavour after canning.

Each variety has its own migration season. length of 'run' and age of maturity, but these facts are well known and it is easy to calculate the dates when the salmon will be returning to the river systems where they were born. Since their movements are so predictable, they are particularly easy to over-exploit. Commercial fishermen now have equipment which can remove almost the total salmon population in a very short time. So catches must be controlled and depleted rivers re-stocked from hatcheries. The major area of salmon fishing is the mouth of the Fraser River, where fish have to negotiate trollers with hooks, vessels with gill nets and private individuals with lines. Upstream the salmon may be threatened for many more days by hundreds of anglers.

Canning of catches has taken place for over a century, though the first canneries had work for only a few weeks each year. At present there are only twenty factories operating, mostly at the mouth of the Fraser, but some at the entrance to the Skeena River. Modern canneries keep busy for much of the year by freezing the fish until required for

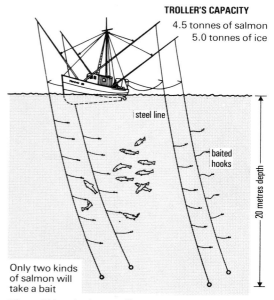

TROLLER'S CAPACITY
4.5 tonnes of salmon
5.0 tonnes of ice

steel line

baited hooks

20 metres depth

Only two kinds of salmon will take a bait

Figure 110   *A salmon troller*

processing. For many fishermen the salmon catch is a very profitable short-season venture, several thousand pounds a month may be earned during the 'salmon run'. However, with the recent development of many other resources, salmon now provide only 1 per cent of British Columbia's yearly income.

Questions

Figure 109 and the account

1. Explain why the run of the Sockeye salmon varies considerably from one year to the next, considering: (*i*) natural changes in climate and river flow; and (*ii*) human intervention.

Figure 110 and the account

2. *a*) (*i*) Describe the method of fishing shown.
    (*ii*) Why do the salmon take the hooks at the river mouth before migrating upstream?

Figure 109   *The life cycle of the Sockeye Salmon*

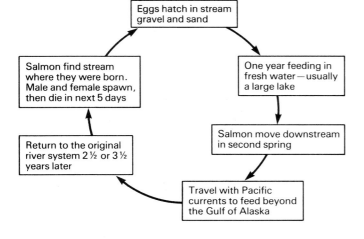

Eggs hatch in stream gravel and sand

One year feeding in fresh water—usually a large lake

Salmon move downstream in second spring

Travel with Pacific currents to feed beyond the Gulf of Alaska

Return to the original river system 2½ or 3½ years later

Salmon find stream where they were born. Male and female spawn, then die in next 5 days

b) (*i*) Would a cannery manager consider the method shown to be efficient? Explain your answer.
    (*ii*) If extremely 'efficient' methods were used what would be the future consequences?

Tables 56, 57 and general

3. *a*) (*i*) Why is so much of the salmon catch canned?
    (*ii*) Explain why the small amounts of frozen, fresh and smoked salmon have such a high value.
  b) (*i*) Construct a bar graph from Table 58.
    (*ii*) Add to the graph 'Atlantic' and 'Pacific' labels, also 'coastal' and 'deep-sea' location of the catches.

Table 56   Processing of Pacific salmon

Canned	637 million tonnes
Frozen	12 ⎫ These 3 make up over 20 per cent
Fresh	2 ⎬ by value
Smoked	1 ⎭
Fish oil, meal	2

Table 57   Total Canadian fish catch, 1975 (£ million)

Lobsters (Atlantic)	£48 million
Salmon (Pacific)	£42 million
Cod (Atlantic)	£29 million
Herring (Atlantic and Pacific)	£27 million
Scallops (Atlantic)	£26 million
Flat fish and soles (Atlantic)	£16 million

TIMBER

The 'recipe' in Figure 111 is for one of British Columbia's best selling products—plywood. The annual income from plywood shipments is about £200 million. However, timber (£1250 m) and pulp and paper (£850 m) bring in much higher revenues.

The claim that 50 cents out of every dollar earned in British Columbia comes from some activity concerned with the forests is probably true. The province has a large proportion of the remaining timber stands on the North American continent, sharing this resource with Washington and Oregon. The long growing season and moist conditions have encouraged the growth of large coniferous trees including Douglas fir, western red cedar and hemlock. The Douglas fir is the prime target of the lumber industry: its tough durable timber serves equally well for harbour jetties, railway sleepers and plywood for the construction industry. However, the 60 years required for a Douglas fir to reach a marketable size is too long for present rates of demand. The British Columbia government controls 95 per cent of the forests, and attempts are now being made to use as many other kinds of tree as possible, to use more efficiently those trees which are cut, and to move away from the heavily logged coastal forests into other parts of the province where the planned extraction of smaller trees is now taking place. Replanting schemes are normally followed in all districts.

In addition, the government is attempting to raise public awareness of the loss of timber by forest fires, many of which are caused by carelessness.

Table 58   British Columbia's forest fires: a ten year record (1960–70)

Causes	Numbers of fires
Lightning	8820
Smokers	3034
Burning of range and scrub (farmers)	2254
Recreational (campers, etc.)	2218
Industrial operations (logging, etc.)	1838

Despite the opening up of the central and eastern parts of the province, the Vancouver Forestry District remains the leading area (Figure 106). Great anxiety is felt for the few remaining mature stands of Douglas fir and hemlock, given the high annual rate of logging. However, the southern coastal region also enjoys several important advantages of position. Georgia Strait and the fiords provide an excellent system of coastal waterways to move logs cheaply to the processing centres. As a result the majority of the large saw-mills and ten integrated pulp and paper mills are located on Vancouver Island and the mainland opposite. In addition the Vancouver area is the main centre for the marketing and export of forest products to other parts of North America and overseas.

Table 59   Sales of British Columbia forest products (1976)

	£ million
Domestic	890
USA	570
Common Market (Europe)	390
Japan	170
Australia	42

Figure 111   *Plywood 'recipe'*

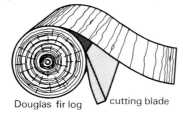

Peel a log into a continuous thin sheet of wood

Douglas fir log   cutting blade

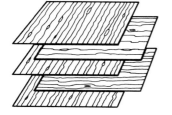

Cut the sheet into large, square pieces, then arrange them into a sandwich of 5 pieces, with the grain of one piece at right angles to the next

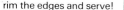

'Butter' the sandwich with waterproof glue, press together and cook in a hot oven for 2 minutes at 140°C

Trim the edges and serve!

Questions

Table 58 and general

1. a) (i) Calculate the total number of fires resulting from work undertaken in and around the forest.
        (ii) In what way do visitors probably cause fires?
        (iii) Which category of fire is not caused by humans?
    b) Why do coniferous trees seem to burn so readily, despite the wet climate?

Figure 108 and the account

2. a) Which district produces most timber
    b) (i) Which two districts show an annual rate of cutting well below current tree growth rates?
        (ii) Explain why the amount cut must remain below the annual rate of tree growth.

Table 59 and an atlas

3. a) Draw a horizontal bar graph to show the markets for timber products.
    b) Write a brief statement opposite each bar to show the probable routes followed.

The account

4. Do you consider that coastal regions will continue to dominate the forestry industry of British Columbia? Argue your case.

The Vancouver urban region

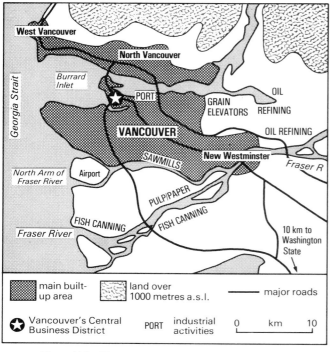

Figure 112   *Vancouver*

Vancouver is Canada's third largest city: including nearby towns, its population numbers about one million. The city has shown rapid growth since 1950 and continues to attract large numbers today. About 40 per cent of the city's population are from other Canadian provinces and 30 per cent are from overseas.

Vancouver has always been a trade and transport centre having an excellent deep water harbour for shipping and command of the Fraser Valley to the interior. The opening of the Panama Canal in 1914 helped the export of local timber and grain from the Canadian Prairies, though it is still over 13 000 km to Europe by this shortened route. Links with the American markets are strongest, but trade with Japan is an important recent development. Copper, coal, timber products and grain are the main exports to Japan, while manufactured goods are the chief imports.

Table 60   Vancouver's trade (annual value)

Country	Exports (£s)	Imports (£s)
USA	6 750 000	6 350 000
Britain	600 000	400 000
Japan	500 000	500 000
West Germany	200 000	250 000

Plate 81   *Port of Vancouver: view looking north*

The main artery of the province, the Fraser Valley, is used by several railways, highways, oil and gas pipelines and electricity transmission lines. The goods brought through this routeway from British Columbia and beyond have led to the growth of manufacturing industry, especially in the southern part of Vancouver.

Site factors have had a very important role in Vancouver's growth in the twentieth century. Suburbs have spread from a 10 km radius from Burrard Inlet in the 1920s to a 25 km radius in the 1970s. Commuting usually depends on the car. Only in the direction of New Westminster has expansion been easy; elsewhere sea inlets have had to be crossed or rivers bridged. The flat land of the Fraser Delta and the Fraser Valley was used for the early growth of Vancouver. However, since 1972 there has been little chance of obtaining government permission to build on good farmland, so that prices of land and houses have increased quickly. Consequently many hundreds of Canadians have bought cheaper houses in Washington State just over the border.

Questions

Plate 81, Figure 112

1. *a*) (*i*) Name three kinds of transport that handle the containers. (*ii*) Explain in what way the operations are mechanised.
   b) (*i*) Name the settlement beyond the water. (*ii*) State two obstacles which have hindered the expansion of settlement in the named area.

Figure 112 and the account

2. *a*) Why was Burrard Inlet a better choice for a port than the Fraser Delta?
   b) Why is little industry situated in the port area itself?
   c) Apart from transport, what advantage did a waterfront location give to the industries named on the map?

The Prairie Provinces

Introduction

The three Prairie Provinces are of roughly equal size and together cover about one-fifth of Canada's territory. In population Manitoba and Saskatchewan number about one million each, but Alberta has almost two million people. Although the northern edge of the Provinces is forested, the greater part is open country and the more developed economically. Farming, originally mostly based on wheat production, is still of vital importance, but mineral exploitation is now creating a more varied economy, especially in Alberta. As a result urban population is growing at the expense of rural, and the traditional image of the Prairies as just a vast grain field is rapidly changing.

Figure 113 *The Prairie Provinces: physical background*

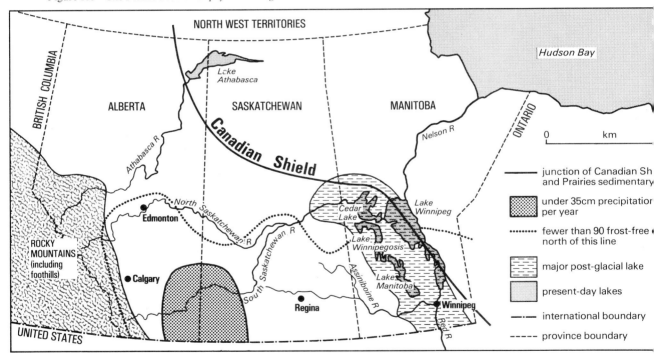

The physical background

The Prairies lie in an area of nearly horizontal sedimentary rock between the Canadian Shield and the Rocky Mountains. The surface has been shaped by erosion over a long period and forms a series of low scarps and gentle vales in the east. Only in the west does higher land appear in a series of foothill ridges below the main ranges of the Rockies.

Minor features, often related to glaciation, give some variety to the landscape. Continental ice sheets left both gravel-based terminal moraines and a mantle of loamy ground-moraine across much of the region. When the ice melted, many level areas in the eastern Prairies were flooded; the present lakes of southern Manitoba are remnants of much larger ones. Since the Ice Age moderate amounts of rain and snow have allowed decaying grasses to accumulate, producing deep, humus-rich soils over much of the region.

The long period of winter cold is a direct result of the location of the Prairies in the northern part of the continental interior. For much of the year the region is under the influence of the cold air masses of northern Canada.

Table 61   Climatic features

	Elevation (metres)	Mean temperature Jan	Mean temperature July	Frost-free period (days)	Total precipitation (cm)
Winnipeg	240	−18°C	20°C	111	50
Calgary	1079	−9°C	17°C	92	44

Often cold waves sweep southwards as far as Texas before being spent. Less frequently Gulf of Mexico air pushes northwards as far as the Canadian Prairies, bringing occasional hot and humid weather in summer.

The most dramatic change in the weather is brought by the Chinook or 'Snow-eater' wind. In Alberta cold Arctic air is replaced by warm Pacific air as the Chinook comes over the Rockies on a few occasions each winter. The air is warmed as it descends the eastern slopes of the mountains and brings a very rapid rise in temperature: from −29°C to 2°C can be recorded in a few hours. Wind speeds reach 80 km/h and the snow cover is rapidly removed.

Questions

The account

1. Explain why the Prairies has a generally level surface.
2. Draw a labelled cross-section to illustrate the *Chinook*.

Table 61

3. What climatic advantages for agriculture does the Winnipeg area have over that of Calgary?

Figure 113 and general

4. Explain why it can be said that the Canadian Prairies are: (*i*) physically isolated from the rest of Canada; but, (*ii*) very similar to neighbouring areas of the USA.

The development of farming on the Prairies

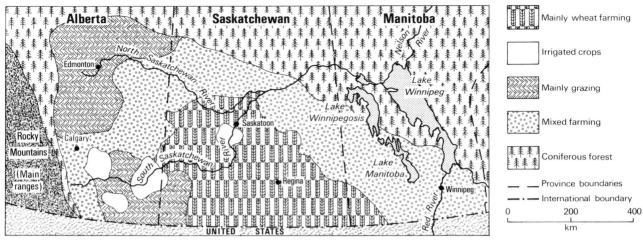

Figure 114   *Farming in the three Prairie Provinces*

A remarkable feature of the Prairies is the regular grid pattern which has been imposed on the land. Since the countryside was practically flat and a straight line (49°N) marked the US border to the south it seemed logical to plan the whole of the Prairies in a block pattern. Roads could then be laid out at 2 mile (3·2 km) intervals and farms spread out evenly along them. With a system that was easily understood, the settlement of thousands of families was rapidly achieved following the construction of the Canadian Pacific Railway.

Huge grants of land were made to the railway companies, and the Hudson's Bay Company was given land to compensate for the huge western area taken from their fur trading territories by the government. These areas were later sold to settlers. A single block of one square mile (1·6 km²) was called a section. In the moist eastern Prairies the farms were allocated quarter or half sections, but in the drier west whole sections or combined sections were the usual size.

With the arrival of thousands of settlers the Prairies quickly became an area of extensive wheat cultivation supplying western Europe with flour for bread. Saskatchewan became the most important producer of wheat, often placing too much reliance on this one crop. Although there have been many changes in the last fifty years, wheat remains a major export product; but today it is usually part of a mixed farming system.

GRAIN GROWING

During a century of wheat growing the amount produced has depended in part on physical factors, especially the

problems of frost and drought, but also on the demand for flour in Europe and, more recently, in Asia. The droughts of the 1930s were catastrophic for most producers, while the 1960s were years of abundant harvests; rarely have there been predictable crops or sales. In order to give the farmers some stability the Canadian government now guarantees the price for the harvest before the new wheat is sown each spring.

The physical factors which favour the production of

Figure 115   *The land system of the Prairies*

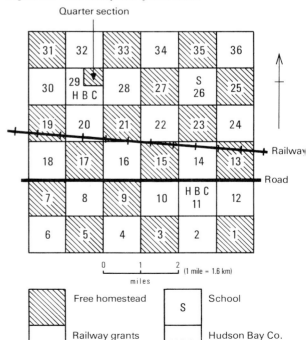

178

wheat are many. In the early period of growth regular rainfall (half the annual total of 40–50 cm) is combined with temperatures which average 18°C. This is followed by drier weather with prolonged sunshine. The extensive plains have rich soils, originally requiring little fertiliser, and machinery can be fully used in all operations. Obviously a good transport system is also needed. Better roads, improved ports and water routes supplement the efficient rail network, giving a variety of export routes. The excellent storage facilities of grain elevators must also be recognised; about two-thirds of the wheat in transit is held in the Prairies region and one-third at ports.

The problems associated with wheat growing should not be ignored, however. The Canadian section of the Great Plains is the northern limit of widespread grain farming and frost is often likely to affect the new shoots in spring or the ears of grain just before harvest time. The Western Prairies have always suffered from unreliable rainfall, and droughts have been frequent. Strips of alternating wheat and grass prevent wind erosion by reducing the areas of exposed soil; the planting of trees instead of crops has the same effect.

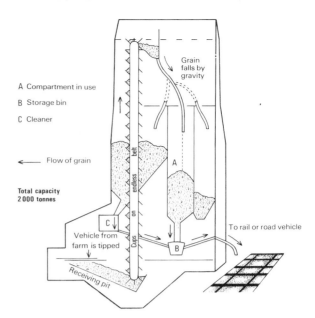

A Compartment in use

B Storage bin

C Cleaner

⟵ Flow of grain

Grain falls by gravity

Total capacity 2 000 tonnes

Vehicle from farm is tipped

Receiving pit

To rail or road vehicle

Figure 116   *A grain elevator*

Plate 82   *Wheat growing district with grain elevators, Lewran, Saskatchewan*

Recently there has been a major expansion in the production of barley, which has become an important food for livestock in the last ten years, and is now the chief crop of Alberta. Demands from home and overseas have increased rapidly and Canada is the world's major exporter of barley. Other types of agriculture which involve irrigation have given much variety to modern farming in many parts of Alberta and Saskatchewan, and ranching is characteristic of areas where rainfall is low and variable.

Table 62   Wheat and barley production on the Canadian Prairies
(Average figures from early 1970s in million kg)

	Wheat	Barley
Stocks in store at the time of sowing of the next crop	21 000	4900
Annual production of Manitoba	2000	2400
Saskatchewan	9300	5300
Alberta	3200	6000
Annual sales of grain within Canada	4700	8200

THE SALE AND EXPORT OF WHEAT

The international reputation of Canadian spring wheat is high, for it is a hard grain rich in protein. European countries take a slightly smaller total than they did 20 years ago, however, partly as a result of EEC arrangements. Russia and China have been important buyers in some years, but only when their own harvests have been poor; Japan is a smaller but more reliable purchaser. In any year Canada is only one exporting nation; there is always competition from the United States, Australia and Argentina.

Table 63   Canadian wheat exports (1976)

Thunder Bay—Great Lakes	63 per cent
Vancouver	31 per cent
Churchill (Hudson Bay)	4 per cent
Prince Rupert (Pacific)	2 per cent

Lastly, Canada donates large amounts of wheat and other high protein foods, such as meat and milk, to assist the poorer nations of the world. In 1977, 400 million kg of wheat was pledged in this way.

THE LIFE OF A WHEAT FARMING FAMILY

Thousands of farming families are still willing to earn their living on isolated farms in the Canadian Prairies. Usually the family runs the farm independently, using hired help only at harvest time. Work in the production of grain takes less than half the year, so it is possible for a family to live in the city for much of the time, or even to migrate in the winter months to Florida or the West Indies.

For the majority who stay on winter is a quiet time when the chief concern is often how long the farm will be snowed in. Visiting the nearest town for shopping, business or pleasure may be hazardous, as may a visit from a doctor or vet. The repair of tractors and combines is done in the machine sheds and when the amount of grain required for the following season is known, plans made for the next year.

Seed planting follows once the ground has dried out. For spring wheat wet ground is not disastrous with modern machinery, but if seed planting is long delayed work must proceed well into the night, using tractor and vehicle headlights, to give the grain a long enough season in which to ripen.

In the summer season the farmer clears weeds and sprays against a variety of pests. Unless drought causes crop failure, the warm weather is a time for visiting summer cottages in the Rockies or the nearby lakeshores. Shopping for special items of furniture or clothing, going to a sporting event or show may take the family on an equally long journey—a round trip of 200 km is not unusual. Late summer brings the busy two or three weeks of harvest. Despite help by hired labour and machines, long hours are worked to gather the crop before the first frost strikes. Once the selling of the wheat has been arranged the family can relax at the end of another farming season.

Questions

Plate 82 and the account

1. *a*) What evidence is there in the present landscape of the original division into sections?
   b) Where and why does a different pattern emerge?
   c) The word 'pool' is written on each elevator. What does this suggest about the way local farmers are organised?
2. *a*) (*i*) Estimate the height of the tallest elevator. (*ii*) Why do the elevators form such prominent landmarks.
   b) What construction work indicates that grain production continues to be important?

Figure 116 and the account

3. *a*) Why do farmers use elevators instead of storing wheat themselves?
   b) Why are different storage compartments advantageous?

Table 62

4. Construct and label horizontal bar graphs to show both the wheat and barley statistics. In each case draw the amount in storage, and then extend the line by adding the totals for the three Prairie Provinces. Make a slight break in the line, then further to the right insert the Canadian demand using the same scale.
5. Answer the following for; *a*) wheat and *b*) barley:
   (*i*) Which province is the most important producer of the grain?
   (*ii*) How does the total annual production from the three provinces compare with the stored amount?
   (*iii*) How does the total amount of grain available compare with the amount required in Canada each year?

Table 63

6. Compile a diagrammatic map to show the export routes of Prairie wheat.
7. Choose the correct response(s) from the four options presented:
   a) Large-scale wheat farming on the Prairies began when:
      (*i*) The fur trading area of Hudson's Bay Company was taken over by the government.
      (*ii*) Free homesteads were made available to settlers.
      (*iii*) The Panama Canal provided a quick route to Europe, via British Columbia.
      (*iv*) At the time of sowing the government made known the guaranteed price for wheat.
   b) Which of the following was an important factor in the full development of wheat growing?
      (*i*) Navigable rivers for the transport of grain.
      (*ii*) Large expanses of flat land, suitable for mechanised farming.
      (*iii*) Fertile, easily worked soil.
      (*iv*) Precipitation of 60–70 cm per year.
   c) Which of the following is *not* a problem as far as wheat farming on the Canadian Prairies is concerned?
      (*i*) Autumn frosts.
      (*ii*) The Chinook wind.
      (*iii*) Wet ground in spring.
      (*iv*) Soil erosion by wind.

A GAME TO ILLUSTRATE SOME OF THE PROBLEMS OF RANCHING

INFORMATION

Cattle ranches are often found in regions of low, unreliable rainfall.
Ranches cover huge areas.
Ranches are isolated from each other.
If insufficient rain falls grazing will be poor and many cattle will die.
The rancher may be able to get extra fodder, or move the stock to more reliable water supplies.

EXPLANATION OF THE GAME

Imagine that you are a rancher in Alberta, with 15 000 head of cattle. Each year the herd increases with the birth of calves. However, the rainfall may not be sufficient to support all the animals and some will die through lack of grass and water. Over ten years some animals will die in any case, but play the game to see what stock you hold at the end of that time.

WHAT TO DO (one die needed)

Make a copy of Table 64 to show ten years. On the given Table three years are shown as a guide.

1. Enter the 15 000 cattle on the top line.
2. Check Table 66 to see how many calves have been born.
3. Record the increased size on line 3.
4. Cast the die *three* times and total the scores, then record the amount of rain from Table 65 on line 4.
5. On line 5 show the number of cattle that the rain will support.
6. If the land will support *more* cattle than you have there are no losses and the total from line 3 becomes next year's starting figure. Carry straight on to next year (line 1). If the land will support *fewer* cattle than you have subtract the number in line 5 from line 3 and indicate on line 7.
7. There are certain choices open for you to try and avoid the *loss*, but there is still a risk:
   a) Buy *fodder* (grass) to save some animals;
   b) Move cattle to a reliable water supply (town supply, well);
   c) Ignore the loss and take next turn with a reduced herd.
   On line 7 state the choice you have made.
8. Shake the dice and use Table 67 to discover the result of your choice; record on line 8.
9. On the last line write the number of cattle at the year end.

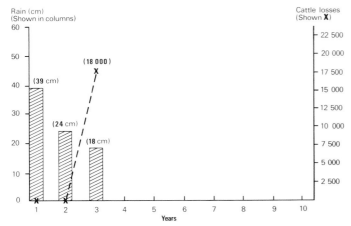

Figure 117　*Graph for the ranching game*

Table 64　　　Ranching game (1)

Line	Year 1	Year 2	Year 3 (continue up to 10 years)
1 Herd at start of year	15 000	18 000	22 000
2 New calves	3 000	4 000	4 000
3 Increased size of herd	18 000	22 000	26 000
4 Rainfall in cm (3 dice shakes)	39	24	18
5 Cattle that rain will support	20 000	13 000	10 000
6 Loss (if any)	—	9 000	16 000
7 State choice made (Table 7)	—	Water supply	Fodder
8 Result (1 dice shake)	—	Saved	+2000 on loss
9 Year end total (after changes)	18 000	22 000	8 000

Table 65　　　Ranching game (2)

Total of 3 dice	Annual rainfall in cm	Number of cattle that land will support
3	9	9 000
4	12	9 000
5	15	10 000
6	18	10 000
7	21	11 000
8	24	13 000
9	27	14 000
10	30	16 000
11	33	18 000
12	36	19 000
13	39	20 000
14	42	20 000
15	45	21 000
16	48	22 000
17	51	22 000
18	54	22 000

Table 66　　　Ranching game (3)

Herd size	New births
Below 10 000	2000
10 000 to 15 000	3000
Above 15 000	4000

Table 67　　　Ranching game (4)
Result of dice shake for expected loss

Dice number	Result
1, 2	Cattle still lost
3	Half of losses avoided
4	Greater disaster—add 2000 to losses
5	If fodder chosen, cattle saved
6	If water supply chosen cattle saved

(*Based on an article in* Classroom Geographer)

Questions

1. a) Did you have more cattle after ten years than you started with?
   b) How did your results compare with those of the other 'farmers'?
   c) Is the game entirely a matter of luck? Explain your answer.
2. Draw a graph of your results as shown in Figure 117. Use columns for rainfall totals and crosses for cattle losses; record at 0 if there are no losses. Join the crosses freehand.

3. Make your own comments on the following:
   a) variation in annual rainfall;
   b) variation in cattle losses;
   c) the relationship of rainfall totals and cattle losses;
   d) the choices offered in a poor rainfall year;
   e) the risky nature of cattle ranching.

Oil and natural gas in the Prairie Provinces

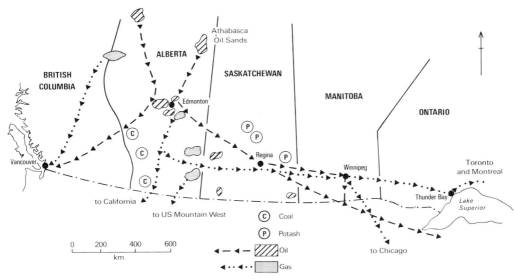

Figure 118   *Production and export of natural gas*

Following the world energy crisis of 1974 Canada was one of the few Western nations not in serious fuel difficulties. The extraction of mineral fuels, based in the provinces of Alberta and Saskatchewan and their transport by pipeline became a profitable operation though exports were reduced to conserve supplies (Figure 118).

Oil is mostly obtained from sedimentary rocks, particularly in the Edmonton area, and will last to the year 2000 or just beyond, at present rates of extraction. Natural gas occurs in great abundance and is encountered in almost every drilling operation. Sulphur must be removed before gas is piped out from the Prairies, but this is very important as a raw material for industry, along with other by-products such as propane gas. Sales of natural gas and its products amount to about 20 per cent of the income from crude oil.

Plate 83   *Mining in the Alberta oil sands*

It is hoped that the full development of 'black gold' in the Prairies will be followed by that of the 'black sands'. The Alberta oil sands form the largest known reserves of petroleum in the world—equalling the total of all other conventional oil reserves. The oil is scattered in minute particles throughout the sands of an ancient river bed, but it is not free-flowing and normal methods of pumping cannot be used. Since 1967 the material has been scooped up by giant excavators and taken to tanks where hot water is added. Eventually the oil floats on the surface and after further processing accumulates as a sediment-free liquid. The lifeless sand can be replaced in the ground, but grass and trees will not easily grow on it. How any oil will be profitably extracted from the lower sands, at a depth of 300 metres, is still a matter of guesswork.

Questions

The account and Figure 118

1. Comment on the movement of mineral fuels from the Prairies.

Plate 83 and the account

2. *a)* What are oil sands?
   b) Why is the extraction so destructive?

Towns and cities of the Prairies

Table 68   Population of Prairie cities (1976 Census)

Calgary, Alberta	469 917
Edmonton, Alberta	554 228
Regina, Saskatchewan	151 191
Saskatoon, Saskatchewan	133 750
Winnipeg, Manitoba	578 217

Table 69   Changing population and employment of the Prairies

1977 Figures		Percentage change in 25 years
Population	3 914 000	+ 53 per cent
Agriculture	232 000	− 32 per cent
Mining and Petroleum	53 400	+149 per cent
Manufacturing	126 000	+ 46 per cent

Until well into the twentieth century Prairie towns remained small but the five centres listed have experienced rapid increases in population, by immigration and by attracting people from local communities. Nationally known manufacturing and business concerns are located there, such as those connected with oil and gas at Edmonton and grain at Winnipeg. Skyscrapers are multiplying owing to pressure on land in the central city districts.

WINNIPEG: GATEWAY TO THE WEST

With a population of over half a million Greater Winnipeg dominates the province of Manitoba. The town next in size, Brandon, has about 40 000 people. The first settlers of Winnipeg arrived in 1811 when Lord Selkirk brought a group of Scottish people to the banks of the Red River. Little growth took place for half a century, but in 1868, it made its first shipment of spring wheat to meet a shortage in Ontario. Shortly after, in 1873, Winnipeg became the first city to be recognised on the Prairies and it experienced tremendous growth during the building of the CPR to the West Coast.

In view of its 'gateway' position it was natural that Winnipeg would become the centre for collecting, grading and packing Prairie produce before it was sent to eastern Canada and abroad. Most processing industries reflect the farming background of the region—flour and feed mills, brewing, slaughtering and meat packing. Clothing, metal manufacture, and the making and assembly of railway equipment, buses and trailers indicate the wide range of industries. Indeed, Winnipeg is the most industrially diversified of all the cities of the Prairies.

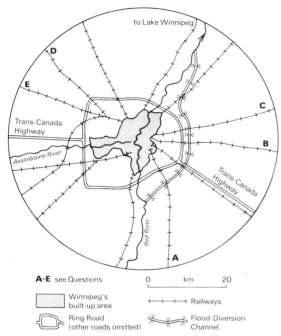

Figure 119　*The site of Winnipeg*

Questions

Table 68

1. Draw the three Prairie Provinces in outline then note the population of each. For the five cities construct a population dot map, using two different sizes of dots.

Plate 84　*A Winnipeg rail yard*

Table 68 and the account

2. Comment in full on the figures given.

Figure 119 and an atlas

3. Draw a large sketch-map of Southern Manitoba to show the 'gateway' position of Winnipeg. Insert Lake Winnipeg, the Red River and the 49th parallel. Mark the railway tracks to: Regina, Saskatoon, Thompson, Quebec via Cochrane, Thunder Bay and Minneapolis.

Plate 84, Figure 119

4. Describe the site of Winnipeg, including both its advantages and disadvantages.

Plate 84

5. List the different types of freight car, and the probable commodities being carried.
6. *a*) Is the marshalling of trains likely to be a 24-hour operation each day? Give reasons for your answer.
   b) (*i*) In which parts of the yard will trains of short length (under 1 km) be marshalled?
   (*ii*) Assuming that the floodlighting posts are 100 metres apart (on the left of the marshalling area) estimate the minimum length of any one of five trains standing nearby.
   c) Suggest why the marshalling area is situated on the edge of the city.

The account

7. Account for the growth of industries in Greater Winnipeg.

Southern Ontario

Introduction

The most southerly part of Canada is very different from the rest of the country. It contributes very little to the export trade in grain, pulpwood, or metals—but it contains over one-third of Canada's manufacturing concerns. Southern Ontario, with a population of seven million people is Canada's major English speaking area; Toronto (nearly three million) is by far its most important centre. Large industrial cities are supported by prosperous agriculture, by water power from Niagara Falls and the St Lawrence River and by the advantages of a peninsula extending into the well developed US Manufacturing Belt. Since 1959 when it was opened, ocean shipping has been able to use the St Lawrence Seaway, linking Ontario directly with world shipping routes.

Nevertheless, the area has its problems. The high density of population on the shores of lakes Erie and Ontario, together with competition amongst industry, transport and recreation for freshwater have caused serious environmental difficulties, especially that of pollution.

The physical background

In Southern Ontario the solid rocks are, for the most part, covered by glacial deposits. However, to the north and east the foundations of the Canadian Shield itself are exposed. There is a prominent north-facing dolomitic limestone escarpment some distance to the south and west, called the Niagara Escarpment. It is over 250 metres high near Lake Huron but it falls to about 80 metres in the vicinity of Lake Ontario.

As the southern edge of the continental ice sheets gradually thawed, the first flushes of meltwater were unable to escape. Huge lakes formed, overflowing by way of the Hudson Valley, until the ice which covered the St Lawrence Valley melted. Although lake levels fell once this occurred, large bodies of water remained to form the five Great Lakes. Flat areas that were once muddy lake floors have developed clay soils, while level sandy deposits indicate old shorelines or beaches. In contrast, ridges and hills of terminal moraine have stony deposits.

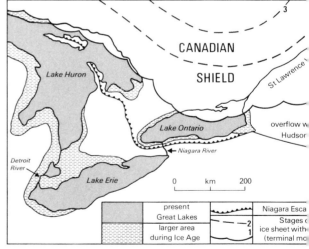

Figure 120   *The formation of the Great Lakes*

Questions

Figure 120 and the account

1. *a*) How has the dolomitic limestone affected the shape of Lake Huron?
   b) In what ways did glacial landforms help to create or maintain large lakes?
   c) Which part of Ontario has clay soils?

The account and general

2. Why does southern Ontario provide so little pulpwood or metals?
3. How are the Great Lakes divided between Canada and the United States?

The Niagara Falls and the Welland Canal

The Niagara River forms the national boundary between the province of Ontario and the state of New York, providing each with a spectacular waterfall at Niagara Falls. As Figure 122 shows, the bedrock lies in horizontal layers, which greatly assists erosion. Even in winter, spray and swirling waters act on the rock face behind the waterfall. Eventually the overhanging limestone breaks away and the waterfall 'retreats'. In two centuries a deep gorge up to 80 metres in height has been created by erosion at the Horseshoe Falls, extending 250 metres along

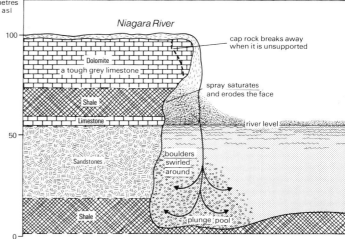

Figure 122 *Erosion at the Horseshoe Falls (Canadian)*

the river. At the same time the American Falls are moving slowly back around the other side of Goat Island.

The Niagara Falls have been retreating upstream since the Great Ice Age, and are now a long way from the original point of descent to the plain of Lake Ontario. At both the Canadian and American Falls attempts have been made to reduce the rates of retreat—at one time the river was diverted away from the American Falls while the rock face was concreted. The diversion of water for HEP is also slowing the rate of erosion.

The full development of Great Lakes water transport had to wait until the Niagara Falls were by-passed. In 1829 the first Welland Canal was completed and in the century and a half which followed, new canals were built to keep pace with larger vessels and increasing traffic. The Welland Canal should be thought of as the first part of the St Lawrence Seaway system, since only a small amount of further deepening was required before the Seaway opened in 1959.

So many more lake vessels (called 'lakers') as well as ocean-going ships started to use the canal that delays became frequent, especially at moveable bridges. Indeed, one railway swing bridge was hit six times in a single season. Eventually it was agreed to build a most unusual feature, a canal 'by-pass', around the city of Welland. An obstruction-free channel, 12 km in length, was completed in 1971 (Figure 121). However, transport by land then had to be re-routed. The most expensive re-routing operation was the diversion of three railway tracks and a major road system under the Townline Tunnel, Welland.

Figure 121 *Niagara River and Welland Canal*

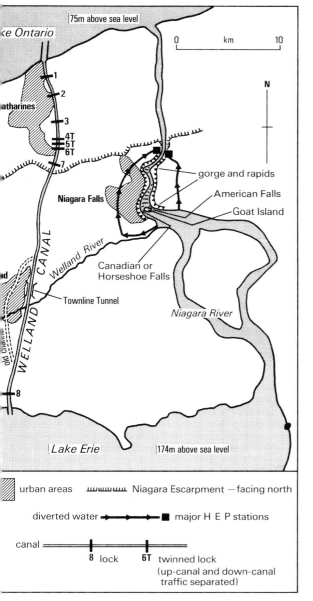

urban areas

Niagara Escarpment —facing north

diverted water

major H E P stations

canal

8 lock   6T twinned lock
(up-canal and down-canal
traffic separated)

187

Plate 85 *Niagara Falls*
Plate 86 *Laker passing a nickel refinery on the old Welland Canal*

Over 64 million tonnes of cargo currently pass through the Welland Canal annually, mostly carried by lakers. These bulk-carrying vessels are compact in shape, low in the water and the largest of them can carry up to 26 000 tonnes—just squeezing into the locks. Maximum efficiency has been achieved in moving, loading and unloading these vessels, but each winter brings navigation to a three month halt as the lakes freeze over.

Questions

Plate 85 and Figure 121

1. *a*) (*i*) In which direction was the photograph taken?
(*ii*) Name the country on the right of the picture.
(*iii*) What is the purpose of the official buildings at each end of the bridge?
b) What evidence suggests that Niagara Falls is a major tourist area? Give a detailed answer.

Figure 121, Figure 122 and the account

2. *a*) What difference in height is there between (*i*) the level of the Niagara River above and below the Horseshoe Falls, and (*ii*) the levels of lakes Erie and Ontario above sea level?
b) Account for the different answers.

3. Explain why the Horseshoe Falls is 'retreating', and where its earlier positions were.

Plate 86 and the account

The laker is 222 metres long and has a crane on deck for self-loading.
5. *a*) How is the vessel's design suitable for an inland waterway system?
b) Explain the major obstacle to canal transport shown on the photograph.

Figure 121 and the account

6. Explain (*i*) the concentration of locks, and (*ii*) the type of locks which occur in the St Catharines area.

Agriculture in Southern Ontario

Farming in Southern Ontario is in many ways similar to that of Western Europe—dairying, livestock raising and the growing of fruits and vegetables. The major activity, the raising of cattle, is supported by crops such as corn, barley and grasses. The farmer's real advantage has less to do with the favourable natural environment than with the proximity of a large urban population; many kinds of agriculture have developed to supply the home market.

Where the growing season is longest specialist crops such as sweet corn and tobacco are grown, or European-type vegetables which ripen early in the season. Often tobacco plants and vegetables are started in greenhouses to give them a few weeks extra growth before they are planted outside. The extra initial cost is recovered by the good selling prices obtained for tobacco and special vegetables. Near the larger cities farmers specialise in milk and poultry production, although the area of supply is quite a broad one. In the cooler northern areas few cash crops are cultivated and beef or cheese are the major products.

Figure 123   *Farming and freedom from frost*

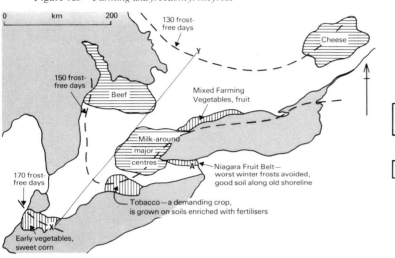

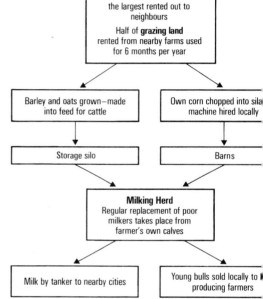

Figure 124   *Operations of small dairy farms*

Questions

Figure 123 and general

1. a) Crossing Ontario from X to Y, explain the decrease in the frost-free period.

b) Account for the northward extension of the 150 frost-free day line.

Table 70 and general

2. a) In the three summer months there is a continuous decline in the moisture content of soils.
(*i*) By what processes is water lost? (*ii*) In which month will the loss be greatest?

b) By September deficiency of soil water totals 10 cm. Explain what this means in relation to the total summer rainfall.

c) How may the farmer counter soil moisture loss, other than by irrigation?

General

3. Discuss the reasons for the success of southern Ontario's farming under the following headings: (*i*) favourable environment; (*ii*) markets; (*iii*) special crops.

Figure 124

4. List the operations of this dairy farm under the following headings: (*i*) machines and buildings used; (*ii*) payments made; (*iii*) income.

Table 70   Monthly climatic averages, St Catharines (location A)

	J	F	M	A	M	J	J	A	S	O	N	D	
Max temp °C	0	0	4	12	19	24	27	26	22	16	8	+2	
Min temp °C	−7	−8	−4	+1	+7	13	16	16	12	+6	+1	−4	
Precip (cm)	5.8	4.5	5.3	6.1	5.4	6.3	6.1	6.4	6.6	5.5	5.4	5.2	Total 69

Industry and power supplies in Southern Ontario

INDUSTRY

Southern Ontario is the leading manufacturing district of Canada and its inhabitants have achieved high standards of living through the sale of their industrial goods. The region leads the nation in the production of steel, motor vehicles, chemical products, industrial machinery, and processed fruits and vegetables. The largest factories, which are located in attractive surroundings near the city boundaries, employ thousands of people. However, there is a major concentration of firms on the western flank of Lake Ontario, part of a built-up area which is similar to the industrialised American states immediately to the south. The population of seven million in southern Ontario provides a compact Canadian market.

Greater Toronto has a large range of companies, whose most important markets are in the area shown in Figure 125. Much of the industry is geared to the consumed needs of the 2·8 million city dwellers; these needs include food, household goods, clothing and transport. Occupations linked with Toronto's role as provincial capital are also of great importance—printing and publishing, insurance and banking.

Windsor is the original home of the Canadian car industry. Branch factories of American firms from Detroit have been established there for over seventy years. The two cities are part of the same urban area and are linked by tunnels and a road bridge across the Detroit River. Since 1964 no customs charges have been made on motor vehicles or parts sold across the border.

Hamilton is Canada's major centre of iron and steel making, producing ten million tonnes a year. Reclaimed land in Hamilton Harbour was used for the early factory expansion but as demands for pipelines and power stations have added to those of traditional metal-using industries, it has been necessary to build a new steelworks next to Lake Erie (Figure 125).

Sarnia was processing crude oil and salt in the last century, but large-scale refining began only when oil was brought by pipeline from the Canadian Prairies. Subsequently, an important chemical industry has developed, producing plastics, rubber and fertiliser.

POWER SUPPLIES

The Niagara River is used to generate two million kilowatts of electricity in the gorge below Niagara Falls, and the harnessing of the St Lawrence and Ottawa rivers adds a similar amount. Even so, demands are such that coal-fired power stations have long been required. American coal is brought across the Greak Lakes to huge

Figure 126   *Hamilton's (H) steel industry and its links*

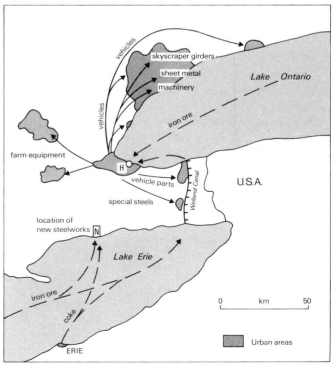

Figure 125   *Power and manufacturing in Southern Ontario*

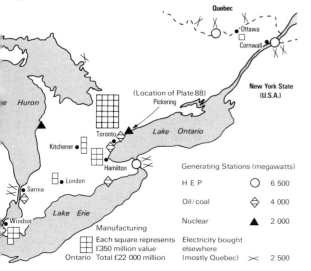

generators situated on the lake shore, the newest on Lake Erie producing four thousand mw each year. Such is the consumption of power that nuclear power stations are now adding their electricity—from Pickering near Toronto (Plate 87) and Douglas Point (Lake Huron). However, demands for power still exceed the supply, and the shortage has to be met by using electricity transmission lines to import power from outside Ontario.

Questions

Figure 125 and general

1. *a*) Explain why HEP production from southern Ontario is not likely to increase significantly.
   b) How may changes of weather or economic activities affect the availability of electricity bought in from outside Ontario?

Plate 87, Figure 125 and general

2. A number of important considerations have to be borne in mind when sites for nuclear power stations are being chosen: (*i*) positioned many kilometres away from built-up areas; (*ii*) good transport links to bring in steel and concrete for the task of construction; (*iii*) sufficient water for cooling during the nuclear reactions; (*iv*) landscape to be little altered; (*v*) solid rock to withstand the weight of the buildings; (*vi*) site large enough for a second station to be added (reducing future costs). Which of these considerations were met at Pickering?

Figure 125

3. *a*) Describe the distribution of:
   (*i*) manufacturing areas; (*ii*) power stations
   b) Do they coincide or not? Give reasons for your answer.

Plate 86 and the account

4. Why is this a good site for a nickel refinery, with regard to: (*i*) electricity for smelting; (*ii*) supplies of nickel ore; (*iii*) metal industries that use nickel?

Figure 126 and general

5. *a*) List at least four towns where steel is converted to other products.
   b) Comment on the position of the new steelworks for supplying these towns.

Plate 87   *Pickering Nuclear Power Station*

Using the Great Lakes to the best advantage

Although the Great Lakes of North America are the world's largest freshwater system, many problems have arisen as different groups wish to use the resource for many and varied purposes. Large industries require water for transport, cooling factory machinery, for many industrial processes, and for waste disposal—if the law permits. Demand is extremely high: for example, a large steelworks consumes the same amount of water as a city of a million people.

The domestic use of water also makes enormous demands both in quantity and quality: the average household uses 360 litres of first-class water each day. Yet again, running water is also used for the disposal of domestic waste. When correctly controlled no major pollution occurs, but if many of the towns discharge only partially treated sewage major pollution of the lakes inevitably results.

The Great Lakes have always had a recreational use, especially as they are within easy reach of twenty-eight million people. Thousands of summer cottages were built by city dwellers, the Lake Erie shoreline being a favourite location. With the reduction of working hours and the gradual increase in wages more demands are being made for large-scale water facilities such as leisure centres and boating marinas. In Toronto a large part of the lakeshore is devoted to leisure features of this kind.

Plate 88   *Ontario Place, Toronto*

AMERICAN-CANADIAN ACTION

In 1972 Canada and the United States signed an agreement to counter the pollution problems which had made Lake Erie and its rivers so notorious. A vivid example occurred in the 1960s, when the bottom of a sampling bucket left too long in a river near Detroit was corroded. New controls ban the discharge of toxic chemicals. Industrial companies now deal with impurities in the factories themselves and use less water by re-circulating it. Steelworks at Cleveland and Detroit made such tremendous progress that thousands of trout and salmon were successfully re-introduced into previously contaminated rivers. Further, the new Canadian steelworks on the opposite side of the lake began operations with a full system of pollution controls.

A programme to give adequate treatment to town sewage also became a priority. About three-quarters of American and almost all Canadian cities had built sewage treatment plants by 1977. Laws reducing the amount of phosphorus in soap detergents also helped to restrict the growth of slimy, dark green algae in the lakes and allowed an increase in quantities of oxygen, measures which helped to increase fish stocks.

Navigators on the lakes also have to observe rigid rules, which forbid the discharge of engine oils, washing out of bilges, or dumping of human waste. Likewise, farmers are expected to keep streams free from farm discharges and not to use toxic insecticides in crop treatments.

In the first five years of the 'clean up' campaign the United States and Canada jointly spent over £600 million, government funds in Washington supplying much of this amount. On the credit side it seems that fishermen have had better catches, recreational centres more customers and the costs of purifying drinking water have fallen. But there is no room for complacency, since the improvement in water quality requires the full and continuous co-operation of millions of people.

Questions

Plate 86 and general

1. *a)* What kind of pollution is shown?
   b) Why must metal refining inevitably create a disposal problem for solids?
2. *a)* The outflow of power station water is sometimes called 'thermal pollution'. Why?
   b) What effects is thermal pollution likely to have on (*i*) the surface of Lake Ontario in winter, and (*ii*) the original fish population?

Plate 88 and the account

3. *a)* Draw a sketch map to show the following localities: Ontario Place recreation area; warehouses and commercial docks; 'downtown' skyscraper blocks; Canadian National Railway Tower (549 metres high).
   b) Explain why there are few open spaces on the lakeshore.

4. Comment on Ontario Place under the headings of:
   a) the kinds of leisure offered;
   b) its access to the people of Greater Toronto;
   c) the chances of having polluted water in this lakeshore area.

The account and general

5. Compile a table of water needs, including quantity and/or quality, for the different kinds of users: navigation by lakers; power station; steelworks; lakeside cottage; any other users.
6. Industrial and domestic forms of pollution were worse on the American side of the Great Lakes than the Canadian.
   a) Does pollution exactly reflect the distribution of population?
   b) Why did the 'clean-up' require a high level of government action?

Southern Quebec

Quebec and the French Canadians

The St Lawrence Valley is both the heartland and economic life-line of Quebec, though it crosses a region with a severe winter climate. Over five million French-speaking inhabitants live here, almost half of whom are found in Montreal. The French language and culture were safeguarded by laws passed when Canada became a nation (1867), but many French Canadians are dissatisfied with their minority status and wish to run their affairs independently.

It is remarkable that French influence has survived, for 'New France' was overthrown over two centuries ago and few French immigrants subsequently arrived to add to the original stock. After the first 260 years of settlement the French-speaking group had reached one million. They produced enough oats, potatoes and animal products to

Table 71   French-speaking Canadians (1971 Census)

	Quebec	Ontario	New Brunswick	Manitoba
Number having French as first language	4 867 250	482 040	215 725	60 545
Percentage of named provinces total population	80·75	6·26	34·00	6·13

make self-sufficient communities possible and developed skills in the spinning of wool, cheese making and the manufacture of tools and equipment. The St Lawrence Valley from Quebec City to Montreal was the chief area

Figure 127   *Land use pattern of French Canadian farms (long lots)*

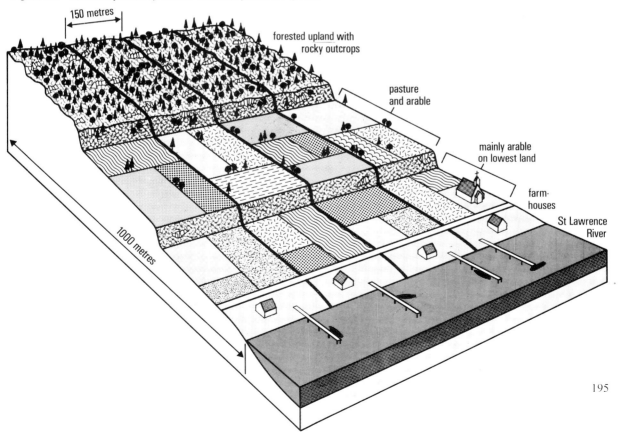

150 metres

forested upland with rocky outcrops

pasture and arable

mainly arable on lowest land

farm-houses

St Lawrence River

1000 metres

195

Plate 89 *Demonstration by French-speaking university students, Montreal*

of French settlement; many of the original 'long lots' remain to the present day.

Following the American War of Independence many British groups immigrated, settling in eastern Quebec and the Ottawa Valley. Later, large numbers of Irish farmers cleared land on the edge of the Laurentian Mountains north of the St Lawrence River. The most important attraction was the port of Montreal, which the Scots and English had used for their business interests since the fall of New France.

As population pressure increased in the last century the French expanded from their base in the St Lawrence Valley. Many families pioneered farming, lumbering and mining activities in remoter parts of Quebec Province, thus ensuring that the rural areas became almost completely French-speaking. In addition, many French groups

migrated to northern Ontario and Manitoba, while smaller numbers established themselves in New Brunswick to the east. However, as soon as French migrants left Quebec they became minorities in English-speaking Canada, where their culture had little chance of survival.

Officially, French enjoys equal status with English throughout Canada. Both languages are used in government documents and in the Ottawa parliament, and, many French Canadians have risen to the highest positions in the country, including Prime Minister. However, there is little doubt that to enjoy such success French Canadians have to become fluent in English, while their English-speaking compatriots have never been under the same pressure to become bilingual.

For many French-Canadians in the urban areas of southern Quebec a serious economic situation exists. In Montreal, for example, English-speakers control much of the city's finance, business and industry, although they form only 22 per cent of its population. In addition, much economic and cultural influence comes from nearby American states. However, since the 1960s there has been a move to use French as the working language, rather than English. The recognition of French has become the official policy of major transport, car manufacturing and aluminium firms, often owned by companies based in the USA and English-speaking Canada. Any English-speaker now in a managerial position will be expected to learn French or step aside.

Recent political events have produced a more dramatic situation. The *Parti Quebécois*, which would like Quebec Province to break away from Canada, has won control of the Quebec parliament and will hold a provincial referendum to test the strength of feeling for separate nationhood. This party believes that Quebec has enough human and natural resources to make independence possible. However, there does not seem to be any way in which the federal government can support the idea and a most difficult problem has yet to be resolved.

Questions

Table 71 and an atlas

1. *a*) By what routes would settlers from the Montreal area reach other provinces listed?
   b) Express (*i*) the Ontario and (*ii*) the New Brunswick French-speakers as a fraction of those of Quebec.
   c) Why do French-speaking families remain in English-speaking Canada although they thereby lose some of their own customs?

Figure 127, Plate 89 and the account

2. *a*) Describe the features of early French settlement.
   b) Why, despite being cut off from its homeland, did French Canada survive?
   c) List some of the French Canadians' grievances at the present time. Do you sympathise with them? Justify your answer.

Alcan

Quebec produces large amounts of that versatile metal, aluminium, making Canada the leading world exporter. In 1925 production began at the Aluminium Company of Canada (ALCAN)'s newly-built smelter in the Saguenay Valley. It was the first industry in the valley to move away from traditional timber processing and it brought a new community, Arvida, into existence. The deciding factor in the siting of the smelter in this remote area was its vast potential for HEP at the edge of the Canadian Shield. ALCAN annually generates enough electricity both to convert 2 340 000 tonnes of bauxite to 1 320 000 tonnes of alumina and to provide for every other electrical need of workplaces and homes in the district. At Arvida a flat terrace provides suitable space for factories employing 6000 people and the town itself with over 15 000 inhabitants. Another important advantage was provided by the Saguenay Estuary, which allowed shipping to reach a point only 25 km from the Arvida works. In addition to bauxite, the processing requires fluorspar (from Newfoundland) and cryolite (from Greenland).

After the molten aluminium has been produced from the bauxite ore it may be sold in a solidified block (ingot) or processed in a number of ways. Continuous rolling produces sheets suitable for making railway coaches or boats, while further thinning gives kitchen foil. By squeezing molten aluminium through different shapes (extrusion) window frames or strands of wire are manufactured. The aluminium castings for internal combustion engines are made by a more specialised process.

Elsewhere in southern Quebec there are other ALCAN smelters at Alma, Shawinigan Falls and Beauharnois (Figure 128).

Questions

Figure 128 and the account

1. *a*) Why was the Saguenay Valley chosen for the production of aluminium?
   b) (*i*) What do the four ALCAN smelting areas have in common? (*ii*) Which smelter has the best position for the sale of its products?

Figure 128 and the account

2. Compile an aluminium flow diagram, beginning in the Caribbean and ending in Montreal.

General

3. Indicate the versatility of aluminium by listing additional products made from it.

Figure 128 *Southern Quebec: physical and economic elements*

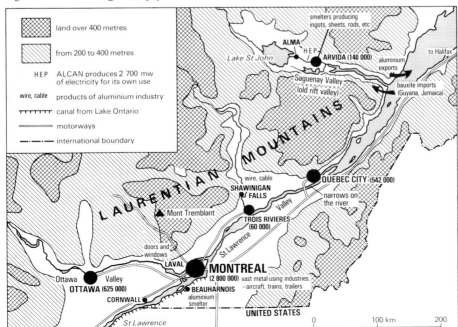

The St Lawrence Seaway

In its widest sense the Seaway is regarded as the whole length of the navigable channel from the Atlantic Ocean to the upper Great Lakes. The St Lawrence River itself (Figure 129) has many falls and rapids, which were by-passed by small Canadian canals in the last century, but by the mid-twentieth century neither large lakers nor small ocean vessels could use these waterways. However,

before a modern navigation system could be created the agreement of the United States had to be given, since some proposed canals, dams and power plants would occupy American land south of the river. Plans also included the regulation of water flows to HEP turbines incorporated in some dams.

In the 1950s a Canadian-American agreement was signed and since it was opened in 1959 the St Lawrence Seaway has provided a channel which is especially useful for the bulk transport of wheat, iron ore and coal. However, a major drawback is that winter navigation has not yet been possible on the Seaway above Montreal, thus lowering the efficiency of the system. Also, the maximum capacity of an ocean vessel using the locks is 12 000 tonnes. Despite increasing traffic paying high tolls the St Lawrence Seaway has not been a financial success.

Table 72   St Lawrence Seaway traffic: cargoes carried through the International Rapids Section (million tonnes)

Before Seaway	After Seaway					
1958	1959	1963	1966	1970	1973	1977
11	19	29	47	49	57	71 40 down 31 up

Questions

Figure 129 and an atlas

1. *a*) (*i*) Name the two American and one Canadian terminal points of the Seaway. (*ii*) How many kilometres is it from Montreal to the most distant terminal? (*hint:* follow the shipping route)
   b) Canada paid two-thirds of the cost of the St Lawrence section of the Seaway. Produce evidence to justify the size of this contribution.

Table 72 and general

2. *a*) Construct a graph of the statistics.
   b) (*i*) Why have bulk cargoes increased far more rapidly than general manufactured goods, including imports? (*ii*) In what way has it now become possible to organise return cargoes for lakers?

Figure 129   *The St Lawrence Seaway*

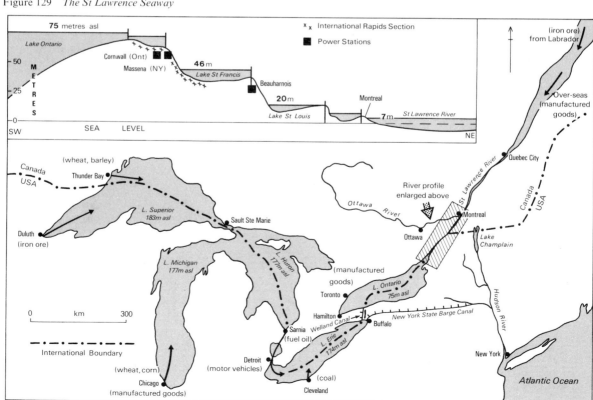

Winter navigation on the St Lawrence River

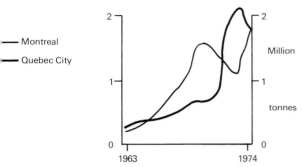

Figure 130 *Winter cargoes at Montreal and Quebec City (1 January to 1 April)*

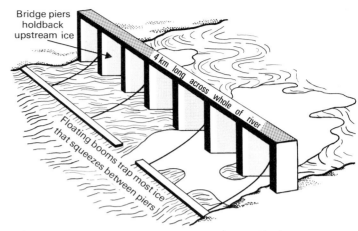

Figure 131 *Ice control 'bridge' (5 km above Montreal harbour)*

In the 1960s successful winter voyages as far upstream as Montreal, by Danish and Russian ships, demonstrated that a closed season was unnecessary. How is winter navigation possible when navigators have always avoided the ice? The answer is that technology has been used to reduce the hazards. Systematic reporting of ice floes gives a computer picture of conditions in the St Lawrence estuary, and icebreakers and helicopter patrols concentrate on the known areas of difficulty. A number of ice-control structures now operate to prevent large sheets of ice breaking away from the shore and becoming dangerous to ships.

Perhaps the worst of the hazards occurs at the Narrows above Quebec City, where the river is less than one kilometre wide. When the temperature falls well below the January average of $-12°C$ this stretch of water is blocked by a continuous cover of jumbled ice, which may fail to break up as the tide recedes. More ice then forms which sometimes creates a barrier for the rest of the winter if left untouched.

Questions

Figure 130 and general

1. *a)* Why do the graphs fluctuate rather widely at this season?
   b) For what reasons is the smaller port of Quebec City able to equal Montreal's total?

Figure 131 and general

2. Describe the hazards of winter navigation.

The account and an atlas

3. *a)* In the past what were the alternatives for supplying overseas goods to southern Quebec in winter?
   b) Suggest reasons for and against the winter use of the ports of the St Lawrence.

Plate 90 *Port of Montreal*

Montreal

A SHOPPING PRECINCT BENEATH THE BUSINESS DISTRICT

'In downtown Montreal it is possible to escape from the deep winter snow and freezing temperatures and enter three miles [5 km] of glittering pedestrian avenues controlled at normal room temperature. The bright, spacious halls have an elegance that makes strolling through them stimulating and delightful. . . . An office worker can meet his wife for lunch, leave her to spend the afternoon shopping, meet her again for a drink afterwards and go on to a play or a concert without either of them venturing out of doors. . . . Perhaps 300 000 people visit these arcades on a busy day, some spending virtually all their time there. You can write a will, have your teeth fixed, take a train, or buy a dog!'

(From *Canada Today*, November–December, 1974)

One of the major reasons for the growth of Montreal is related to its command of routeways. In the railway-building period Montreal gained control of links between Ontario, Quebec and Atlantic Canada and southwards to New York. Montreal developed into a most important rail hub, housing the headquarters of both the Canadian Pacific and Canadian National Railways. Quebec City, then almost equal in size, attempted to compete, but its location was unsatisfactory. When highways were improved in the present century Montreal strengthened its dominant position and developed the best road links in eastern Canada, including many motorway systems.

During its 300 years of growth Montreal has spread northwestwards over two islands and, to a lesser extent, eastwards across the St Lawrence River. However, the major harbour keeps closely to that first selected, although the amenities are continually being modernised. Quite near the harbour are many large warehouses and the main commercial district of the city. Older houses and small factories surround the business district, except for the open spaces and high quality homes of the Mount Royal area.

Although there has been much renewal of old buildings in the city many modern industries have been erected in

Figure 132   *Site of Montreal*

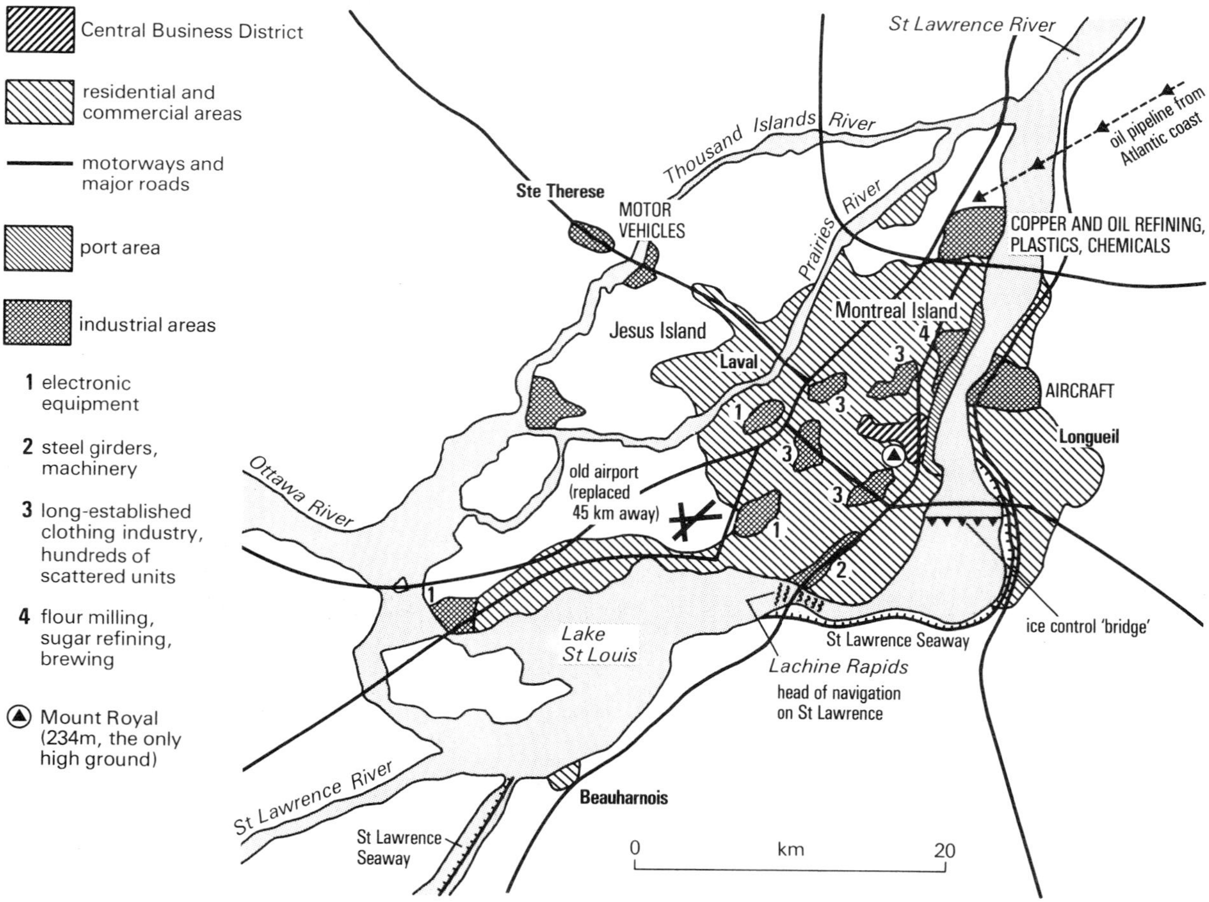

rural settings, particularly where road links are good. Figure 132 shows most of the important manufacturing industries of the Greater Montreal area. Nearly one-sixth of Canada's factories are situated here, employing 263 000 people. There is intense rivalry between Montreal and Toronto for first place in Canadian manufacturing.

Table 73   A comparison of Montreal and Toronto industries

	Greater Montreal	Greater Toronto
Number of manufacturing firms	5 243	5 684
Total number of workers	263 313	294 140
Value of goods shipped (£m)	3 450	4 323

Questions

Figure 132 and general

1. a) Other than car manufacture, which industries shown require large amounts of open space? Why?
   b) Explain in full the advantages of being (i) near the docks (00), and (ii) spread across the city in small units (00).

The account and an atlas

2. What physical advantages enabled Montreal to become of major importance in land and water transport?

Plate 91 and general

3. The view shows the first car factory in Quebec. It was built in 1965 and employs 2500 workers. Suggest why the American company thought it worthwhile to begin production near Montreal.

Plate 90, Figure 132 and general

4. a) Using map evidence verify that the view is from the north-east.
   b) Why was the St Lawrence Seaway not built on this side of the river?

General

5. Write an explanatory account of the importance of Montreal

General

6. A simple method of estimating the importance of a city is to record the number of routes converging on it. The city shown scores 12 points.

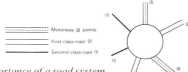

Motorway ③ points
First-class road ②
Second-class road ①

Figure 133   *The importance of a road system*

For selected cities on Figure 133 if actual roads are scored the results are: Montreal 33; Quebec City 23; Ottawa 16; Arvida 8.
   a) Using the system shown make route counts of four or five urban centres in your own locality.
   b) Draw two columns, then list the towns in decreasing order of size in the first one. Record the route score in the second column; then comment on the relationship shown.

Plate 91   *General Motors, Sainte Therese*

The Atlantic Provinces

Physical background

Atlantic Canada shares with New England the difficulties of steep slopes and glacial soils. Areas of fertile lowland are small in comparison with the rugged and mountainous districts which rise to over 500 metres in central New Brunswick, Cape Breton Island and northern Newfoundland. The coastline shows great contrasts. On the Atlantic side offshore islands and rocky inlets are characteristic, while the head of the Bay of Fundy is an area of extensive mud flats, the result of a spectacular tidal range of 15 metres, one of the highest in the world.

The region lies on the track of year-round depressions from the Great Lakes. Summer may bring temperatures as high as in the St Lawrence Valley, but rain or Atlantic mists soon end the hot, dry weather. Snowfall is heavy for one-third of the year and freezing rain is common even when the winter temperature rises above normal. Also, pack ice is present in many sea areas and completely envelopes Newfoundland's west and north-east coasts.

In the moist climate a mixed forest, dominated by spruce trees, has developed across the region. However, great contrasts exist between the hardwood forests of the lowlands, developed on glacial soils, and the swampy and infertile Barrens of Newfoundland where trees grow with great difficulty.

Figure 134   *The Atlantic Provinces: land and sea resources*

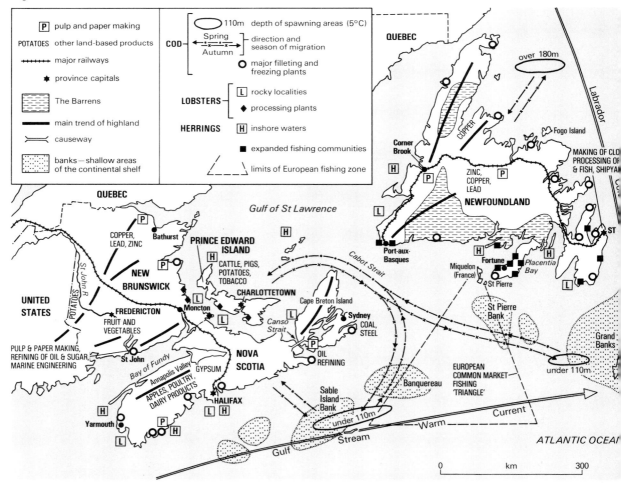

Table 74　Selected climatic factors of Atlantic Canada

Region	Average temperature Jan °C	July °C	Frost-free period (days)	Annual precipitation cm	Probability of fog
S.E. Newfoundland	−16	16	70	127 (15% as snow)	One day in three throughout the year
St John Valley	−10	19	120	99 (30% as snow)	From Bay of Fundy in summer

Questions

Table 74, Figure 134 and the account

1. Describe and account for the frequency of cloudy weather in the Grand Banks area.

2. Describe the climate of S.E. Newfoundland and that of the St John Valley. Explain any differences noted.

Gaining a livelihood

FARMING AND INDUSTRY

Despite early prosperity connected with trade and ship-building, gaining a living in Atlantic Canada has always been difficult. Sales of its forest, mine and farm products are limited by fierce competition from other Canadian regions and a local market of only two million people. In farming there has been a gradual decline of employment throughout the twentieth century, even in productive Prince Edward Island, but in coal and iron-based occupations the loss of jobs has been much more rapid. Many families have moved from the Atlantic region to central Canada or the USA in search of employment, giving the eastern provinces a reputation as a depressed area. Only in a few centres, particularly large ports, are long-term job prospects attractive.

Prince Edward Island is the only Canadian province where farmland is more extensive than forested land.

The low-lying island has no coal, oil, or swift rivers for HEP and is marginally placed for Atlantic fishing. Hence farming has been carefully developed on the gently sloping land, where there is good quality sandy loam.

In the early days of agriculture, tidal mud, oyster shells and seaweed were spread on the fields to increase the fertility, but this is now maintained by farm manure and chemical fertilisers. Careful management also built up good-quality production of cattle, pigs and poultry. Potato growing has been important for many generations, although tobacco has recently become the most valuable crop for some farmers. However, farm output is not reaching the level that it could if more convenient markets existed, and the population of the island seems unlikely to increase.

Although appearing to have sound prospects based on

Table 75　Farming in the Atlantic Provinces (early 1970s)

Province	Total land area (in thousands of hectares)	Area of farmland (in thousands of hectares)	Improved land (drained, seeded) as fraction of area of farmland	Farmland as percentage of total land area
Newfoundland (Island only)	10 666	25	One-third	0·2
Nova Scotia	5286	538	One-third	10·2
New Brunswick	7212	542	One-third	7·5
PEI	566	314	Two-thirds	55·5
Total	23 730	1419		6·0

coal and steel (Figure 134), the Cape Breton area of Nova Scotia has been unable to support its population. Out-migration since the 1950s has removed a quarter of the 15–24 years age group. Coal and steel, the two major industries in Sydney, cater for a few thousand workers, but prospects are uncertain.

In the coal industry over forty mines have closed since 1920, and only four, including one recently opened, remain in the extreme north of Cape Breton. With current demand high, the main advantages are the huge reserves near to the port of Sydney, much of which is either good coking coal or suitable for the generation of electricity. Disadvantages are the high cost of pumping out the coal workings under Cabot Strait, and the fact that many seams are quite thin and the coal is often sulphurous. Since output is not expected to rise above three million tonnes per year few young miners are being trained to replace the ageing work force.

The other large employer is the iron and steel industry, which was developed early in the twentieth century. However, supplies of iron ore from Newfoundland ceased in the 1960s when the mines closed, and increasing quantities of coking coal had to be imported. Only 15 per cent of the rods and rails are sold in Atlantic Canada. The works have long been subsidised by both the Canadian and Nova Scotia governments, but modernisation has not yet promised a secure future.

In contrast, the southern end of Cape Breton Island has experienced much new growth, mainly because Canso Strait is easily able to accommodate supertankers. Two oil refineries, a large dock area, two power stations and a pulp and paper works have recently been constructed.

Questions

Table 75 and general

1. Explain why farming on Prince Edward Island is not typical of the Atlantic Region.

The account and general

2. Explain briefly why Cape Breton's coal and steel industries cannot compete with their North American rivals.

TRADITIONAL FISHING: THE GRAND BANKS

One of the world's greatest fishing areas occurs over the 'banks' of the continental shelf, the best known of which is the Newfoundland Grand Bank. The area has been fished commercially since the seventeenth century, cod forming the mainstay of the catch until modern times.

The Atlantic cod is restricted to a narrow temperature range and water conditions, but it must move with its food supply of smaller fish such as herring. Figure 134 shows the most important spawning areas, where the eggs are laid and fertilised in the spring. Each female produces about five million eggs, many of which become larvae and ascend to feed off plankton in the warmer surface waters. Next the 'small fry' stage is spent in deep water, but on maturity the surviving cod seek out precise temperature and light conditions for the remaining fifteen years of their lives. Seasonal migrations take place to and from the banks. If there are cloudless skies and clear water in the summer, the shoals leave the inshore waters temporarily.

'Cod was the gold that brought the white man first to those heaving grey waters lying between Newfoundland and the coast of Nova Scotia. Cod is still the gold that causes men to sit hunched with cold in little boats scores of miles off shore, scores of miles from the mother ship that put them there. They sit and watch their hand lines and hope the cod will bite. They hope the price will be good. They sit and hope that, should a sudden storm change the slow Atlantic swell into a foam streaked hell, they'll live to see land again. They often do.'
(From K. M. Wells, *Colourful Canada*, Jarrold & Sons Ltd.)

Cod traditionally provided the chief source of protein in the local diet and had the great advantage of being easy to dry or preserve in brine. No matter how poor the farming potential of the land, villages could be established wherever the sea would yield a rich harvest. Line fishing still provides the income of some families, though trawling is now the major fishing operation.

By tonnage, herring and cod are most important, but by value lobster easily exceeds either one. Lobster trapping occupies only the warmer months of the year, so that other employment is necessary. However, those fortunate in taking the earliest spring catches may earn thousands of pounds in a hectic week or so of the setting and collecting of traps. Large lobsters are marketed live, often being kept in huge tanks in which sea water circulates. Small specimens are canned or sold as chilled lobster, though there is a minimum size to protect the future lobster fishing industry.

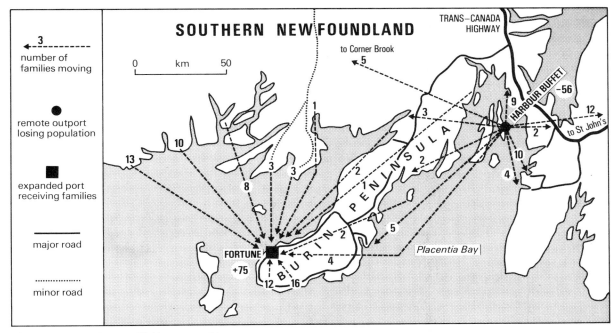

Figure 135 *Resettlement of fishing communities*

MODERN DEVELOPMENTS IN FISHING

Since the 1950s attempts have been made to provide frozen and filleted fish for the markets of North America and Europe. This has meant concentrating modern fishing fleets on the best harbours available and constructing processing plants served by good roads. In such 'expanded villages' the provision of electricity and water supplies has provided a great improvement in living standards for many families. Also, for every job at sea, five more have been created ashore. In Newfoundland the 'expanded village' policy involved widespread changes of home location, sometimes even the house itself being moved. Between 1954 and 1973, when the schemes were completed, over 300 small fishing communities had been completely evacuated and 27 000 people had moved, at great government expense.

Plate 92 *Traditional fishing village, Fogo Island*

Plate 93 *A house being towed across water to its new location, Dover Cove, Newfoundland*

The complicated pattern on Figure 135 shows the importance of individual choice, despite the government's financial control of the resettlement. Many families moved to be near relatives and some to remain with the same religious denomination. A strong minority were reluctant to move at all and tried to remain self-reliant despite the attractiveness of the resettlement schemes.

In recent times Atlantic fishing stocks have shown signs of exhaustion as a result of over-fishing. The major competitors to Atlantic fishers are the numerous foreign vessels. Common Market trawlers are particularly attracted to the area south of the remaining French territory of St Pierre and Micquelon, where Europeans have their own zone. Also, fishers from Quebec province have long-established rights in the Gulf of St Lawrence; they take one-tenth of the Canadian Atlantic catch.

Canadian fish catches have declined since 1965. Vessels from the USSR, Poland, Japan, Spain and Portugal have together taken more fish than local boats. In 1971 Canada instituted a quota system to restrict catches of traditional table fish, such as cod and haddock, and also extended its own fishing limits to 12 nautical miles (21 km), measured from 'headland to headland'. By 1976, however, foreign vessels were taking twice the catch of Canadian boats and further controls became necessary. In 1977 quotas for foreign boats were reduced to 340 million tonnes of flatfish. Even more dramatically, in the same year Canada extended its territorial waters to 200 nautical miles (368 km). Within these limits only Canadians are permitted to fish, foreign vessels being excluded unless Canadian quotas are not fully taken up.

Questions

Figure 135 and the account

1. Comment on the advantages of the continental shelf to the shoals of cod.

Figure 135, Plate 92 and the account

2. Justify the 'expanded village' policy in terms of (*i*) employment, and (*ii*) services.

The account and general

3. Is the 200-mile sector claimed by EEC countries a productive one for cod? Explain your answer.
4. What do you conclude about the size and type of vessel that the Russians and Japanese are using?
5. Explain why the 'headland to headland' baseline gives the best possible advantage to Canadian fishermen.

General

6. Do the Atlantic fisheries offer a good livelihood for the future? Give reasons for your answer.

Halifax : Atlantic Canada's premier seaport

Halifax has long attracted population from rural areas in Atlantic Canada and is now the region's largest city, containing a quarter of a million people. The Canadian government has recently given financial help to create more employment and to maintain the city as a growth point for the region. Halifax is the capital of Nova Scotia, the eastern office centre for many business firms, and a major NATO naval base.

Many of the industries shown on Figure 136 are long-established and are the result of a favourable position on an eastern peninsula of Canada. In the period of wooden sailing ships Nova Scotia was a world leader in both ship-building and the carrying of goods. Today, shipbuilding continues in the Halifax harbour area, but the industry has also diversified into items such as offshore oil-drilling platforms.

Like many other ports, Halifax has seen a transformation in methods of handling cargoes, as containerisation and bulk handling have rapidly developed. A first step in containerisation of goods was the move to

Figure 136   *Halifax Harbour*

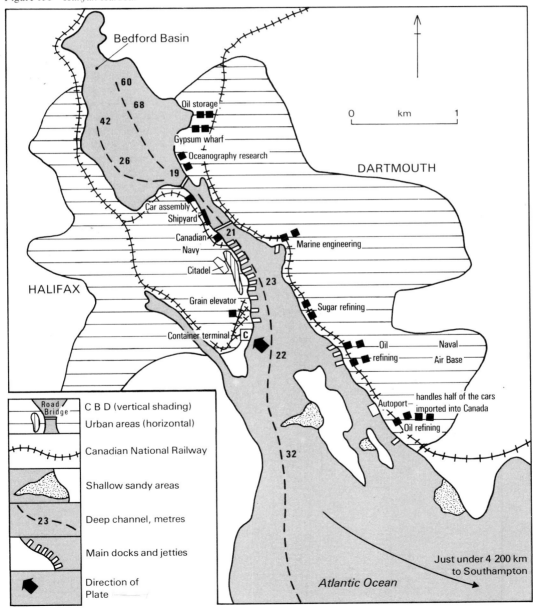

standardise sizes on an international basis: thus easy stacking on ship, lorry and rail flat-car was achieved. In southern Halifax an area of 23 hectares with Canadian National rail links, new large cranes and carriers give an exceptionally fast rate of transfer from one form of transport to another. Unloading of ships which used to take up to two weeks can now be completed in two days. In addition, many ships have been specially built to carry large lorries and wide loads, so that the vehicles can use their own power to drive on and off.

Table 76   Annual cargo at the major Canadian ports (thousands tonnes)

	In containers	In bulk	General cargo
Halifax	1700	11 300	700
St John	400	4 000	1400
Quebec City	800	12 500	500
Montreal	1800	19 500	2200
Vancouver	900	35 000	2300

Questions

Figure 136

1. Classify the industries of Halifax harbour under the following headings: (*i*) storage and handling facilities; (*ii*) industries which process imports, and (*iii*) the remaining activities.
2. Discuss the site of Halifax-Dartmouth considering: (*i*) its advantages as a harbour, and (*ii*) problems on the land-ward side for goods, and the work force.

Figure 136 and an atlas

3. Comment on the position of Halifax with reference to
   a) its strategic value to NATO navies;
   b) the importance of the nearby continental shelf;
   c) its distance from Europe compared with its main Canadian and American rivals.

Plate 94 and Figure 136

4. *a*) Describe the position of the container terminal.
   b) Why was it situated there rather than elsewhere?

Table 76

5. *a*) Convert the figures into a multiple bar graph.
   b) (*i*) Name the port which has the highest percentage of containerised traffic, and (*ii*) account for its lead in this type of traffic.

General

6. Do you think that 'general cargo' will ever be completely containerised? Why?

Plate 94   *Halifax container terminal*